MUSKA MOSSTON

Rutgers, the State University of New Jersey

TEACHING PHYSICAL EDUCATION

From Command to Discovery

Charles E. Merrill Publishing Co.
Columbus, Ohio
A Bell & Howell Company

ISBN 0-675-09842-4

Library of Congress Catalog Number: 67-10472

5 6 7 8 9 10 11 12 13 14 15-76 75 74 73 72 71

PRINTED IN THE UNITED STATES OF AMERICA

To my Juniors at Rutgers who motivated me to find out more . . .

and

To my teacher and friend, Dr. Richard C. Anderson, who led me through the cognitive barrier.

To my wife, Leora—now I know why authors thank their wives.

ACKNOWLEDGMENTS

I wish to thank the administrations and faculties of the schools in the following communities for permitting my students and me to test the results of our work in styles of teaching.

East Brunswick, New Jersey

Franklin Township, New Jersey

Highland Park, New Jersey

Madison Township, New Jersey

New Brunswick, New Jersey

North Brunswick, New Jersey

New Jersey
1967

Muska Mosston

INTRODUCTION

Professor Mosston has written an exciting, stimulating, frustrating and finally, subtlely provocative treatise on how and what to teach. The book is written primarily for physical education instructors but there is no doubt every teacher or potential teacher will be emotionally affected by reading it. His analyses of the spectrum of styles of teaching and the position where the reader places himself as well as his students on it, cannot help but be upsetting. When this occurs, learning and changing can potentially follow because conflicts between what we previously believed and are now exposed to through this book must be resolved. Professors Mosston and Festinger call it cognitive dissonance but the reader will find himself either re-reading this book many times or else trying to repress what is read.

I want to amplify in the following paragraphs what was meant by describing this book as "exicting, stimulating, frustrating and finally, subtlely provocative." The book is exciting because of the author's painstaking logical dissection of the methods teachers utilize in instructing students from the unfortunately usual command style, through guided discovery, problem solving, to the ultimate goal, creative teaching and learning. Example after example in physical education helps to illustrate Professor Mosston's ideas and also serve as models for the reader to try out for himself. It is a fine companion work to his "Developmental Movement" because they are "learning how to" books.

Professor Mosston stimulates the reader by carefully examining the strengths and weaknesses of command teaching which is the usual mode of instruction in physical education and most other subject courses. Essentially the command style consists of teacher demonstration, explanation, student execution or imitation and finally teacher evaluation. The closer the student is to the model the more approval and higher grade he achieves. Mosston shows how reaching the model level is too difficult for most students and therefore physically and emotionally does not lead to individual student growth. Equally important, the physical education teacher feels he has not had a positive impact on his class except for the physically talented. The author points out the obvious but painful truth that teaching a class of 30 to 100 an activity such as the running broad jump involves all students waiting on line most of the time. To find out that there are alternatives (such as small groups of students doing many different *parts* of broad jumping according to their needs, at the same time), *has* to stimulate the reader.

The book is frustrating and perhaps somewhat discouraging to read. It is frustrating because as one reads the methodical presentation one begins to feel overwhelmed. For example, in the chapter on Guided Discovery Professor Mosston shows simply and clearly how to guide the student to the principles of the fast break in basketball. There are 34 questions and at least twice the number of clues in the form of verbal questions which inevitably lead to a complete learning along the four channels described by the writer, namely: physical, social, emotional and intellectual. What is frustrating and discouraging is the amount of reading, thinking, planning, testing, and modifying necessary to develop guided discovery methods. This writer can think of no book in the field of education in recent times which could affect the reader as deeply as this book. Dare the reader compete with Professor Mosston to develop the necessary guided discovery questions to understand the principles of swimming, handstands, personal hygiene, etc.? This method is related to the programmed learning methods developed by B. F. Skinner. The writer has shown how it can be adapted to physical education and in fact to all subjects that are taught in or out of school.

This last statement plus the enormous range of ideas presented—from how the teacher can free himself from the bonds of setting an example by demonstration concentrating on discipline and being distant from the student, to planning for the student to work and evaluate himself—is overwhelming emotionally. Utilizing the teachings of Professor Mosston profoundly alters the role of the teacher to one of creator, planner, observer and expert advisor openly encouraging the student to extend and surpass himself. The teacher in turn finds himself being stimulated by the student's new ideas as he has stimulated them by his new approach to them. Reciprocal learning is always the most gratifying experience for teacher and student since both give and receive. The book will be a classic in the field of physical education and will influence and shake the entire field of education in the years ahead.

Before closing I want to add a few personal words concerning Professor Mosston. We met in the summer of 1963 in the mountains of New Hampshire where we had both gone with our families for a rest from intellectual activities and to climb mountains. I remember hearing the ideas presented in this book as we stood by a lake, drinking hot soup heated by a Sterno stove at 2 a.m. We both became so excited by the similarity of our ideas developed in widely disparate professions that we were yelling at each other in excitement. We decided that whenever we would write books on our theories of teaching or behavior the other would write the introduction. Professor Mosston finished his book first and I am proud to have written this introduction and so be associated with this creative treatise.

New York, N. Y.

Dr. Selwyn Lederman, *Psychoanalyst*
and former Lecturer in Psychology,
Hunter College

FOREWORD

Inspection of some recent literature in physical education makes it apparent that the former "how to do it" field is truly striving to become academically oriented. Passing from a philosophical to a research emphasis within the past three decades has produced well grounded theories about man in action which support changes in methodology. While several recent authors have been content to merely synthesize research and to point theoretical implications arising from their compilations, fewer have had the courage to attempt to bridge the gap between research findings and program change. It is believed that this text forms a portion of that much needed weld. Mosston presents framework which should result in a happier marriage between theory, anchored on data, and applications on the playfield.

Some university and college teachers and researchers caught up in a struggle for their existence in the academic community look with some disdain at the applied, clinical "portion" of their discipline called physical education. The fact remains, however, that this part of our calling remains the main reason for our existence and is the primary outlet for our graduates. To better educate is a noble aim, and the writer of this text seems to enoble it further by the sensitive approach presented on the following pages.

In *Teaching Physical Education: From Command to Discovery*, Mosston's personal dynamism and creative energies are transmitted to the reader in a text which brings a synthesis of educational psychology to the teaching and learning of movement. Mosston translates such terms as creativity, cognitive development, and self-realization into concrete suggestions for interactions between the teacher and learner.

It is to be expected that readers from a number of disciplines will read and be influenced by the concepts presented by this master teacher. Although the framework he presents might only cause a ripple within the community of physical educators, it is more to be expected that a medium size tidal wave might result as workers in the field inspect the content.

Mosston places emphasis upon *becoming*, rather than upon *performing*—upon *flexibility*, rather than upon *rigidity*—and upon *change* rather than upon *dogmatism*. Education is viewed as a planned series of dynamic behavioral interactions between teacher and child. The starting point is the kind of behavior one might wish the child to evidence in a free society. Mosston outlines how this behavior may be elicited through exposure to movement tasks in a variety of sports skills to which every physical educator can readily relate.

Learning is not described in the usual sugar-coated terms, but rather is presented as a struggle to be resolved—and in the resolution comes the realization—the personal triumph of the learner. By skillfully blending concepts advanced by Maslow, Skinner, Bruner, and Socrates into meaningful and workable formulas, a flexible framework is offered to those sensitive enough to grasp it. It is suggested that true learning is only accomplished by carefully transferring decisions formerly made by teachers to the learner.

Some of these goals are familiar to us. Mosston, however, translates platitudes into exact operational procedures familiar to the physical educator. Detailed descriptions of methodology in gymnastics, soccer, basketball and football should provide anchoring points for all. Mosston does not simply suggest that we throw open the doors, and somehow free the student's creative energies by doing so—rather he leads the reader by the hand toward this objective in precise ways, pointing to specific kinds of movement experiences which free the intellect.

The author suggests that children and youth should be treated with respect, as rational beings capable of gaining the ability to formulate decisions for themselves. He states that by artfully manipulating the quality of decisions we ask of people, and by increasing the complexity of the situations in which we place them, their powers of cognition will likewise improve. The older learning principles of gradual progression toward difficult ends—and of reinforcement— are wedded to newer concepts emphasizing self-discovery and creativity. The base of Mosston's pyramid of success thus rests upon stones inscribed with such phrases as "classical learning theory," "workable motivational techniques," "knowledge about group interaction" and "respect for the dignity of man."

The assumption of the style of teaching suggested by this gifted author will require courage on the part of many readers—the courage to admit that perhaps there might be better ways of working with children in an educational setting. To change takes the courage to admit that in the past one has perhaps not quite grasped the essentials of the situation in which he has been operating—and Mosston is attempting to change the reader!

The author nurtures his readers as he would have them offer succorance to their charges—taking them from "Command to Discovery—" discovery of the sensitivity of the self—of the realities of the learning process—of workable ways to stimulate youth—and discovery of the nobility of the human spirit. Mosston pleads and reasons with those whose needs for dominance may obliterate their sensitivity, and by the final pages he has perhaps persuaded them that some of their decisions might better be transferred to their students. Upon those with the courage to follow Mosston into his simple yet complex labyrinth will fall the mantle of success . . . success based upon the knowledge that they have had a part in increasing the ability of a youth to make meaningful decisions about his own destiny.

Los Angeles, California

BRYANT J. CRATTY, *Director*
Perceptual-Motor Learning Laboratory
Department of Physical Education
University of California

PREFACE

The concept of styles of teaching emerged from the need to identify and clarify the structure of teaching behavior. It is conceived as the bridge between the structure of subject matter and the structure of learning.

The identification of each style, its premise, its operational design, and its implications strengthen the teaching process and elevate it to the level of consciousness and deliberation. Deliberate teaching is good teaching.

Styles of teaching physical education offer teachers on all levels an evolutionary process of teaching physical activities which consistently increases and develops:

A. The individualized learning process.

B. The cognitive process which is fundamental to all learning.

The interaction of these two processes—towards individualization and the cognitive development—is described, analyzed and demonstrated in the construct of the Spectrum of Styles. The teacher who wishes to lead the student toward independent learning and better performance will find that the variety of examples in the many sports clearly illustrate this process of individual growth.

The Spectrum of Styles reflects a philosophy of education which promotes independence in decision making, independence in seeking alternatives, and independence in learning.

Each style has its rationale and way of teaching supported by current studies in the behavioral sciences and the psychology of cognition.

Teaching physical education is a road toward creative physical responses, toward enhancement of self concept in a changing environment, and toward clearer use of the thinking abilities.

This book was designed and written for the students in physical education who are puzzled by the question, "How am I going to teach;" and for the teachers who are already in the field experiencing and experimenting with new ideas in teaching styles.

All the proposed styles have been successfully used by students and professors in teaching all grade levels (elementary level through graduate school) in a variety of activities in many school systems.

It is the author's hope that this work will serve as a contribution to more effective teaching of free students and indeed will lead the learner from command to discovery.

MUSKA MOSSTON

TABLE OF CONTENTS

TEACHING
PHYSICAL EDUCATION
From Command
to Discovery

1

The Premise

In recent years several publications in education and in psychology have renewed discussions of how people learn and how curricula should be adjusted to implement new knowledge about the learner. The 1962 yearbook of the Association for Supervision and Curriculum Development, *Perceiving Behaving Becoming* (64),[1] proposed to present a new focus on the self concept of the student, to encourage the student's concept of himself as one whose main purpose is to emerge, to become a "fully functioning" person. This publication was preceded, in 1960, by Bruner's *The Process of Education* (17) and followed by his *On Knowing: Essays for the Left Hand* (16). Both of these books stirred a great deal of interest and experimentation in two major concerns of education: the structure of the child's thinking process and the structure of subject matter areas in various disciplines.[2]

Bloom's *Taxonomy of Educational Objectives* handbooks (11, 50) on both the cognitive domain and the affective domain shed renewed light on what we are attempting to do in education. *The Teacher and the Taught* (39) and *The Structure of Knowledge and the Curriculum* (34) strengthen our current realization of the need to view education and learning in new ways—philosophical, sociological, and psychological. To crown this vigorous discourse on the role, development, and con-

---

[1] Numbers in parentheses are those of references listed on pp. 231–234.

[2] Since the writing of *Teaching Physical Education: From Command to Discovery,* Dr. Jerome S. Bruner has published a new book: *Toward a Theory of Instruction* (Cambridge, Mass.: The Belknap Press of Harvard University Press, 1966). Like many of Dr. Bruner's previous works, this one sheds a brilliant light on contemporary education and reaffirms the need for a construct as reflected by the Spectrum of Styles.

1

tribution of the cognitive process to education has come Anderson and Ausubel's book, *Readings in the Psychology of Cognition* (5).

Several works have drawn the field of physical education closer to the other areas of education. Diem in Germany (30) and Morrison in England (55) have introduced the concept of discovery and innovation in movement. Andrews (6) has proposed a variety of program ideas in this direction. Cratty's *Movement Behavior and Motor Learning* (25) offers a vast review and classification of research which strongly points to the need to strengthen physical education by deeper study of psychology and sociology.

The common characteristic of all these works and many others (excluding the majority of books on methodology, which really concern themselves with organizational and administrative issues rather than with the core issue of methodology: teaching and learning) is their focus on the structure of learning and the structure of subject matter. The third structure, equally important, either is lightly mentioned or is completely ignored in most works. This third structure is the *structure of teaching*.

Discussions of the structure of learning are concerned with *how* a person learns. The structure of learning involves the matrix of psychological and physiological constructs which offer explanations about learning behavior. Study of the structure of subject matter presents an attempt to relate components of knowledge in logical and meaningful ways. Now, let us assume for a moment that we know everything that there is to know about the structure of learning and the structure of all subject matter—how do we connect the two entities? How should teachers behave—how should they teach—so that all this intricately related and integrated subject matter will be learned, understood, and internalized by the student?

Should we leave the problem to anyone's hunch or whim? Should we leave it to the individual teacher's mood or personal opinion? Doesn't the lack of a clear concept of the structure of teaching create a serious gap between the structure of subject matter and the structure of learning? Is it enough to expound philosophically on the merits of individual learning—and to substantiate its possibilities by research in cognitive strategies, in strengthening the self image, and in social intercourse—without actually suggesting operational ways to accomplish it? Shouldn't one be able to propose operational ways to bridge the gap between student and subject matter and thus to evolve a fresh and fruitful relationship, a relationship based on the involvement and interaction of three main participants: the teacher, the student, and the subject matter?

The teacher brings to the process of bridging this gap his total self

—his cultural background, all his biases and personal limitations, his own needs for self-assertion, and his value structure—and this largely dictates his behavior and the conduct of his teaching. The chain of decisions he makes about the student and about the handling of subject matter is a projection of these conditions, enhanced by a personal belief about what the teaching-learning process should be. This teaching behavior is a cumulative chain of decision making—of deciding among known choices. The absence of decisions about various aspects of a lesson also reflects decision making—*a decision not to make decisions about* some aspects of the lesson.

The student also arrives with a complex background, which includes his level of physical ability, emotional complexity, social attitudes, mores, and his intellectual capacity.

From the first meeting the teacher and student interact. This interaction can be on a maximum, minimum, or in-between level; but interaction *does* occur. Many, if not all, of a student's decisions are closely interrelated with his teacher's decisions. This interrelated behavior exists in a minimum-maximum dimension. Whether the student's responses are in total correspondence with the teacher's judgment of what should be done, how fast, how well, and so on, or whether they are quite different, these responses are still a reflection of the kind of decisions the teacher made.

Now, neither teacher nor student can make decisions in a vacuum. Decisions are always made about something. *This "something" is the subject matter of teaching and learning.* Pitching in baseball is subject matter; pole vaulting is subject matter; the relationships among players in a given game strategy are subject matter. The attitudes of team members towards a player of an ethnic minority are subject matter. The way a student feels about himself in various situations and under varying stress conditions is subject matter. Regardless of what the subject matter is, decisions about it must be made. Decisions *are* being made in every single lesson.

Several fundamental questions arise about the teacher–student–subject matter relationship:

1. What are the decisions to be made?
2. Who makes these decisions?
3. How do they affect the teacher's behavior?
4. How do they affect the structure of subject matter and curricular progress?
5. How do they affect the growth and development of the individual student and his interaction with his culture?
6. What is the direction of this growth and development?

This book offers some answers to these questions, and it delineates observable teaching styles. These styles already exist in the reality of many teachers' experiences. But instead of describing them in a random way, this book proposes to show how they can be deliberately used in developing teacher-student interaction in the decision-making process and to define the role of the teacher and the role of the student in this process. (Childs, in his book *Education and Morals* [21], discusses the role of deliberate action and the responsibility of the adult in this effort.) Teaching in all communities is deliberate; we really want to repeat our successes and avoid our failures. But if we do not know what we do and how we do it we can accomplish neither.

What kind of deliberate action does a teacher use? How does use of deliberate action affect the ability of the student to learn? How does this influence the student's pre-disposition to learning? Is it possible to approach optimal learning conditions for the individual student?

The description of the *anatomy of each teaching style* proposes operational steps to answer these questions; and the styles will be related to one another in a way which reflects an evolutionary process of decision making concerning physical responses, social interaction, emotional growth, and intellectual involvement. These four areas are the basic developmental channels through which students progress. The phrase "developmental channels" conjures a sense of action and mobility—of process—rather than the static implication of the terms "physical, social, emotional, and intellectual *objectives*."

As he moves along the channel of physical development the student seeks to explore and identify his physical capacities and limitations. He seeks his movement preferences in a variety of situations; he seeks the experiences which help him develop to higher levels of physical security, physical expression, and joy. He is freed from single physical standards pre-determined and constantly controlled by others.

A developmental-channel approach to social interaction connotes freedom of association in and outside school. This approach involves a process of re-examining the interpersonal and intergroup practices in both the school and the community.

The emotional developmental channel, in the context of physical education, involves the physical self concept of the child, his ability to accept himself in the pursuit of excellence and in facing deterring physical limitation. The physical education teacher can aid the child's emotional development if he helps the child develop *his own* physical image rather than forcing him to reach for an image developed *for* the child. This facet of the development of a physical self image is intimately related to the total process of evolving an acceptable over-all self image.

The intellectual developmental channel involves that very private, very personal faculty—the ability to think; to assemble data; to weigh, judge, and organize information; to remember; to project; to draw conclusions; to imagine, to dream; to invent. This developmental channel involves all these wonderful intellectual streams which so uniquely and mysteriously flow during the life of each person. Shall we dam these streams by physical control, emotional inhibitions, and social prejudices of any sort? Or shall we poke, intrigue, stimulate, and free these capacities so that each child will feel and say, "This teacher is teaching *me!*" "*I* am a person. *I* am important. *My* thoughts matter!"

The concept of development involves a *process*. In order to study a process it is necessary to identify direction, since any process means moving from one condition to another. One can move from *minimum* toward *maximum* on any one of the developmental channels discussed above. One can be stationed at any point on any of the channels.

If we identify the theoretical "maximum" point on all channels with the target *independent decision making*, then we can say that the theoretical minimum point will be the farthest from the target. Thus evolve the *theoretical limits* of the developmental channels (see Figure 1).

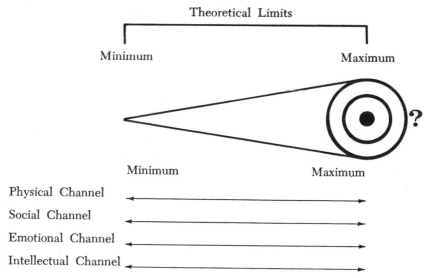

Figure 1. *The Four Developmental Channels*

Suppose we examine the point which gets closest to minimum in this schema. What does it mean to be close to minimum on these developmental channels? What kind of behavior does a teacher manifest at this point? What kind of behavior does a student manifest at this stage? Will he be able to make decisions concerning his movements when a new situation arises, or will he *need* to respond to an external stimulus —a decision made by someone else (teacher, coach, peer, etc.)? Will this student know that there *are* alternative movement possibilities? Will he know how to judge and select the appropriate alternative? Will he be able to make the decision by himself and execute it by himself? Even a team effort is based on the cumulative appropriate small decisions and actions of each individual, and only when each individual is capable of making decisions can the team advance to a higher level of performance.

Behavioral alternatives are needed to increase decision-making alternatives in all dimensions of behavior: physical, social, emotional, and intellectual. Teaching alternatives are necessary to create a different variety of interactions among the behavioral dimensions.

The literature in the behavioral sciences is quite rich in proposals concerning the emotional state of the learner, alternative psychological theories of learning, studies in perception and self-concept constructs. We know more about how people learn; we know more about how people perceive their environment. A variety of mediational theories attempts to explain the role of cognition in interpreting the perceived data.

The paramount question remains: How does all this affect teaching behavior? What is the role of the teacher in promoting alternative styles of learning? What are some of the operational and behavioral adjustments that must be internalized to affect alternative relational patterns between teacher and student? We know more about how people learn; now we need to know more about teaching styles. What are the alternative teaching styles which transcend organizational patterns and personal idiosyncrasies? What are the alternative teaching styles which even transcend the personality of the teacher? Can we identify in the teaching process those variables and components which are intrinsic to the process of the style and not to the individual teacher? It is not proposed to diminish, curtail, or ignore the unique genius of the individual teacher who inspires, motivates, and leads his students to great moments in learning by conscious or accidental use of his intellectual abilities and personality attributes; rather, it is an attempt to draw teaching styles closer to learning styles. It is a proposal to view teaching as a conscious behavioral pattern which can be learned. *Teachers can learn to behave in alternative styles* and thus affect change in learning styles and gradually. propel the student to greater individuality in physical response, social awareness, emotional strength, and intellectual productivity.

What do teachers actually do and say? What do they *not* do or say? How do teachers' behavioral patterns affect the progress of students along the developmental channels? What kind of teacher's behavior brings, or helps maintain, the student close to the minimum level? What can a teacher say or *not* say, do or *not* do in relation to the given subject matter to move the student toward the maximum achievement in the developmental channels? Are there only two extremes? Are there any teaching styles in between?

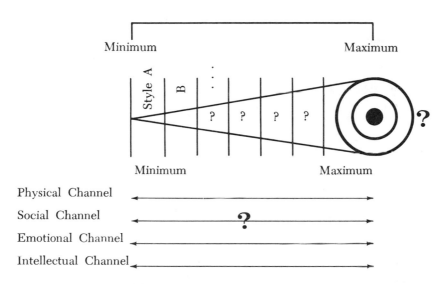

Figure 2. *Are There Only Two Extreme Styles? Is There Anything in Between?*

The concept of the SPECTRUM OF STYLES proposes a theoretical construct and an operational design of alternative styles of teaching which gradually move *both* teacher and student along all four developmental channels. A SPECTRUM is proposed because the shift from one style to another is sequential in terms of the identified behavioral variables and components. Thus, by holding all variables (and components of the variables) constant *except* one, a *new* style evolves—a style which is *similar* to its predecessor yet *different* in its contribution to the developmental freeing process.

Each style in the spectrum has its own operational structure—described in the section on the anatomy of teaching style—which defines and describes the behavioral role of the teacher and its influence on the student's behavioral role. A style of teaching, in essence, is composed of all the decisions that are made during the teaching-learning process to induce a particular style of learning. Two main dimensions are constantly and consistently observed and developed in the use of the spectrum of styles. One is the individualized response dimension, reaching its peak in the various designs of *individual programming*. The second is the dimension of the cognitive process, which blossoms fully under the guidance of those teaching styles which help the student go beyond the *cognitive barrier*; these are styles of teaching which evoke the discovery capacities of the student and strengthen his problem-solving abilities.

Only after this stage of the teaching-learning process is well developed will one reach, in the spectrum of styles, the level of education at which creativity predominates—a level at which one's energies are self-perpetuating, his imagination is ever seeking, and his achievement is never ending.

ANATOMY OF A TEACHING STYLE

We need to know now how to construct these different behavioral patterns. We need to identify the variables involved in the anatomy of a teaching style and then, by manipulation of the variables, identify or create *alternative* styles along the spectrum.

What is the first behavioral variable? What do all teachers do? It is proposed that the first variable is *pre-class* decisions. All teachers do *something* before the class begins. Some are more involved, and some are less involved; but *all make decisions* about the next phase of their teaching behavior. This variable of pre-class decision making is made up of several components. *Each component represents a different area of decisions*—decisions about the selection of subject matter, about quantity, about quality, and so on.

Let us delineate and examine the various components of the first variable:

1. *Decisions concerning the* selection *of subject matter.* Have you ever questioned the curricular practice of spending such a long time teaching basketball? Wrestling? Gymnastics? Other activities? Has this selection of subject matter helped the student learn more than he knew before?
2. *Decisions concerning* quantity *of an activity.* Have you ever questioned your quantity standards? Are they the same for all students?

Are they different for some students? How do you differentiate standards? Do you consider individual differences? Do you make *conscious* provisions for these differences? If you believe in the need to differentiate, do you know how to individualize standards of quantity? Do your students *know* about individual standards? Do they learn to accept themselves and others who may be higher or lower in ability?

3. *Decisions concerning* quality *of performance.* Which standard of quality are you seeking to meet? Your own? The Olympic standard? The principal's? The student's? Would you agree that this phase of decision making is important? It can affect your entire view of teaching and can affect the student's view of himself, his relationship with you and with his peers. Have you ever questioned, for example, the straight hand-stand? Who decided that the hand-stand must be straight and that it looks better that way? Kinesiologically speaking, it is more profitable for acquisition of balance to learn a variety of curved and combined hand-stand postures.

4. *Decisions concerning the degree of the* teacher's *own involvement.* What phrases are you going to use? Which ones are you *not* going to use? How much are you going to *tell* your students? Do you want your students to respond by executing the movement that you demonstrate? Do you want something else? What?

5. *Decisions concerning the degree of your* students' *involvement.* What kind of involvement do you seek? Do you want your students to evaluate your decisions and statement before they move? Do you want your students to learn to produce their own decisions? Do you want your students to *discover* ways to execute their motor decisions, and do you want them to learn to evaluate these decisions in light of the requirements of the given situation? Are you secure and confident enough in your knowledge to permit your students to explore alternatives?

All these questions and probably many others are answered *by the teacher* before the lesson begins. The answers depend entirely on the teacher's philosophy of education. They stem from the teacher's view of what constitutes his role and the student's role in the teaching-learning process. Awareness of the anatomy of teaching style will help the teacher make the kind of decisions which are most appropriate to his beliefs about education.

The pre-class decisions are carried out from the very moment the teacher makes contact with the class. In fact, some of these decisions are carried out by the students in the class even before contact is made;

which decisions these will be depends upon either the impact of the previous lesson or the pre-arranged "contract" with the class. (In physical education classes, evidence of pre-class decisions by the students is seen when the class is lined up when the bell sounds, without any signal from the teacher. Such evidence is present also when the students spontaneously discuss or practice a particular detail of a sport according to suggestions presented in the previous physical education class.)

After the moment of contact between teacher and students the second variable begins: *execution*. Here again, all teachers *do something*. Some do more, some less; some teach in one way, others in another. But all are engaged in the execution variable. This variable consists of many behavioral components, which reflect the variety of decisions made by the teacher during this phase of the lesson. These components are:

1. *Organizational decisions*. Where should students stand? Should they sit? Do they stay on the same spot at the beginning of every class? Why? Is this the only way? What are the alternatives? Are the alternatives desirable? Why? Are they more efficient in terms of time spent? Do they affect discipline in a particular way? What way? Is this the "kind" of discipline you want? What kind is it? Can you define it? Have you considered the implication of this kind of discipline? Is there another kind of discipline?

   Do you want the class in squads? Why? Is this arrangement relevant to the activity that follows? Or is there another reason? Do you want the class in a circle? Why? Is it because a red circle is painted on the gymnasium's floor or because there is a need to stand in a circle? Have you considered other geometric forms? Must the class follow a particular geometric form? Why? Why not? What does a geometric form do to enhance the quality of a lesson? Does it hinder any aspect of the learning process?

   How do students line up? Randomly? By height? Alphabetically? Why?

   Let us examine the tradition of lining up by height. Whenever people line up there is always a "first" and a "last," regardless of the direction of the line. When the criterion for this arrangement is height, who is first, the tall or the short? Who is last? What happens to a student who, by genetic coincidence, is always last? Is lining up by height a real organizational necessity, or is it merely a traditional arrangement based on a false aesthetic value?

   A similar analysis can be applied to alphabetical arrangement, convenient as it seems. Who stands at the head of the line, the student whose name starts with *A* or the one whose name starts with *Z*? What happens to the child who has been standing at the end of the line quite frequently through his school career because his name starts with *Z*? Often standing at the end of the line means being far away from the teacher, unable to see or hear, unable to *be* seen or heard.

There must be alternative organizational patterns which are efficient for attendance taking, checking of attire, and the like and at the same time are non-offensive in their socio-emotional implications. (See the proposals in the alternative teaching styles.)

2. *Time decisions.* When do students *begin* to move, to exercise, or to practice a particular shot in basketball? The starting time seems to be an important component about which teachers make decisions. Here, too, several alternatives exist—all students can start moving together when a particular signal is given, or they can start moving one squad at a time, or individuals can move when they feel like it. The point is that this matter requires a decision.

3. *Decisions about the* duration *of an activity.* Most commonly teachers will say, "Do fifteen push-ups," or "Swim twenty-one laps," or "Ten minutes for practicing the hook shot," or "Fifteen minutes practicing techniques of tackling." Is there another way of handling the duration component? Can all students do the same amount of work in the same amount of time?

4. *Decisions about the* rhythm *of the movement.* Since people are different in their physiological make-up and in their psychological needs, *whose* rhythm shall the teacher follow? That of the slowest mover? That of the fastest? That of the average? Can one determine the average? Is it desirable to impose a single rhythm on all? All the time? Sometimes? What happens the rest of the time? Is there intrinsic merit in externally imposed rhythm (a count, teacher's hand-clapping, drum beat, or a record) as compared to self-determined, inner rhythm? When is group rhythm desirable, and when is it unnecessary or even detrimental to other primary purposes of movement? A decision which affects the behavior of both teacher and student is needed.

5. *The decision of when* to stop. Do the students stop moving when the teacher has to make a comment? Do all stop or only those to whom the comment is directed? Do all students have to stop at a *single* signal? Why? Do students stop when the task has been fulfilled? Can they stop to rest? Can they *not stop*, despite the teacher's signal, because they are interested in what they are doing? Why?

A schematic summary of the preceding discussion will be helpful here.

Teaching Variables	*Role of Teacher*	*Role of Student*
1. Pre-class decisions	1. Selection of subject matter.	Involved?
	2. Quantity of subject matter.	Not involved?
	3. Quality of subject matter.	To what
	4. Teacher's role.	degree?
	5. Student's role.	?
2. Execution	1. Organizational matters.	
	2. Time—when to start.	
	3. Duration of activity.	
	4. Rhythm.	
	5. When to stop.	?
	6. Mode of communication (oral? visual? both?).	
	7. Can you think of other components of behavior which are common to all teachers at this phase of the teaching-learning process?	

A word about the mode of communication: You can use an oral mode alone. What do you say? Do you deliver the facts? How many facts do you present? In what sequence do you present them? Do you ask questions? What kind of questions? In what sequence? Are all questions relevant? Can *you* continue this list of questions about the issue of questions?

You can choose to use a visual mode. Do you show a film of the expert performer? Of the poorest performer? Do you demonstrate movement on the mat, the football kick, other activities? *Can* you demonstrate? Can you tell your students that you cannot demonstrate because of your physical limitations? Are there other ways of using the visual mode of communication? Is it always the best way to communicate? Is there a time *not* to show? When? Why?

The next behavioral variable which is common to all teaching is *evaluation*. All teachers evaluate their students. Some do it well; some do it more frequently than others; some base their evaluating statement merely on momentary observation, while others prefer using a variety of validated testing devices. Evaluation can take the form of immediate verbal reinforcement or a comparative measurement of cumulative achievement. In any case, a decision of what to do and how to go about it must be made. This variable has the following components.

1. Teacher evaluates the student. The teacher can offer verbal reinforcement when he sees a student performing well. This is an *ongoing* evaluation process.
2. Teacher evaluates the student by use of a testing device. The testing device can be either an unannounced test or an announced and prepared-for test. Testing can be done at a variety of time intervals: daily, weekly, monthly, at the end of a semester, and so on.
3. The teacher can evaluate each individual *according to group norms*.
4. The teacher can evaluate the student *according to his own growth and improvement*.
5. The teacher can evaluate the class in relation to itself, other classes, state norms, etc.

The teacher can use all these evaluating procedures during the class period, or he can do the evaluation after the class period. The teacher *must* decide which of these ways is to be used in various situations.

Schematically, the anatomy of a teaching style looks like this:

Teaching Variable	*Role of Teacher in Decision Making*	*Role of Student in Decision Making*
Variable 1 Pre-class decisions	Decisions about the following components:	
	1. _____	_____ ? _____
	2. _____	_____
	3. _____	_____
	4. . . .	
Variable 2 Execution decisions	1. _____	_____ ? _____
	2. _____	_____
	3. _____	_____
	4. . . .	
Variable 3 Evaluation decisions	1. _____	_____ ? _____
	2. _____	_____
	3. _____	_____
	4. . . .	

We know now some of the questions which the teacher needs to answer in each phase of the teaching process (behavioral variables). The decisions to act in a particular way depend upon the philosophy of the teacher, his cultural environment, his practical experience, his self concept, and his ability to adapt to new behavioral dimensions and styles of teaching.

Some teachers cannot shift their styles of teaching and remain frozen in one particular style despite the need and readiness of the students to be taught and to learn in alternative ways. Such a freeze-up may result from many causes—for example, personal limitations in teaching ability, habit, emotional rigidity, and intellectual inability to examine alternatives beyond one's own experience. It may result from learning isolation or inadequate knowledge of the operation and implications of the spectrum of styles.

A thorough analysis of the anatomy of a teaching style and the examples proposed in various activities and sports should provide the teacher with further insights into his own teaching behavior and the teaching-learning process. The anatomy of a style proposes a delineation of expectations of students' behavior.

When a teacher communicates with a student, the student's responses are closely related to the kinds of stimuli emitted by the teacher. Changes in the teacher's behavior will cause changes in the student's responses. The anatomy of each style attempts to anticipate and describe these. Thus, as the teacher deliberately moves along the spectrum of teaching styles, the student makes adjustments along the developmental channels, ever approaching the state of being an independent individual.

In summary, it can be said that the anatomy of a style is a framework of relationships in which the role of the student is defined and described. It is related intricately and in specific ways to the behavioral role of the teacher and results in a special process of communication. The style a teacher uses reflects his philosophy of education, interpreted in an operational design; results in changes in the learning process; and has implications for behavior adjustments.

Any teacher who might consider moving along the spectrum of styles needs to consider all the implications of a change in style and anticipate the possibility that he will have to adjust his philosophy, his daily teaching operations, and his values.

Let us start with a chart of possible implications (Figure 3). The purpose of this chart is to raise questions concerning various areas of behavior which are part of the daily teaching-learning process. The arrows which connect the style with its implications are double headed, indicating the reciprocal relationship which exists between the decision to use a particular style of teaching and the behavioral element which might need adjusting. For example, if you choose Style A as your avenue of communication for today's lesson, then, among other things, you must make a decision concerning the organization of the class on the gymnasium floor. It is possible that style A requires a very meticulous, formal organizational arrangement. Conversely, this kind of organization creates the need to use style A as a way of teaching.

You will have noticed that the areas of implication in Figure 3 are not completely enclosed. The implications are open ended; there are more questions to be answered and acted upon in each area. Indeed, the implications of the spectrum of styles are vast and intriguing. A very functional way of using this chart is to review it after reading about each style and then use the chart as a guide when that style is used in teaching physical education.

TOWARD INDIVIDUALIZATION

The process of moving from one teaching style to the next one on the spectrum calls for an increase in the quantity and quality of decisions made by the student. Where does this lead us? What happens to a student who approaches the maximum limits of the four developmental channels? What kind of person is the student who knows how to select and produce the desirable physical responses? What kind of person is the student who approaches the maximum limit of the emotional development channel? Is he not a person with a relatively clear self concept, who can re-establish his emotional stability in the face of new circumstances of decision making? And what kind of person is the one who knows how to perform in new social climates and make decisions about new social interaction? Who is the person who knows how to observe, gather information, judge, and draw conclusions, to think and evolve new ideas?

Who is the person manifesting these admirable qualities? He is a free man. It is the free man whose unique individuality is sought and developed. It is the free man whom a free society wishes to produce through its education—education for a society of independent people. Independence implies the ability to make choices among convictions; it connotes the strength to act and pursue the chosen convictions. It requires the courage to be different and to accept the different. Independence requires the ability to interact with others so that they, too, re-

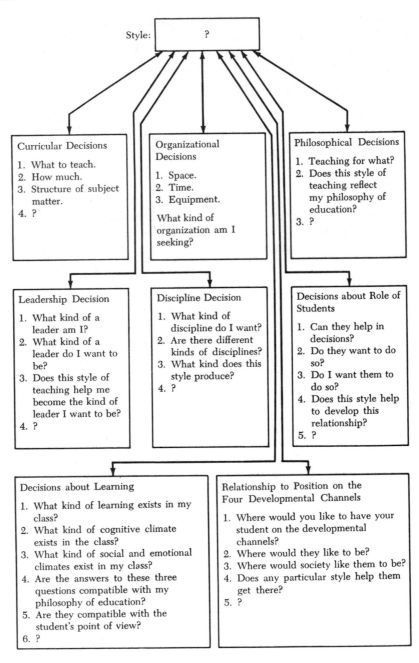

Figure 3. *The Implications of a Style of Teaching*

main independent. Independence means that one can learn to be free—free of physical limitations, oppressive social forces, emotional prisons, and intellectual dogmatism.

The education of the free, independent person must be a *freeing process*, a process so deliberately and elegantly developed that the student's dependency on the teacher gradually diminishes until the free student emerges.

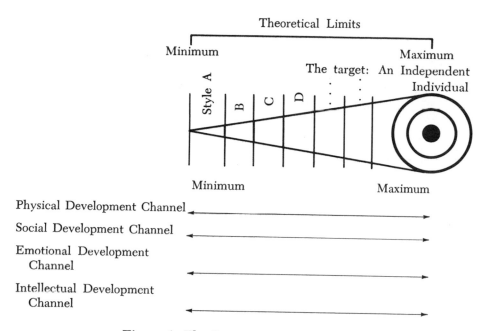

Figure 4. *The Spectrum of Styles*

2

Teaching by Command

The first style in the spectrum to be described and analyzed is the *command style*. It has a long history of use in physical education, as mentioned by Weston (82), and is perhaps the most prevalent style of teaching now used in physical education, particularly with large classes. Like all teaching styles, this one is based on certain assumptions and has a certain structure and certain implications.

First let us examine the purpose and assumptions of command teaching. The purpose of the command style is to elicit a response or many responses from one or more persons in a given subject matter. Specifically, it means that a teacher may want his fifty students to run half a mile, or swim twenty laps, perform the handstand, or spend fifteen minutes in practicing the hook shot in basketball. For the students to exhibit these responses, there must be something that initiates the action—some stimulus must be offered. An assumption underlying command teaching is that when certain stimuli exist, the desired responses will occur. Consequently, the teacher learns to present the kind of stimuli which will (in most cases, in "normal" situations) produce the expected responses. Thus, a teacher can say, "Today you will run half a mile!" or "We shall start our swimming lesson with twenty laps—slow laps!" or "When you perform the handstand today, note the place of your shoulders, make sure they are placed over the base. Also, avoid an excessive arch at the lower back!" We observe that in these statements the stimuli, the commands issued by the teacher, may take the form of either a general announcement of the selected subject matter or detailed directions for the students to follow.

The important principle involved here is that the sought responses and the stimuli used to produce them are results of decisions made by the teacher. This principle is based on another fundamental assumption

19

which undergirds the command style: the role of the student is to respond to the teacher's stimuli. Theoretically, the student should respond in all cases, in all subject matter. This is based on a traditional view of the teacher-student relationship: since the teacher possesses knowledge and is experienced, his role is to tell things to others; the role of the others is to listen, to absorb, and to comply.

Whenever the process of stimulus-response functions well, one can identify the following features in a given lesson:

1. Organizational patterns are well executed. When the command to line up in a particular geometric form is issued, the response is practically immediate.
2. When attention is called for, it is there! (In the command framework of assumptions this behavior is referred to as good discipline.)
3. Any command for motion is followed (instantly, in most cases) by a physical response—performed either in unison or individually, primarily depending upon the nature of the activity or the traditional way in which this activity has been carried out.
4. A meticulous teacher will offer group or individual corrections (if the response was "wrong" in the light of his preferences). This is often done by stopping the entire class (Stimulus: "Hold it!" "Stop!" blowing a whistle, or any other agreed-upon signal. Expected response: the class stops the activity!), whereupon the teacher identifies the error, states the correction, and then gives the command to resume the activity.
5. When the lesson is over, the teacher's command stops the activity. Then follows some sort of end-lesson ceremony: a particular formation, a cheer, an announcement concerning the day's achievements, a preparatory statement about the next lesson, or the like.

In these five features of the lesson, the closer the student's responses to the teacher's stimuli (in time and in accuracy), the more perfect the lesson. The closer the lesson is to perfection, the more it substantiates the validity of the fundamental assumptions of the command style. Reciprocally, the stronger the teacher's belief in these assumptions, the more nearly perfect is the execution of the lesson taught in this style.

The assumptions underlying the command style include also the expectation of progress and growth along the four developmental channels. Physical development will occur as a result of fluent participation in the activity directed by the teacher. Social awareness will result from the student's adherence to the rules and specifications imposed by the teacher. Emotional growth will occur as a result of the individual's assumed acceptance of his role as a member of a group as perceived and evaluated by the teacher. Intellectual development is assumed, since the student's acceptance of what the teacher offered and his performance of what the teacher requested both require some cognitive involvement and understanding of what the teacher wants.

This framework seems to be rather pure and perfect in form; perhaps it does not exist in actual experience. However, only when a framework is as complete and pure as theoretically imaginable does it become possible to understand its function, its contributions and limitations.

The step by step operation of the command style is described in outline form below.

ANATOMY OF THE COMMAND STYLE

	The Role of the Teacher	*The Role of the Student*
Variable No. 1: Pre-Class Preparation	1. Pre-determines the objectives of the lesson.	Not involved.
	2. Pre-determines the activity which will help accomplish the objectives.	Not involved.
	3. Pre-determines the order of the activity—or motion sequence.	Not involved.
	4. Pre-determines the approximate quantity of the activity (four minutes marching, twelve minutes warm-up exercises, etc.).	Not involved.
	5. Pre-determines the quality of performance expressed by either measured standards or by a set of values which fixes the quality or the "rightness" of performance.	Not involved.
	6. Pre-determines the organizational pattern of	Not involved.

The Role of the Teacher	*The Role of the Student*
the class which will help accomplish Items 1–5.	
7. Pre-determines the kind of discipline which seems to suit his needs and convictions concerning learning climate.	Is made aware of the discipline standard.

Variable No. 2: Execution	8. Conveys the information about the activity or explains the details of the activity. This can be done *verbally* or *visually by a demonstration* of the activity. Sometimes both means of communication are employed.	Listens (passive involvement); listening leads to some degree of comprehension. Observes the demonstration and establishes a standard of what is "correct" and "good."
	9. Determines the starting time.	Follows the instructions.
	10. Determines the duration of each segment of the lesson.	Adheres to instructions and participates in the activity.
	11. Determines the pace and rhythm of motion.	Follows the external rhythm.
	12. Determines the termination time.	Stops participating.
	13. Uses techniques of motivation.	May or may not be motivated.
Variable No. 3: Evaluation	14. Observes the performance of the class or individuals.	Usually continues to perform while being observed.
	15. Periodically offers corrections either for the whole class or to individuals.	Receives the teacher's comments and attempts a correction of the error.

16. When he chooses to comment on good performance (random reinforcement), may do so in front of the entire class or on an individual level.

In either case, hears the encouragement and continues to perform.

17. May use the variety of testing procedures administered on a group or individual basis.

Responds to the requirements of the testing procedures.

FOCUS ON THE TEACHER AND SUBJECT MATTER

Command teaching has been called by various names: the teacher-centered approach, dictatorial teaching, formal teaching, regimented teaching, and so on. The command style (or the parallel lecture style in strictly academic areas), by definition, is the style which focuses on the teacher and the subject matter. The teacher is the only one who may make decisions concerning physical activities; he is the one who determines the social-emotional climate in the class. Most often he seems to be the only one who is involved in some measure in the cognitive process or in cognitive activities. The student is expected to adhere to the physical limitations set, determined, and controlled by the teacher. *This physical limitation* imposed on the student may take any one or all of the following forms.

Organization

The student may have to stand on a particular spot in the gymnasium as assigned by the teacher. The rationale usually given for this requirement is that it fulfills the organizational needs of the teacher: "It is more efficient for roll-call purposes," or it seems efficient for a variety of tasks which require identification of students in a large class.

Limitations may be imposed when students change positions on the floor, when they move from one activity area to another or from one "station" to another. For reasons of discipline, this aspect of the lesson's organization is very often highly controlled by the teacher. The teacher determines when the change will take place (and signals the change by the sound of a whistle, a handclap, etc.), where each group shall go, what the direction of movement should be, and what formation should be used while students move to the new destination.

These aspects of the organizational phase of a good lesson are adhered to in varying degrees of precision, depending upon the teacher's concept of what constitutes discipline and control and upon the *teacher's* need to assert central leadership. Regardless of degree, these aspects of control are exhibited in most physical education classes and constitute the first level of physical limitation imposed upon the student. Alternatives to these procedures will be apparent in the discussion of organizational responsibilities involved in other styles of teaching. However, the controlled organization is consonant with the definition and anatomy of the command style and is carried out by the teacher who is trained in the use of this style and is comfortable with its procedures.

It must also be said that under certain conditions—physical or social in nature—it may be *necessary* to employ this style and these control procedures.

Movement

Limitations may be imposed in the teaching of movement. ("Movement" is used here as an all-embracing term which includes sports, games, gymnastics, etc. Movement is the essence of our subject matter.)

When a teacher uses the command style and conceives his role as that of a conveyor of information, a transmitter of knowledge, the following statements tend to be fairly common in his physical education class (these examples are drawn from the teaching of a variety of different activities to illustrate the similarity in teaching procedure despite the diversified subject matter).

In teaching warm-up movement or developmental movement, the teacher may say: "To straddle position. [pause] Jump! Hands on hips. [pause] Place! To count No. 1, bend down and touch your left foot with your right hand. To count No. 2, straighten up to the starting position. To count No. 3, bend down and touch your right foot with your left hand. To count No. 4, straighten up to starting position. Ready. [pause] Begin!" At this point the *entire* class will begin to move and follow the teacher's rhythm: "One, two, three, four!" and the class will continue until the command "Stop" or "Hold" reverberates in the gymnasium. The precise teacher will demand exact adherence to the beat and rhythm which he originated and controlled.

In teaching the serve in volleyball, a teacher may make statements like the following: "Have the ball rest on your left palm (facing up) while your left foot is placed ahead of your right. Swing your right arm from behind your body forward and hit the ball with the heel of your right palm, using an upward motion. The ball will fly in a high arch and will go over the net."

In observing a lesson on throwing the discus one can hear statements like the following: "As you swing the arm holding the discus backward, twist your trunk in the same direction and follow through with your head. At the same time bend both knees while you turn in the toes of the leg opposite the throwing arm. This combined motion will bring you to the beginning phase of the throw itself. From this phase the following occurs . . ."

In vaulting or in diving one can hear such statements as: "Keep your body straight, head up, and point your toes!" or "As you go up in the air, when you reach the climax of the flight, tuck your head and body and prepare for . . ."

These examples and thousands of others merely illustrate the *common* behavioral pattern of the teacher: he *tells!* Teachers may differ in their tone of voice, the length of their speeches, or their use of gimmicks; but, essentially, whenever information is delivered as described above, the style of teaching behavior is the same. Consequently, the role of the student in the relationship remains the same—a reflection of the teacher's commands with as close adherence as possible to the standard of performance demanded by the teacher.

THE DEMONSTRATION

The demonstration merits a special discussion because of its importance in teaching physical activities by the command style. Understanding this aspect of teaching will help one to understand why it is not present, why it *cannot* be present, in some alternative styles.

A demonstration of a physical activity executed by a good performer has an enormous impact on the observer and has psychological implications for the learner. A good demonstration has the following strengths:

1. It presents an holistic image of the activity.
2. It presents a visualization of the various parts of the activity and the integrative process of movement.
3. It creates a sense of admiration and can serve as strong motivation for learning.
4. It fortifies the position of the performer as an expert or an authority.
5. It can inspire a sense of the beauty of human motion.
6. It can draw the learner's attention to details that seem to be impor-

tant in the activity (the position of the fingers on the grip of a tennis racket; the position of the feet against the starting blocks; the curve at the lower back, or lack of it, in the handstand).

7. It points to a success level. It may motivate the learner to try for his potential level of performance.
8. It may save time. Explanations often seem to be too long, too tedious, or unclear. A neat demonstration tells the whole story quickly.
9. It seems to be efficient. All that is needed is to "show and tell," and then it is left to the learner to emulate the demonstrator.
10. A demonstration by a good performer can show an exact starting position in a given sport: the start in track, the lineman's stance, the serve position in tennis, the balance position on skis, etc.
11. A demonstration can illustrate the desired initial movement toward a desired purpose: the first step after the start in the dash, the movement of the arm in serving a volleyball, the forward lunge in fencing, etc.
12. It can show the series or sequences of movements which are employed in a given activity.
13. It can focus on the precise results of performance (as in, for example, the performance of an accomplished pool player, an expert in marbles, or a sharpshooter).
14. It can impress the learner with the smoothness, suppleness, and grace of coordinated human motion. One must stand breathless at the skill of a spinning dancer or a lithe gymnast.
15. It can affect the perceptions of the learner. (For an intensive study of perception and motion see Cratty [25]).
16. It presents to the students the standard of what the teacher considers to be "right" or "good."

For those who believe that children need and want to be shown the way, the correct standard is a vital tool of teaching, control, and evaluation of achievement; it is consistent with the definition of command style. The teaching obligation, in this view, is discharged by the act of demonstration. While a teacher is illustrating, the student must observe; repeating the demonstrated data is a common imperative in learning, and it keeps the learner under control. Assessing the learner's performance against the demonstrated standard supplies the teacher with an evaluative procedure which presumably helps motivate the student and helps maintain the kind of discipline needed for the execution and use of the command style.

The demonstration is not unique to the field of physical education. Very often mathematics teachers demonstrate solutions to students; physics teachers do the same. English instructors demonstrate the aesthetic elation they feel when they read a poem, and social studies teachers demonstrate their knowledge concerning the political and social issues in our civilization. In all cases this teaching behavior is designed to achieve prescribed and limited goals.

It must be said that when the demonstration is used well, learning can be achieved, learning of what is prescribed. It is a particular kind of learning, and it occupies an important position in the traditions of our public schools. It is needless to give a bibliography of method books in physical education that use the demonstration. Practically all use this famous "quadrivium":

> Step 1: Demonstration
> Step 2: Explanation
> Step 3: Execution
> Step 4: Evaluation

It is important to note that the influence of a demonstration is mainly external. The student is the passive recipient of all this powerful matrix of stimuli and influences; all he has to do is *accept* and *emulate* the performance. Acceptance and emulation seem to be the purpose of teaching as reflected by the command style. The focus is on the teacher and his standards and on the performance repeated by the student.

IMPLICATIONS OF THE COMMAND STYLE

It is necessary to raise a few questions at this stage so that the teacher will be able to clarify his position in terms of the ever-evolving purpose of American education, individual development. Is it not true that in most physical education classes one observes a fairly large number of students? Is it not true that the students attending the same class are of an incredible variety of shapes and sizes? Do they not possess an impressive variety of physical abilities? Are they not held back by a range of performance limitations in agility, strength, flexibility, coordination, and the like? Do they not, moreover, represent the whole spectrum of human temperament and readiness? Yet, this motley crew are expected to respond like one man to a single stimulus, to adhere to a single rhythm, to attempt performance fashioned by a single standard, and to try their best to attain the standards determined by one person.

Does this make sense? Does this way of teaching movement help reach the desired goal of individualized development and learning? Is this the best we can do more than half a century after the American physical education profession sought to shake off influences of foreign cultures which revolved around the axis of central control in education, family life, government, and so on? During the last century and at the beginning of the present one, stormy attacks were launched by the leaders of American physical education (see Weston [82]), who became very critical of the teaching style used by foreign teachers, a style which is identical in its behavior components with the command style described here; and yet half a century later we find this behavior pattern in most of our schools.

Let us examine now the limitations command teaching imposes upon the individual in other developmental channels. What do you suppose happens emotionally to a young person who constantly has to obey others—more specifically, the adult authority? What do you think happens to the self concept of a young, growing person who has to accept all the decisions which are made for him by others? What kinds of strengths will such a person develop? Will he develop any besides the ability to obey and to do what others tell him to do? Have you considered the weaknesses which this person will manifest when a situation demands self-assertion, a decision? (It is interesting to note that even in the military, a structure which can survive only with a clear, rigid system of subordinates who do not make frequent decisions but are well trained in executing other people's decisions and orders, new procedures of training officers have emerged, procedures which include alternative decision making rather than just execution of a pattern "according to the book."

Now, what about the channel of *social development?* Does not the phrase "learning social freedom" connote learning to relate to others, learning to make judgments when one is in a group situation, learning to exchange ideas, learning to evaluate exchanged ideas, learning to communicate with others, and learning to establish the self in new social frameworks and conditions without hesitation and fear? How is it possible for anyone—a young child or an adult—to experience fruitful and meaningful social intercourse when the opportunity to associate and communicate with others rarely occurs? This concern is fundamental to the success of the teaching-learning process in a democratic society. It is necessary for the teacher to recognize that satisfactory social development can be encouraged, not by stating social freedom as an objective, but by *putting it into practice daily.* One does not learn how to use freedom when he is in jail. In order for a child to learn *how* to be free in a social situation he must experience the sense of *being* free and experiment with this freedom; he must have the opportunity to find out about the limits of freedom within the social structure. This concept is very important in physical education. Within the command style of teaching (when it is executed well, with all controlled well by the teacher) do we provide for this positive socialization process? Or is the teaching behavior pattern which has been identified as the command style inimical, in its very essence, to the socialization process?

Is it possible to teach children social freedom when their physical and emotional freedoms are curtailed and often nullified on the gymnasium floor? Can we teach them how to engage in social intercourse—in the exchange of opinions, thoughts, feelings—when the discipline climate in which they learn calls for obedience, silence, and non-communication?

Is it possible to develop in the youngster a sense of responsibility without providing him with a *choice* of responsibilities, without giving him the opportunity to try alternative social solutions, and without granting him the right to make errors? The very essence of the command style does not permit these things to be done.

Now let us examine the limitations command teaching imposes in the *channel* of *intellectual development*. No teaching procedure in a democratic society can be called education unless it provides for, develops, and encourages individual intellectual growth and individual decision making. Elimination of thinking, questioning, inquiry, doubt, imagination, and experimentation with un-orthodox ideas—and these are some aspects of the cognitive process—produces intellectually sterile individuals. The command style in physical education inhibits and prevents growth of cognition. When an entire way of teaching is built upon the principle "I say or show; you do it!" not much is left for the student except, of course, to obey and perform to the teacher's satisfaction.

Whenever the command style of teaching is employed to its fullest, regardless of subject matter, it imposes limitations in all four developmental channels. In examining the content of physical education, one observes that when this style is employed by a teacher, the tendency is to teach everything—warm-up exercises, the techniques of a ball game, the details of a tumbling sequence, or a given strategy of a game—this way. All decisions are made by the teacher and conveyed by the teacher to his students, who are expected to listen, obey, and execute.

This analysis of the command style is offered in an attempt to sharpen the reader's insight into a teaching behavior pattern which is quite common, quite accepted, efficient, and seemingly successful in accomplishing its objectives.

It has been argued that judging a way of teaching only by observing and evaluating the performance results is an incomplete view of an educational process. There is a gap here; a link is missing. In order for us to identify the nature of the missing link it is necessary to examine each step and every component of the command style in light of the purpose of American education. It has been proposed that the development of independent individuals is the aim of our educational processes. If full development in the four channels discussed is the criterion of such independence, then the command style needs to be re-examined, and new decisions need to be made about its use—its quantity, quality, and frequency—in physical education classes.

Insight into this behavior pattern might help teachers to understand why they do what they do in their classes and might elevate the teaching act from a mechanical level to a more conscious one. This insight might help the teacher become aware of a conflict between what he really does (on the daily, functional level) and what he proclaims he would like to do (on the philosophical level). In turn, this conflict—if strong enough—will need to be resolved, and a search for alternative styles of teaching will begin, a search for styles which isolate the missing link, identify it, and do something about it.

It is suggested that the missing link is the *process* which must take place between the stimuli sent by the teacher and the random responses given by the student—a process which is reflected in organized development of the physical performance, in deliberate experiences for social growth and judgment, in continuous emotional strengthening, and in a chain of situations and problems which elicit the cognitive powers of imagination, discovery, and decision making. It is a process of becoming a freer man!

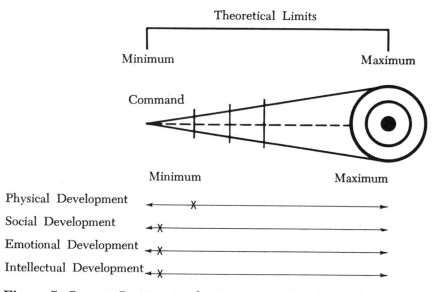

Figure 5. *Present Position in the Spectrum of Styles and the Channels of Development*

3

Teaching by Task

A SHIFT IN DECISION MAKING

To free his students gradually, the teacher must decide which element of the command style can first be taken from the role of the teacher and made part of the role of the student. Let's turn to "Anatomy of the Command Style" (pp. 21-23), review the role of the teacher, and find the one variable which requires the teacher's control (decision-making) the *least*. If we can identify this variable, then we can try to shift the focus from the teacher to the students in this variable only and for a short time in each lesson until the students develop sufficient strength and responsibility to carry out a small task on their own.

Let us seek that variable. In *preparation,* all components must be decided upon by the teacher in order to maintain control over subject matter, organizational patterns needed for a successful lesson, and the discipline or social climate that suits the teacher's set of values. Now we are at the stage of the *execution* of the lesson; all the preparations by the teacher are over, and the lesson begins! Once the class is organized in the desired pattern, the next teaching act is delivery of the task. This is done, as we have seen, by demonstration, by explanation, or by both. We are still clinging to the command style, *but* when we reach the component of *doing,* of performing the activity, the students can be taught to perform on their own.

We can see how we may effectively introduce this new element in the performance of developmental movements. The command style requires control of all variables and uniformity of standards; consequently, movement can commence only when the teacher gives the signal, and movement is performed to a cadence controlled by external

31

media: the teacher's voice, handclapping, a drum beat, a record, or the like. Then, of course, the movement stops when the appropriate signal is delivered. It is suggested that at this point an alternative behavior can be introduced, which will start the process of weaning the students from the command style. Once a task in physical performance has been explained and demonstrated, most students are independent enough to *start* the movement on their own, perform it a certain number of times or for a certain duration, and *stop* on their own.

It may seem like an obvious step in the teaching procedure, but it is *crucial* to be able to identify the difference between self-motivated performance of a *small task* and the performance of the same task under the control of the teacher. Cadence control, which is so important to so many teachers, seems to be based on an aesthetic consideration—that it looks better when many people in a group do the same thing at the same time to the same beat. This may be a valid consideration if the intention of education is to produce *sameness*. It is an absurdity, however, in view of proclaimed educational objectives which so highly value the *individual* as a special and unique entity. Shaw (70) presented a strong condemnation of "sameness" in various activities presented to people who are so different.

This is not only a matter of educational philosophy, it is a serious physiological and psychological issue. Is it not absurd to require the tall and the short, the fat and the slim, the energetic and the phlegmatic to follow as one man the drive of one person—the teacher? If we recognize that individual differences exist and that these differences produce a variety of explicit or implicit needs, then should these needs not be satisfied and treated in a manner other than a communal one?

Permitting the students—in fact, requiring the students—to learn to execute the movement tasks on their own will achieve several goals:

1. Because of the teacher's new behavior, the student will begin to change.
2. This partial shifting of focus to the student may develop more responsibility for his individual performance.
3. Self-motivated execution of the task may suit best the individual's ability, temperament, and aspirations.
4. Individualized learning begins to emerge.
5. Independence from the teacher begins to evolve.
6. Since, at this stage, the student learns to be independent and to control his own performance in small tasks, the teacher's position in decision making and control is not jeopardized. On the contrary, the teacher may gain new strength by using the time of the students'

self-directed performance for observation, for individual corrections, or for individual reinforcement.

7. *The Teacher* begins to gain new freedoms for himself. When he uses the command style, the teacher *must* be at the controls at all times. This can become rather tiresome and is so often wasteful, since the teacher must concern himself with so many irrelevancies. (Occupying one's mouth in counting one to four during a considerable part of one's career is really irrelevant to the noble process of teaching and learning. Moreover, this boring procedure may have an ill effect upon the teacher's personality.)

Teaching by task creates opportunities for new relationships between the teacher and the students and permits the teacher to develop and assume a new role for himself while the students enter a new phase of self-development.

ANATOMY OF THE TASK STYLE

Let us examine the anatomy of this style. (Compare with the anatomy of the command style, pp. 21-23.)

	The Role of the Teacher	*The Role of the Student*
Variable No. 1: *Pre-class* *Preparation*	1. Pre-determines the objectives of the lesson.	Not involved.
	2. Pre-determines the activity which will lead to the accomplishment of the objectives.	Not involved.
	3. Pre-determines the tasks which are the sequential parts of the activity involved. (See below, p. 43, the discussion on insight into subject matter and task determination.)	Not involved.
	At this point Items 4, 5, 6, and 7 in "Anatomy of the Command Style" shift	Beginning to affect the decisions made by the teacher. The stu-

	The Role of the Teacher	*The Role of the Student*
	to the next aspect of teaching, the execution of the lesson. *Decisions* about these elements are beginning to shift and *involve* the student; therefore, they cannot be fully pre-determined by the teacher before the teaching-learning experience begins. These can be better determined and observed while *contact* between the teacher and the students is developed.	dents' varying abilities—differences in performance levels, pace of performance, and quality of performance—are beginning to be *considered*. More direct contact between the students and the teacher begins to evolve.
Variable No. 2: Execution	4. Quantity decisions can be made only in general terms. Differentiation in quantity decisions must consider the levels of individuals in the class or the levels of the ability groups in the class.	Students' abilities affect the *amount* of activity. (Amount of activity can be established either by individuals or by ability groups. See below.)
	5. Quality of performance is not "fixed" on a single standard. Existence of quality differentiation is not only *accepted* by the teacher, it is deliberately expressed by the teacher in order to reinforce those who are "below" the standard the teacher hopes the students will eventually achieve. (See below, p. 45, the discussion of the range of tasks.)	The students understand that there is a place for their present level of performance. The student begins to develop insight into his different level and may begin to feel accepted *despite* the difference between him and the rest of the class.

Comment: Perhaps this is the crucial point which differentiates the task style from the command style. The teacher, by presenting a more flexible task structure, demonstrates a more *accepting* behavior pattern, which has an effect upon the self image of the student as a performer of physical tasks and as an accepted member of a diversified group of peers. This facet of teaching probably exists naturally in some situations. It is suggested here, however, that this be done more frequently, consciously and with deliberation. (The reader is referred to an incisive discussion of deliberate education, in Childs' work [21].)

6. Organizational patterns are less rigid. The differentiations mentioned above necessitate more flexible organizational arrangements which *permit* the students to select the area on the gym floor or on the field. In fact, the student is asked to select the appropriate place for the execution of the task.

The student begins to learn to make decisions concerning his location in relationship to the task at hand. The student becomes less dependent on the teacher in respect to space orientation and space relationships to other members of the class. Certainly a greater degree of responsibility and self-discipline must be developed to do this effectively.

7. Decisions about the kind of discipline vary with the degree of self-discipline and responsibility demonstrated by the class. This means that the *teacher is ready* to help the class develop a kind of discipline which is different from that used in the command style, a discipline which is less rigid and less dependent

The student has the opportunity to exercise a more responsible, self-conducted experience, which leads him to assume a more independent role in the learning process. Even though this occurs only in small tasks or a short sequence of tasks, *it is* the beginning of a

The Role of the Teacher	*The Role of the Student*
on an *external force*, the teacher.	different kind of discipline.
8. Conveys the task information by means of a demonstration, an explanation, or both. Since this style (by definition and concept) shifts some consideration to the ability levels of the students, a more *careful analysis* of the subject matter is needed in relationship to the *class* at hand. General subject matter decisions are inadequate here. For example, inclusion of a given technique of a ball game in a lesson just because it has traditionally been taught at a certain grade level is out of place in this style.	By the nature of the task differentiation process, more students in a given class become more involved in learning the subject matter. More students have the opportunity to relate to some level or some part of the subject matter presented.

Comment: It is common in observation of classes of physical education to hear the teacher complain about the failure of the class to reach the standard of activity performance presumably suited for that grade level. Rather than complain, however, the teacher needs to develop new insights into the structure of the subject matter and the tasks involved in *relation* to the *present* performance level of the class or individuals in the class. This conflict is rather common in school and is, no doubt, a result of a rigid acceptance of graded materials which at best were arbitrarily decided by various experts. One must note that this conflict does not exist when the command style is used. By definition, in the command style subject matter decisions are pre-determined, and if the class does not adhere to the standard or does not reach the expectations of the teacher, then the conclusion is rather simple—since in essence it is also pre-determined—that the *class* must be below standard.

9. Starting time for activities can vary from student to student—not all need to start together at a given signal; since readiness for activity varies, the starting time can vary too.

The students start the activity on their own without waiting for a *specific* starting signal.

10. The duration of performance varies according to the present abilities of students. A general statement to stop action can be given to conclude the tasks in which they are engaged.

When the statement to stop is given by the teacher, the students complete their assigned task and then get ready for the next phase or step in the lesson. Ending time will not be the same for all (within reason, all should stop within a two- to three-minute interval, perhaps), since different students are engaged in different tasks. Some students always need more time to complete an assignment.

Comment: The teacher can utilize the time interval for correcting and reinforcing comments to various students. It may "feel" peculiar in the beginning, since some teacher classes are so accustomed to a tradition of uniformity, but in time one can learn to relax and adjust to the alternative arrangement.

11. It follows that the teacher is not engaged in *counting* numbers as a rhythm support to developmental movement, nor does he count the number of turns in basketball

Once the students understand the task presented to them by explanation or by demonstration, they can proceed on their own, performing the move-

The Role of the	*The Role of the*
Teacher	*Student*

shooting practice or the like. (This is not a disparagement of the need to teach rhythms. An argument against using a single rhythm for all, all the time, however, was developed previously. See p. 27.)

ments at their own pace and to their own rhythm.

Not needing to count (or to use other means of rhythm support) *frees* the teacher to move about, observe, make corrections, offer evaluations, or just talk to the students. It is a most rewarding experience for both teacher and students. The teacher may have the opportunity to listen to what the *student* has to say.

Any student will appreciate a periodical direct, quiet comment by a teacher. The physical proximity of a teacher can have a fine effect on the student who is accustomed to being talked to in a "broadcasting" fashion by a remote teacher. The student may have the opportunity to talk directly to the teacher, in a personal manner.

12. Termination time of the task was discussed under Item 10.

13. In this style of teaching something important happens to an unfathomed dimension of learning—motivation. At present, we are not attempting to discuss the relative merits of different kinds

of motivation. This is merely to describe the change in motivation when the student is on the way to independence.

In the command style, the motivation is primarily promoted by the very kind of relationship that exists between the student and the teacher. The authority of the teacher, if accepted by the student, provides the bulk of the motivation; the wish to please the teacher is a common motivational force. It is necessary, however, to acknowledge the existence of self-motivation. When command is used, forces such as the need to excel, the need for recognition, and the like serve as tremendous motivations for success in learning. There is no doubt that extrinsic motivation can produce magnificent results.

Since, however, the premise of *Teaching Physical Education: From Command to Discovery* is that education should encourage the process of growth, the process of emerging and becoming independent, it is imperative to *identify* the kind of change in motivation which occurs when one

The Role of the Teacher

The Role of the Student

moves along the spectrum of styles.

In teaching by task, subject matter is presented with more consideration of individual differences; the source of some motivation *shifts* from the teacher to the students. More students can see themselves as *successful* performers at some level of the task. The variety of tasks presented *is within reach.* Furthermore, the *accomplishment* of the task *is* the motivating agent which is most powerful and most enduring.

The assumption is that if this occurs frequently enough the motivation becomes internalized or intrinsic, and this in turn adds a dimension to independence. (For a fuller discussion on motivation the reader is referred to Cratty [25], Chap. 8.)

It is imperative to exercise a greater degree of patience, even if some students *do not* perform their tasks initially; they will come around. *Teachers and students alike need time to learn the use of a new style.*

It has been observed that when students are given a *range of tasks* within their abilities to perform, a greater interest in the activity evolves as a result of successful attempt at performance. Equally important is the factor of *choice* of alternative standards which is inherent in the concept of a *range of tasks.*

The students begin to realize their limitations and perhaps to accept them. The opportunity to try out tasks at varying levels is usually welcomed by students of all levels of accomplishment.

It must be emphasized again that the teacher's offering alternatives and behaving in an *accepting* way only *initiate* the students' new look into their own actions and reactions. The students will be seeking a consistent

		teacher-behavior pattern and will need periodic reassurances to continue their self-controlled learning process.
Variable No. 3: *Evaluation*	14. Determines dismissal time or carries out the general school policy for dismissal time.	Follows the dismissal procedures.
	15. Although the greater part of evaluating performance remains in the hands of the teacher, the teacher *begins to differentiate* evaluation standards to comply with the differentiation of the *range of tasks.*	A degree of self-evaluation begins to develop in a meaningful way, since the student has to learn to select the tasks which are within his ability to perform.

SOME SUGGESTIONS FOR PROCEDURES

The purpose of using alternative styles is to teach the student to increase his capacity for decision making. This increase seems to occur step by step as new kinds of behavior are understood and assimilated by the student. It is important to develop a variety of techniques for each style in order to inculcate in the students the essence of the anticipated behavior. The structure and purpose of a teaching style determine the specific techniques that are best suited for carrying it out.

Organizational patterns on the floor, the vocabulary used, and the social-emotional climate in the class are all tools in the hands of the teacher. It is not by chance that a list of specific command terminology has evolved in physical education. This vocabulary is not designed for general communication purposes; it aims at a particular *kind* of communication which clearly defines the role of the teacher and the expected role of the students as described in "Anatomy of the Command Style." Teaching by task, however, presupposes a different kind of relationship between the teacher and the students; therefore, communication techniques, as well as organizational patterns and the social-emotional climate, must also be treated in a different manner.

It is not difficult to find alternatives to a rigid organizational pattern. Random organization on the floor proves to be satisfactory for almost all activities. "Spread out in the gymnasium!" is a common way of telling the students to position themselves in this way. You might need to add, at first, some suggestions, such as "Make sure you do not touch your neighbor when you move around." You will find that when you request a random spread from classes that are accustomed to a specific pattern, the members of the class tend to congregate in one part of the gymnasium, usually rather far away from *you*, the teacher. On a second attempt, they will form a semi-circle around you. Don't despair! Ask the class once more to spread out and fill all the empty spaces on the floor. Remember that this random arrangement in the gymnasium may be new to them.

Random organization improves communication. If you choose to demonstrate, you have a better chance of being seen by all when the students are randomly organized; the straight line arrangement usually curtails the field of vision; and if you choose to demonstrate on a higher platform (vaulting box or the like) so students standing in a straight line can see you, you are removed even farther from the class.

One of the best techniques of demonstration is to tell your students to come near so that they can really see every detail of the demonstration; just call them to come close to you. This technique has been used by coaches for years with great success. *The physical proximity* adds a human dimension to the process of communication.

There are more advantages to this technique. When your students are close to you, you talk to people, specific people, not to a crowd. You can see their reactions, their responses. Certainly, this physical proximity has an important effect on the second avenue of communication: the verbal explanation. All you need to do is talk to your students, using your normal voice, your natural voice modulation, facial expression, pauses for thought, and so on. It is amazing to observe the kind of relationship that can develop as a result of this personal contact. There is really no need to stand away from the group and use the commonly heard "projected voice." Talk to your students; don't shout at them!

Now, to class procedure: First, assemble the students close to you. Then demonstrate and explain the tasks (preferably one at a time). Next, ask the students to resume their positions on the gym floor and perform the desired task. While performance goes on, *move about; observe individuals;* offer comments to individuals. Here is time available for just that. Before long you will have communicated individually with most or all of your students (even in larger classes). It may take two or three lessons before you get to everyone, but by that time your students will realize your genuine intent to establish individual contact. They will continue to assimilate the value of this manner of teaching. When the task seems to have been completed by most or all students, call them back to you (and you may be at a different point in the gymnasium) and proceed with the next task. The dispersement and assembly, in addition to aiding communication, helps break the monotony that is present in traditional organizational patterns.

You will find that the random organization on the floor can be used as a diagnostic tool to identify more quickly individuals who need your guidance in physical performance. In accord with the premise that physical inadequacy creates a degree of emotional discomfort when physical performance is called for in public, you will find that those who are for some reason insecure will tend to seek the more remote corners of the gymnasium. In one extreme case of such insecurity a successful athlete, when asked to perform a new physical activity, chose the hall leading to the gymnasium as his "spot" on the floor. This kind of identification of a need for guidance cannot occur as frequently when students are told where to stand or perform. These incidents are clues to more complex behavior patterns, and a keen observer can pick up these broadcast signals and use them as guides in his educational relationship with the student.

TASKS IN A GIVEN SUBJECT MATTER

The division of subject matter into tasks can take the following forms:

1. A single task for the entire class.
2. A sequence of tasks for the entire class, leading to the accomplishment of a given movement or activity.
3. A range of tasks within the single major task, of varying degrees of difficulty and based on analysis of the parts of the subject matter (see Mosston [56], Chap. 1). This is an excellent device for individualization of performance. The range of tasks accommodates the novice as well as the advanced performer.

You will recall that the command style limits recognition of individual differences by presenting to everyone, and by demanding that everyone reach, a single standard. In order to aid the individualization process, the concept of a range of tasks is very valuable. It calls for presenting the class with several tasks which permit everyone in the class to participate according to present ability. The range of tasks to be used is determined by task differentiation to suit the range of abilities which exist in every class. Examples in various areas of activity will follow. Let us talk some more about the values derived from this concept. Suppose you present your class with a range of tasks in developmental movement, basketball, volleyball, etc.; your initial tasks are on three or four different levels of performance (quantitatively and/or qualitatively); and each individual has to select a level for performance. What kinds of decisions may *each* student make?

1. The student may decide *not* to be involved in this operation at all.
2. The student may decide to attempt this process of self-decision (within the framework that you proposed).
3. The student may try to discover his present level of performance by attempting the task at the level that he thinks may be presently possible for him. If the level tried is satisfactory, then this is the level at which the student performs before moving to the more advanced task. If, however, the attempt is not successful, the student will need to try the next-lower task in the range. In either case, the process of self-assessment is begun, and the need to learn to accept oneself within one's present limits becomes real to the student. The important aspect of this realization is that in this style of teaching there *is* a place for *each* and *every* student. It has been observed that students who rarely participate with any degree of zest or enjoyment and usually drift away from most activities are slowly drawn back to the class when the task style of teaching is used. They seem to have found a place for themselves within the range of tasks, a place which is recognized and accepted by the teacher and by the student's peers.
4. The last decision that the student must make is to carry out the task. This overt behavior, the actual performance of the task, is a basic objective in education, is it not?

Let us now speculate on the results of the decisions which were made by the student. If the decision was not to take part in this operation (Decision 1)—which, of course, could also happen within the experience of teaching by command—then you must make decisions concerning the reasons for this behavior and how to treat this response. In most instances this can be best handled individually after the class, when a one to one relationship can exist. If Decisions 2, 3, and 4 are in evidence, then, it seems that the following steps in learning *have actually occurred:*

1. The students have accepted your new teaching role. Your behavior has opened up new avenues of freedom for your students, and they

have learned to accept you in your new role; they are ready to anticipate similar behavior next time.

2. The students have learned that *being different* is not a crime! In fact,
they have learned that you recognize individual differences by presenting them with *a choice*.

3. The students have learned to see themselves as different—they may
have even begun to accept their difference (or the different).

4. Each student has had to begin to learn to assess his abilities, accept
his present limitations, and operate within them, without necessarily
competing constantly with some of his peers who are more
advanced.

5. Chances are that because the student has found a place for himself,
reinforcement, rather than dissolution, is at work.

6. By performing on his own level, the student has learned to execute
and enjoy the activity which otherwise might be out of reach.

7. Having experienced the enormous pleasure of success, the student
has learned that he *is* capable of learning; and he may be motivated
to learn again, to learn more.

These are important accomplishments in the educational process, leading the individual toward greater independence.

DESIGNING THE RANGE OF TASKS

The range of tasks in a given activity for a given class can be based
on *quantitative* measures or on *qualitative* standards. Results of certain
activities can be measured with concrete numerical units: ten laps
around the field, twenty-five push-ups in a given position, one mile
under five minutes, ten out of twelve shots in basketball. These quantitative measures can serve as guides to the establishment of a range of
tasks in certain activities.

Other activities are usually measured by qualitative standards which
are observable: A compact roll can be evaluated only after various
qualitative standards have been established for the given class, school,
etc. Standards can vary from quality decisions made by the students
themselves to Olympic standards. The important point is that *a* standard or *several* standards have been established to form the basis for a
range of tasks, so that a beginning performer may try to reach a simple
level of performance which involves relatively few controls, while the
advanced student in the same class may try to reach a higher level of
performance.

"Quality of performance" ("form" in traditional terminology) refers to
the performance of a *given movement* in a *particular way*. In fact, this

particularization of a movement—which is pre-designed and pre-determined by the performer, by the choreographer, or by the Olympic Gymnastics Committee—is the device closest to "objective judgment." It is important to recognize both the qualitative and quantitative avenues of evaluation because both can be used in designing the range of tasks. It is even possible to use the qualitative measures where usually only quantitative measures really count. An example that comes to mind is foul shots in basketball. Suppose you establish a range as follows:

Objective Level No. 1: five goals out of ten shots (using "your" most convenient shot)
Objective Level No. 2: same as No. 1 twice (with a short interval while others shoot)
Objective Level No. 3: five out of ten using a different shot

Now, determining the level of a student will depend only on a quantitative fulfillment of the requirement, as if the student answered the question: How many? In a *real* game situation this is what counts! However, for learning purposes, in order to heighten concentration and present a greater challenge, you may establish the following tasks:

Objective Level No. 4: five goals out of ten shots—counting only the *clean* baskets
Objective Level No. 5: five *consecutive* goals
Objective Level No. 6: five *consecutive clean* goals

Here you find the added qualitative measure, which is operative in conjunction with the qualitative measure. This combination is applicable not only to ball games; it can be used in gymnastics, where usually the qualitative measure dominates the evaluation:

Objective Level No. 1: Perform a forward roll with one leg bent and the other fully extended.

The evaluation here is qualitative in nature, since we are looking for the execution of a particular movement in a specific manner. By introducing the quantitative measure the level of this task rises:

Objective Level No. 2: Perform the roll *three consecutive* times.

This quantitative addition affects the quality of performance, thus demanding more of the performer.

Certainly *changes* in the qualitative *and* quantitative demands will create a whole range, or perhaps series of ranges, of tasks in the activity to be learned. It is necessary to remember that this manipulation of subject matter is supported by the following beliefs:

1. A breakdown of subject matter promotes easier learning for more students, perhaps for all!
2. Interest and motivation will increase, and more frequent success in performance will occur.
3. New insights by the student as well as the teacher into the structure of subject matter tend to evolve.

EXAMPLES OF RANGES OF TASKS
IN VARIOUS ACTIVITIES

Developmental Movement (Quantitative Differentiation)

Suppose that one of the purposes for a given lesson or a group of lessons is to develop strength in the arms and the shoulder girdle and that the selected movement which will help accomplish this purpose is the push-up; then the next step is to establish various tasks to accommodate and challenge all members of the class. It must be understood that it is more realistic to establish the range when the limits (minimum and maximum) in the given class have been established. This can be determined in one or two lessons by testing the class in the performance of the selected movements.

The following might be included in a range of tasks for the push-up:

Task No. 1: Try to establish your *maximum*—maximum number of push-ups in a given position. Example: Hands under the shoulders, at shoulders' width. The body remains straight throughout the movement.

The chances are that each member of the class will have reached a different maximum (M). This M, then, can serve as a task for subsequent lessons until members of the class are asked to test themselves again in order to find a possible new M, an indication that strength development has occurred.

Task No. 2: The next possibility is to practice the push-up with *less* than maximum effort and thereby establish a different task for the individual.

We learn in physiology that the repetition of movement with less than maximum load is desirable for strength development. This offers us a clue to the kinds of tasks possible. By repetition of a fraction of the maximum one can be led from task to task. Suppose student A's maximum is twenty push-ups; then he can practice "sets" containing only one-half maximum $\left(\dfrac{M}{2} = 10\right)$, with short intervals of rest between sets. It has been observed that practicing for strength in sets of one-half maximum is rather comfortable for most students. The number of repetitions of the set will vary with the development of strength. After a while the M will change. More ambitious students may choose to practice tasks which consist of two-thirds M or four-fifths M and repeat these sets several times every lesson.

This approach virtually establishes the task on an individual level, which is in concert with the philosophy of individualized learning.

Task No. 3: If, however, the teacher finds it rather difficult to conduct the class on this individualized basis, another possibility exists: *arbitrary task differentiation*. Let us assume that the preliminary performance test shows the limits of your class to be ten and forty-two. That is, at least one student could perform only ten push-ups, and at least one could do forty-two. The rest of the class is in between. Now, you may suggest to your students to practice *one* of the following tasks: (1) five to ten push-ups, (2) eleven to fifteen push-ups, (3) sixteen to twenty, (4) twenty-one to twenty-five, and so on, up to forty-two.

The division of tasks by intervals of five is arbitrary. You may try other rank ordering. In presenting this range to your class, you will find the class instantly divided into ability groups. You may ask them to stay and practice on this present level for several lessons before attempting the next level.

Task No. 4: Another possible change is to vary the position of the body and arms for the execution of the push-ups. Example: By moving the supporting arms more to the side (or front, etc.) one changes the base for the push-up and thus, kinesiologically, creates tasks which are more difficult and challenging to the more advanced students (56).

With this new task you can incorporate some or all of the previous possibilities. Thus, you manipulate one movement in a quantitative way to accommodate the concept of range of tasks of a style of teaching which strives to recognize and reach more individuals.

Another example in developmental movement is the assignment of quantitative tasks in the strengthening of the abdominal muscles. Sup-

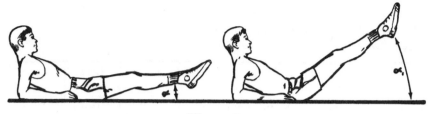

Figure 6.

pose we take the common movement of leg lifts while the upper part of the body is in a slight back-leaning position supported on the forearms. Two major factors at this position can affect the development of a stronger abdomen: (1) duration—holding the position longer (or performing a variety of leg movements through the duration of the "hold" position) and (2) height. The height to which the legs are raised off the supporting base affect the degree of difficulty of the position or the movements in the given position. The higher the legs the *easier* the position.

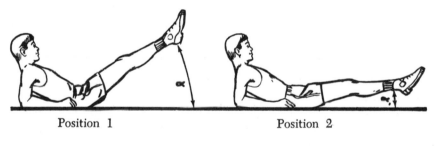

Position 1   Position 2

Figure 7

Position 1 is easier than Position 2. (For a fuller discussion on degree of difficulty, see Mosston [56].)

Now, these two factors actually help us determine the kind of tasks possible here and the range of tasks. A table of tasks might look like the one on page 50. The table of tasks, of course, should be adjusted and designed according to the ability of the class or group you teach. This approach to task differentiation provides the teacher with endless task possibilities. The teacher can start with the minimum-quantity task for the weaker ones in the class and increase the maximum (Levels 3, 4, 5, etc.) for the stronger ones.

These tasks can be presented to the class orally or in a written form. If a Mimeographed form is used, the student can check off his achieve-

Table of Tasks

Purpose: Development of abdominal strength

Suggested Movement: Position as shown

Task	Developing Factor	Kind	Level 1	Level 2	Level 3
No. 1	Duration	Static (isometric)	20 seconds	30–40 seconds	Your decision
No. 2	Duration	Dynamic (isotonic)	Vertical Scissors 20 times	30 times	Your decision
No. 3	Height	Static	20 seconds at 45 degrees	at 30 degrees	Increase no. of seconds. Decrease angle of legs.
No. 4	Height	Dynamic	Vertical Scissors 20 times; legs at 45 degrees	at 30 degrees	Your decision

ment and progress after every class, and this record can serve as a check list and an evaluation tool for the teacher.

A very important feature of this style of teaching is the need to develop better insight into the structure of subject matter. In attempting to design the table of tasks, the range of tasks, and the levels within the task, the teacher must study the task, review its purpose, judge its appropriateness, and determine what factors or variables affect the determination of levels of performance. Often, one must rely on kinesiological analysis of the task and seek support in current physiological findings. (For example, the issue of massing *vs.* distributing practice affects the task distribution in a lesson or lessons. For further discussion and research references, see Cratty [25] Chap. 12.)

Another quantitative table of tasks in a developmental movement appears on p. 51.

Developmental Movement (Qualitative Differentiation)

In developmental movement the qualitative standard of a movement is determined by what the teacher considers to be fair, good, or better

Table of Tasks

Purpose: Development of flexibility of the trunk (laterally)

Suggested Movement: At a straddle position, with varying positions of the arms—lateral bending of the trunk

Factors Affecting Flexibility Quantity at This Position: (1) Duration—the number of repetitions in bending. (2) Extent—the distance the segment of the body "travels" toward the end flexible position (See Fleishman [33]). (3) Fixation of the base. The more fixed the base, the more difficult the bending movement. (4) Lever effect. It changes by moving the arms from the hip to extension above the head.

Task	Developing Factor	*Level 1*	*Level 2*	*Level 3*
No. 1	Duration	Alternate sides (6 times to each side)	Alternate sides (12 times to each side)	?
No. 2	Duration	Hands on hips (6 times to each side)	Hands on hips (12 times to each side)	?
No. 3	Extent	Bend to the side until you feel that the muscles on the other side pull.	Bend to the side (slowly!) beyond the point of feeling the pull.	Determine the next extent. *Do not exaggerate!*
No. 4	Base fixation	Perform the above bending movements in a straddle position, each leg at 45-degree angle to the base.	Perform the above with a wider base.	Approach *your* maximum in straddle; perform the above.
No. 5	Lever effect	Perform the above with hands on hips.	Place your palms behind your neck.	Extend your arms above your head loosely.

performance. Performance tasks can be assigned with this differentiation in mind. It offers varying degrees of "goodness" to the student and follows, in principle, the concept of this style of teaching.

Suppose we examine the forward roll and determine the different *controls of performance* which the performer is required to execute in order to be considered a good performer. First, we must decide on the details of the *correct form* of the forward roll. This, as mentioned previously, demands an understanding of this movement, what it is, its purpose, its intrinsic structure, and the possible variations. An examination of this specific movement leads us to the realization that it is a forward rotary motion which can be performed with the following variables affecting its details:

Variable 1: Body posture. *Variations:* (*a*) Compact (minimum posture)—all joints bent. (*b*) Extended (maximum posture)—all joints approaching extension, with some fully extended. (*c*) In between—combinations of *a* and *b*.

Variable 2: Plane of motion. *Variations:* (*a*) All segments of the body move in one plane. (*b*) One or more segments move in other planes.

Variable 3: Speed. *Variations:* Speed variation on a continuum, from the *slowest* to the *fastest* (within the safety limitation!).

Variable 4: Rhythm. *Variations:* (*a*) Fluent unified motion. (*b*) Fluent un-unified motion. (*c*) Non-fluent unified motion (staccato); (*d*) Non-fluent un-unified motion.

This analysis of the forward roll is offered merely to point out the many possibilities of performance and *good form*, depending on the criteria of goodness. Thus, the learner can be observed and evaluated in performance of this multiple-task approach to the forward roll, and the teacher can, of course, select the tasks or range of tasks to suit his students' qualitative levels of performance (see p. 53). These variations serve as important psychological factors in motivation in addition to contributing to better neuromuscular control of performance.

Track and Field (Quantitative Differentiation)

Activity (event): running broad jump; *purpose:* to achieve maximum distance in the jump.

Here again, the first step in establishing the tasks which will aid the jumper is the analysis of the broad jump. One needs to understand the components of the broad jump, the variables involved, and the possible variations in movement which will lead the performer through a range of experiences until he reaches his optimum performance.

The variables in the broad jump are:

Variable 1: The approach run. *Variations:* (*a*) Change of distance of approach. (*b*) Change in speed. (*c*) Change in rhythm.

Variable 2: The take-off posture. *Variations:* (*a*) Left foot take-off. (*b*) Right foot take-off. (*c*) Changes in the leaning angle of the body.

Table of Tasks

Task	Variable	Variations
1	Body posture	Compact roll, all joints bent (minimum).
2	Body posture	Compact roll, all joints bent *except one.*
3	Body posture	Compact roll, all possible joints extended (maximum).
4	Body posture	Compact roll, extended joint or joints on one side.
5	Body posture	Compact roll, alternate the side of the bent and extended joints.
6	Plane of motion	While in forward roll (select any of the previous tasks) move one of the body segments in a different direction. Example: Extend your left leg sideways while rolling.
7	Plane of motion	Alternate sides and parts of the body.
8	Plane of motion	Change the angle of the direction.
9	Speed	Perform any of the previous tasks in slow motion.
10	Speed	Try *your* slowest! Maintain the accuracy of all the details of the task!
11	Speed	Try a variety of speeds and find out the comfortable ones for you and those which seem to disturb your performance.
12	Speed	Try your fastest forward roll, performing any or all the previous tasks (observe safety).
13	Rhythm	Perform the whole movement in one continuous fluent motion. Keep the whole movement unified in speed.
14	Rhythm	Perform a part of the roll fluently in a given rhythm, (example: relatively slowly) and fluently combine with the next part of the roll with relative speed.
15	Rhythm	Perform a small part of the roll (just bending down towards the mat) and *stop* for a fraction of a second; then continue with another part of the roll (the first half of the roll so that you can stop on your back) and stop again. Continue, complete the roll, and get up.
16	Can you figure out another variable?	Can you design other variations which will make you aware of each aspect of the movements?

Variable 3: The posture in flight. *Variations:* (*a*) Compact (minimum). (*b*) Extended (maximum). (*c*) In between, or combination of *a* and *b*. (*d*) Positions of the appendages in the air.

Variable 4: The posture in landing. *Variations:* (*a*) Compact (minimum). (*b*) Extended (maximum). (*c*) Combinations.

Now, each variation in each variable can serve as *a task* to be learned and practiced *independently*, in *varying combinations*, and in *sequence* until the best possible sequence produces the best results for a given performer. The learning process on the way to this best achievement calls for the manipulations of the above variables and variations by each individual performer. The following is a quantitative table of tasks for the *learner* of the broad jump (it might also apply to the expert performer who might need improvement of a *small aspect* of the jump and by manipulation of variations he may find the way to improve).

Table of Tasks

Activity: Broad jump

Task	*Variable*	*Variations*
1	The approach run	*a)* Run a short distance (5 steps) and take off.
		b) Increase the distance to 10 steps and take off.
		c) Change of speed: Increase the total speed over the entire distance.
		d) Change of speed: Start faster and end faster at take-off.
		e) Change of speed: Start rather slowly and increase the speed to almost maximum before take-off.
		f) Change of rhythm: Increase the speed *gradually* during the approach run.
		g) Change of rhythm: Start fast, slow down for a few steps and go back to original speed toward take-off.
		h) Try *your own combinations* of speeds.
		i) Any other variations of the approach run?
2	The take-off position	*a)* Try all the variations proposed in the first variable and use your left foot for take-off.
		b) Repeat the above and use the right foot.
		c) Try a short approach run (approximately 10 steps) and use a *very short last step* before take-off. This will affect the angle of the body in relation to the ground during the take-off. Study its effect on the jumper.
		d) Repeat *c* with a longer last step and study its effects on the jumper's take-off. (You could measure each jump, or several jumps with the *same* last step, and compare the results.)
		e) Now try the same approach run with a *very large* last step. Obviously the body angle will change considerably at take-off, and the entire jump will

		be affected. *Experimentation* with these variations will help you find the optimum last step for optimum jump.
		f) Repeat this procedure with varying *distances* of the approach run and varying speed until you discover the *correct* combination for your jumper.
3	The posture in flight	*a)* Compact (minimum): After take-off, raise your knees as close to your chest as you can; extend your arms forward.
		b) Extended (maximum): Immediately after take-off, reach with your arms upward and extend your body as if you were hanging in the air. (You could use a horizontal rope, hung at various heights, as a target for touching while in flight.)
		c) The pike: Immediately after take-off, while you hang in the air, start moving both legs close to a pike position in the air and complete the flight in this "sitting in the air" position.
		d) Vary each one of the above positions by *changing* the position of *one* segment of the body while the body is in the air (example: Send one arm midways, or bend your head in one direction). *These* variations will help the jumper identify the *effect* of superfluous motion on the flight, and they may help the jumper find *his* best form. This proposal for awareness of body orientation in the air may in many instances be superior to the natural form that the beginner exhibits on his first attempts.
4	Posture in landing	*a)* Compact: From *each* of the previous flights try landing in a *low* squat position.
		b) Try a slight knee-bending position as landing posture.
		c) From the previous flights try an extended-body landing. (Make sure you land on a very soft spot!)
		d) Vary the legs' position in any of the suggested landing postures and find out the one for you.
5	Combinations	This task is the most advanced in the range. It requires of the jumper to try various combinations of the suggested variations in all the variables. This will end with the best possible integration of variables for a most successful jump.

This table of tasks is an example of the detailed possibilities that an analytic coach and teacher could use in order to gain greater understanding of the jump itself and at the same time create a great variety of interesting situations for the *various* performers, all designed to stimulate the neuromuscular process and develop the performance.

Comment: The variations of the body posture in flight and in landing may appear to require to a qualitative judgment, since it is difficult to measure them; however, they are really quantitative differences if one considers them with the degree of mechanical difficulty in mind.

Rope Climbing (Quantitative Differentiation)

Here again, the first step is to analyze rope climbing. Which is the most obvious variable? Is it not the kind of climb, with or without the aid of the legs? This is a primary factor in rope climbing; it separates the novice from the advanced, the weak from the strong.

Since the main purpose of rope climbing is to develop strength of the arms and the shoulder girdle, this differentiation can serve as the first step:

Variable 1: The number of points of contact between the body and the rope
Variable 2: Height: from the lowest to the highest
Variable 3: Weight: (*a*) with added external weight, (*b*) with change of body position
Variable 4: Speed: from slowest to fastest or vice versa

Each variable can serve as a *different task* for different ability levels in the class, and variations within each variable will illustrate the range of tasks (see first Table of Tasks, p. 57).

Gymnastics (Qualitative Differentiation)

Activity: the handstand. (See second Table of Tasks, pp. 57-58.)

Variable 1: The kind of ascent: number of legs used in the swing-up, position of the swinging legs, no momentum—"the press."
Variable 2: The degree of support: from handstand against a wall (or a partner) to free handstand.
Variable 3: Posture: compact to extended, change in the vertical line.
Variable 4: Base of support: narrow to wide, various levels, various planes.

The examples given throughout this chapter of different tasks and ranges of tasks will provide the teacher with opportunities to accommodate all levels of ability and success in the class. Other tasks can be added or deleted to fit the qualitative level of performance of individuals in the class.

Table of Tasks

Task	Variable	Variations
1	Number of points of contact	*a)* Climbing up *and* down using both hands and feet. *b)* Using *both* legs and one hand only. (This task will require more strength in the legs and knowledge of the techniques of using the legs.) *c)* Use two hands and one leg.
2	Height	*a)* Start with each of the previous variations and climb a few "steps" upward. The weakest student can start from no-step. Just hang for a few seconds in the particular hold. (Variable 1, all the variations.) *b)* Gradually increase the number of "steps" or feet (if exact measurement is sought). *c)* On reaching the maximum height of the available rope, when you climb down *do not* get off the rope! Instead, start upward again a few feet. Develop this until you can climb the rope twice without touching the floor.
3	Weight	*a)* Add external weight—Wear a knapsack with some weights in it. *b)* Hold a medicine ball (various weights) between your ankles.
	Change of body position	*c)* Raise your knees as you climb. *d)* Climb in L position. *e)* Climb in V position. *f)* Climb in other body positions you may invent.
4	Speed	*a)* Climb very slowly—your slowest! *b)* Climb the fastest you can! *c)* Climb in "half" your speed. *d)* Other fractions of your fastest speed. *e)* You can use *speed* by decreasing the time interval between climbs: 15 seconds rest between first and second attempt, 30 seconds between second and third climb. *Vary* the length of the intervals.

Table of Tasks

Task	Variable	Variations
1	Kind of ascent	*a)* One-bent-leg swing-up. *b)* One-straight-leg swing-up. *c)* Two-bent-legs swing-up. *d)* Two-straight-legs swing-up. *e)* "Press" from squat position—bent arms. *f)* "Press" from squat position—straight arms.

Task	*Variable*	*Variations*
		g) "Press" from straddle—bent arms and legs.
		h) "Press" from straddle—bent arms and straight legs.
		i) "Press" from straddle—straight arms and straight legs.
		j) "Press" from standing position, feet together—arms? (your decision); legs?
2	Degree of support	*a)* Execute a handstand against the wall.
		b) Repeat with only *one* foot touching the wall.
		c) Alternate foot support with momentary "hesitation" in the air.
		d) Repeat *a*, *b*, and *c* against a partner's hand.
		e) Repeat against *less* than a full hand: partner's three fingers, two fingers, one finger! (Observe *safety*—Do not use with beginners!)
		f) Try against a wall; but first hesitate and stay in the air for a short while, and only when you lose balance, lean against the wall.
		g) Free handstand.
3	Posture	*a)* Using each of the previous ascent possibilities and each of possibilities of degree of support, keep your body in a compact position.
		b) Repeat with more body extension.
		c) Repeat with full extension.
		d) Try with all joints bent.
		e) Try with all joints bent at approximately the same angle. (It is great fun to try a handstand with 90 degree angle at the elbows, knees, hips, and so on —quite a challenging task!)
		f) While in handstand position move one leg away from the vertical line.
		g) Repeat *f* with both legs away from the vertical line.
4	Base of support	*a)* Both hands on the floor at shoulders' width on the same line (plane).
		b) Hands at shoulders' width, one hand ahead of the other.
		c) Same plane, narrow the base.
		d) Same plane, hands touching each other.
		e) Same plane; widen the base!
		f) Same plane, the widest base!
		g) Change planes and widths.
		h) High degree of difficulty: repeat *a–g* and use the fingers instead of the palm.
		i) High degree of difficulty: repeat *a–g* and use the flat part of the fists as a base.

ORGANIZATIONAL APPROACHES

The task style of teaching can be used with all levels and with small or large classes. In fact, teaching by task is a very useful way of teaching large classes because the *teacher is freer* to move about, observe students in learning their tasks, and communicate with students on an individual level. The degree of freedom which is accorded to the student in return frees the teacher from sitting at the controls all the time.

When this style is in good operation, the teacher can afford to be at any point of the gymnasium, communicating with one or a few students, and be assured that the rest of the class is engaged in performing the task. It has been observed that when a class learns to be more self-reliant, the *discipline* problems in large classes are reduced, and learning and accomplishments increase.

This style can be executed on the following organizational levels: (*a*) mass level (a large class), (*b*) levels of ability groups within the class, (*c*) individual level.

The Mass Level

When you use this style with the entire class, present to the class *one* task at a time and let the students perform it according to each one's ability. Then you present the second task, and so on.

You can present two, three, or four variations of the task at a time (range of tasks) and let each student select the variation he can perform. You will see your large class in action, with many different individuals doing many *seemingly different* things but actually performing variations of the same task. The uninitiated may find this sight a bit confusing in the beginning; but if the concept of individualization is strong, then it is possible to get used to this sight. The learning which results and the zest of participation outweigh any need for unified group performance.

It is important to discuss the advantages of this style with the students. The teacher must explain to the student the shift in his behavior and in the kind of expectations he has for *their* behavior. Students who are accustomed to the command style, especially in large classes, may interpret the shift to task teaching as weakness and laxity on the teacher's part, unless the concept is explained and followed through. It may be worthwhile to try it at first for only a few minutes and to use an activity in which the students feel rather comfortable. If success is achieved in this initial conduct of the style, the class should be reinforced, and the advantages of this style should be again pointed out to the class in *conjunction* with their achievement in the given activity. *Since this behavior is new to the class, they must learn the basic behavior before they can use it in learning an activity.*

Levels of Ability Groups Within the Class

In large classes heterogeneity is quite notable, and the concept of the range of tasks is very useful. The procedure here will determine the organizational pattern of the class:

1. The teacher presents (by explanation, demonstration, or both) the range.
2. Each student selects his appropriate task. (Most students know what they *can* do. Those who do not will try to find out.)
3. The teacher assigns an area on the floor for each task.
4. The students move to the area of their task choice.
5. At this point the class *is divided* into ability groups.
6. The students in each group proceed to perform their task.
7. The teacher, after observation, may recommend the necessary adjustments in group membership.
8. The groups are ready for the next step in their respective tasks.

The advantage in the arrangement is the feeling of group membership which develops on *all* levels. There is, also, the opportunity to learn to accept people who are on different levels of performance.

Another advantage may be observed in the development of group competition. This phase, though, must be carefully observed and guided by the teacher to avoid excessive admiration of the most advanced group or groups, which can destroy the very purposes of teaching by task. The first step has been made toward differentiation, individualization, and acceptance of oneself in a new role.

The Individual Level

For a discussion of teaching at the individual level, see Chapter 6, "The Individual Program."

SOME IMPLICATIONS OF TEACHING BY TASK

Implications for Use of Equipment

Since the essence of this style is full participation—everybody participates in some suitable level of activity—it becomes necessary to examine the impact of this style on the distribution and use of equipment during the physical education class. Here again, a shift from the patterns customarily used when the command style is employed is necessary. The command style rests on the concept of the teacher's full control; when it is used, one can observe situations like this: Thirty elementary school children stand in a circle. The *teacher*, in the center, holds *one* ball; and one by one the children receive a pass from the teacher and are asked to throw the ball back. There is no need to discuss here efficiency of learning—the lack of it is quite obvious. The use of equipment is determined by the degree of freedom accorded to the students and by the degree of control needed by the teacher. When the teacher uses *one* ball as the center of action, all students *must* observe the teacher, listen to the teacher's instructions, and follow his commands.

This procedure is *not* uncommon in high schools. In fact, too frequently one observes long lines of students assembled near the basket, the parallel bars, the mat or any other piece of equipment. All stand there and wait in orderly fashion (in orderly schools) for their *infrequent* turn to shoot a basket, perform one mount on the bars and so on. This procedure is *incompatible* with efficient learning, motivation, and discipline.

The use of the *task* style, particularly the use of the *range of tasks*, provides the teacher with opportunities for the efficient use of equipment, space, and time.

As you recall, the backbone of the range of tasks concept is avoiding one standard for all; now, by developing new insights into your subject matter while you design the tasks, you will find that you *can* use more of your available equipment and space. The use of one ball for an entire class is not often a result of school poverty; it is rather a result of a governing concept. Most or perhaps all schools have more than one ball. Presenting the class with various tasks will provide you with the opportunity to use your balls more frequently and more efficiently. Your students will learn more and will perform better.

Similarly, one can use *all* the available mats for a range of tumbling tasks so that the principle of maximum activity per student per unit of time will become a reality on the gymnasium floor. When this procedure is used, the students, because they use the equipment frequently, learn the real meaning of safety rules. They have the opportunity to understand, observe, and execute the safety procedures; moreover, it is worth their while to observe these rules because they usually want an opportunity for frequent performance.

The diagrams on the next pages suggest some samples of use of equipment in relation to this style of teaching. (Observe the use of floor space and use of the walls.)

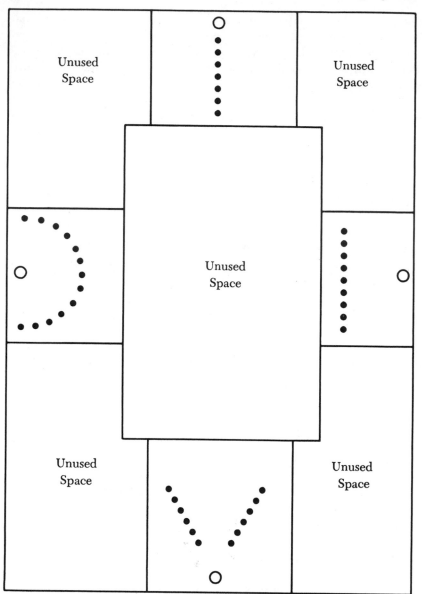

Figure 8. *Basketball—Common Equipment and Space Organization (Four Baskets in the Gymnasium)*

Search your equipment room and closets and get out the rest of the balls—*any balls:* basketballs, volleyballs, playground balls, etc.—and instead of the arrangement shown in Figure 8 try the one in Figure 9.

The arrangement shown in Figure 9 provides frequent opportunities for all students to shoot. The nine tasks shown are designed with the *range* in mind, and *small* groups rotate from task to task. Figures 9 and 10 will provide the teacher with a guide to alternative use of space, equipment, and tasks in teaching basketball. Similar arrangements can be adapted to baseball, soccer, hockey or other ball games. The teacher can design many of these alternatives to fit the local conditions of space, equipment, and the task level of the class. When such alternatives are employed, the time available is utilized more efficiently.

Before a similar analysis and alternatives are offered in gymnastics, it is necessary to identify the framework of gymnastics in terms of physical prerequisites to the work on the apparatus. One needs to develop the qualities of agility, balance, flexibility, strength (and others) *before* and *during* the experiences on the apparatus. This certainly applies to the novice in our schools. Therefore, concurrent with the tasks on the apparatus, students—instead of sitting and waiting long minutes for their turn in a *single* performance on a piece of apparatus —can and should be engaged in developmental movements which will help them progress in the areas that need improvement.

Here is an excellent opportunity for developing a rather extensive range of tasks. For example, some students may need extensive work in the push-up family of exercises in order to develop the kind of strength needed for support of the body even in a simple parallel bar sequence. These students should be involved in this development instead of sitting near the parallel bars doing nothing.

One more comment before the diagrammatic proposal for alternatives is offered: It might be a very revealing experience for the teacher to time the actual waste of time which occurs in the traditional arrangement in the gymnastics unit for large classes. Select two or three students, follow them through the lesson, and record the *actual* time spent passively and in motion on the apparatus. You will discover that most of a student's time is spent in sitting, waiting for his turn to go on the apparatus. Obviously, this calls for an alternative arrangement.

In many schools (with large classes) you will find unused spaces in the gymnasium, as shown in Figure 11, because the students are grouped according to the number of pieces of gymnastics equipment. With large numbers of students and small numbers of pieces of equipment the *frequency* of experience is *low*, and development of agility, balance, strength, etc. is *insignificant*. Because of infrequent experiences at the apparatus, many students are not only poor performers in the techniques of gymnastics, but they usually lack the physical prerequisites for such activities—they lack the strength, the flexibility, the endurance to pursue a successful gymnastics program.

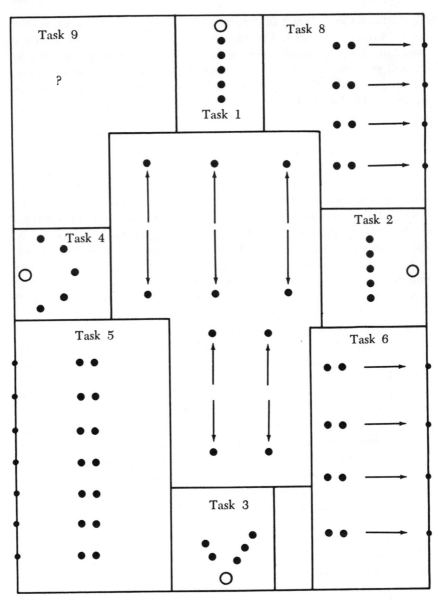

Dots on Sidelines: Marked Targets on Walls for Practicing Accuracy and Arch Control of Shots

Figure 9. *Basketball—Alternative No. 1 (A Single Skill—Shooting)*

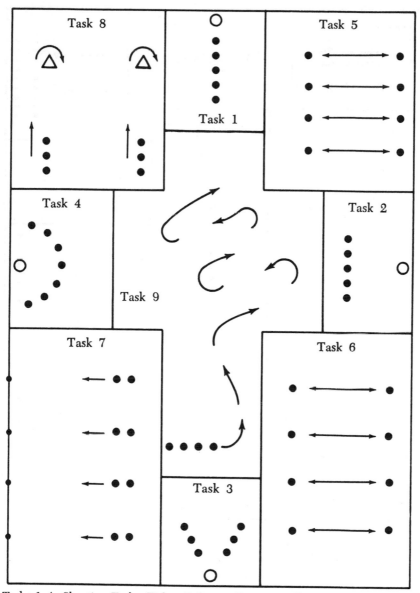

Tasks 1–4: Shooting Tasks, Either Different Shots or Different Tasks within the Same Shot

Tasks 5–6: Passing Tasks (with a Partner)

Task 7: Passing Practice against a Wall (and *Use* of Targets)

Task 8: Dribbling Practice

Task 9: A Dribbling Course (Changing Direction)

Figure 10. *Basketball—Alternative No. 2 (Multiple Skills)*

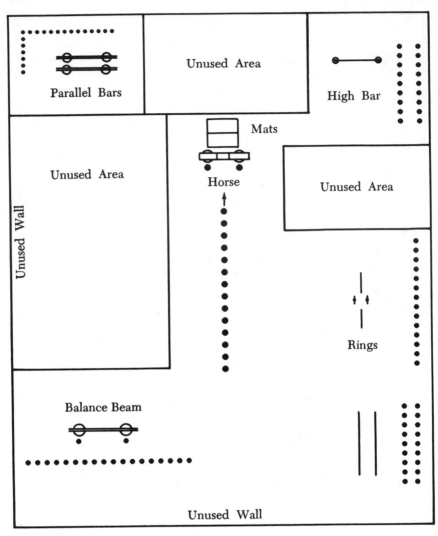

Figure 11. *Gymnastics—Common Equipment-Space Organization*

By using the empty spaces on the floor and the walls, you actually add equipment to your program. Present the class with a program of a range of tasks in activities relevant to the gymnastics unit, and your student will be engaged in developing the required qualities and the techniques of gymnastics. It is important, though, to explain to your student the connection between the variety of tasks on the floor, the development of the body, and its application to better performance on the apparatus. It is helpful, for example, for the student to realize that various push-ups and a variety of other support activities (there are many simple games in the support position which could serve this purpose) are absolutely necessary for the development of the muscles of the shoulders, arms, and chest and that this development is vital in parallel bars performance because the great majority of movements and sequences of movement are performed while the body is *constantly supported by the arms.* (To be more precise, the bulk of the body weight is usually above the base of support in parallel bars sequences). Conversely, the rings and the high bar provide the performer with situations in which the center of gravity is below and above the base of support; therefore, the muscles involved in the hanging position must be developed to a level which permit the performer to "hang" in comfort and without effort for some duration.

All these supplementary activities can be done in any regular class by using the alternative floor plan and time-activity sequence. The gains of such an arrangement are rather impressive, because even the weakest student can show significant progress.

Figure 12 shows a sample of alternative arrangement of equipment-space relationships. A teacher may Mimeograph the floor plan, with the tasks written in the various spaces so that each student has a guide for his tasks. This can save a great deal of time and eliminates the need for repetitive explanations. It *frees the teacher* to move about, observe, correct, and offer reinforcement.

The areas designated as unused space in Figure 11 are used in the organization shown in Figure 12 for *relevant* activities necessary for the learner of gymnastics. The principle of maximum activity per student per unit of time is observed here. The assumption is that more frequent experiences for each student in gymnastics movements helps learning, development, and enjoyment.

A word about the use of time: Let us figure out what happens to the *time dimension* in the arrangement shown in Figure 11. Let us assume that fifteen students flock around the parallel bars and that the lesson lasts for thirty minutes. If we allow thirty seconds for a short sequence, that means that it will take seven and a half minutes to conclude one "inning." During the entire lesson each member of the group will have the opportunity to be on the parallel bars four times for a total of *two minutes. For each*, therefore, there will be *twenty-eight minutes of inactivity.* Suppose we cut the time on the parallel bars in half (fifteen seconds); each participant will then be on the bar eight times—a rather

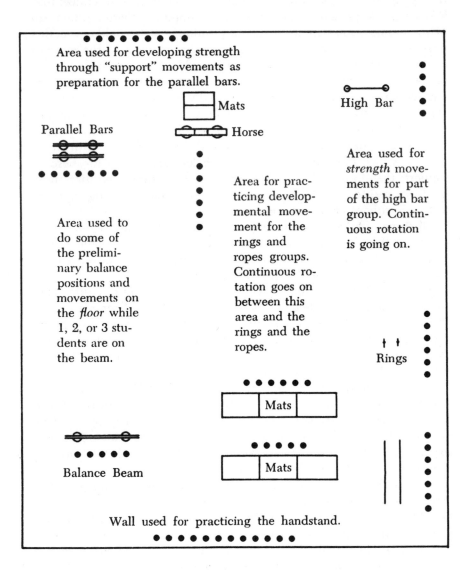

Figure 12. *Gymnastics—An Alternative Equipment-Space*
Organization

unconvincing argument for the contribution of gymnastics to the development of each individual. This calculation applies to any activity or unit that employs this kind of equipment-space-time relationship. Those lost twenty-eight minutes can be used more efficiently. It seems

SCHEMATIC SUMMARY OF TEACHING BY TASK

(The Position of the Variables and the Components in the Anatomy of the Task Style)

	The Role of the Teacher (in decision making)	*The Role of the Student (in decision making)*
Variable No. 1: Pre-class Preparation	*Components:* Selection of subject matter. Preparation of subject matter. A particular kind of relationship with subject matter.	
Variable No. 2: Execution	*Components:* When? How? How much?	The student is beginning to learn to make decisions about the execution of the task without *direct stimuli* emitted by the teacher.
Variable No. 3: Evaluation	*Components:* Self concept.	The *individual* student begins to *emerge!* He begins to see himself in a new, freer role! He is more than a mere *responder* to external stimuli. *Self-evaluation* begins during self-placement on the range of tasks.
	Assessment by peers. Evaluation by teacher.	

that it is not a lack of time which deters the teacher from developing successful programs; rather, it is the way the time is used.

It is worth repeating, in conclusion, that the use of this style of teaching by task, with the *range of tasks* concept, accommodates greater efficiency of participation, more learning, and growth toward greater independence.

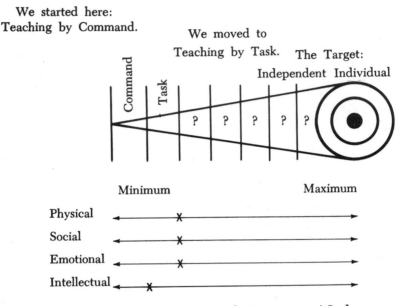

Figure 13. *Present Position in the Spectrum of Styles and the Channels of Development*

4

Reciprocal Teaching—
The Use of the Partner

Now—what is our next step? We need to identify the variable and the components that will free the student further and will lead him a step closer to independence.

The execution variable was the one transferred to the student's column in "Anatomy of the Task Style." Let us now examine the possibilities in manipulating the evaluation variable. At this stage of the development of the concept of teaching styles it will suffice to delimit the concept of evaluation to just error corrections, helping a student follow and perform a series of tasks and offering frequent reinforcement following proper execution of the tasks. Other aspects of evaluation, such as assessing total improvement, the teacher's role in evaluation, teacher-student relationships, and effects on the self concept of both teacher and student, will be discussed and analyzed as the new style emerges.

Presently, it is proposed that since *one* teacher cannot observe and evaluate the *immediate* performance of an entire class, even during the execution of simple movements, this component of the evaluation variable can be relegated to the student.

Once, when I told a class of third graders, "I have only two eyes; I cannot see all of you when you move, and therefore I cannot tell many of you how well you do the movement. What can we do to see more of you when you move?" the immediate response by several children was, "We can watch each other." And indeed they could and did. It is logical that a one-to-one relationship can be very helpful during the learning process. The buddy system has been used before for various purposes—for example, safety in the water, spotting on the apparatus, and ball passing in various games. All these situations, though, offer the partner only a secondary role, in some cases only the role of a crutch. Important and necessary as these are, they do not match the values (primarily social, emotional, and intellectual) that can be derived from a teaching role performed by the partner. The teaching role proposed here involves entrusting the partner with the observation of the performance of a given task and supplying the partner with information about the "rights" and "wrongs" of the given task. If students know *what* to look for and *how* to correct *observed* errors they gladly and successfully can perform the role of an observer and a corrector.

The anatomy of this style, reciprocal teaching, will include the delineation of the teacher's behavior, including what *not* to do and say, and an analysis of the role of each partner.

The anatomy of this style will be introduced in *three cycles*, each cycle more advanced in its task complexity and more advanced in the degree of freedom for both partners. Each cycle will also involve a mode of communication which is freer of the teacher's direct delivery of task instructions.

Cycle Number	Task Complexity (Freedoms increase)	Mode of Communication
1	A single task at a time.	Oral, visual or both.
2	A series of connected tasks concerning the same activity.	Task card (things to look for).
3	A program of tasks concerning a variety of activities (could utilize the concept of range of tasks).	Task sheet.

You can observe the similarity here to the design of the previous style, teaching by task. The added dimension, of course, is the involvement of *a partner* in the role of an observer, a corrector, and a reinforcer. Cycle 1 serves as a training exercise for both partners to get used to their new roles. Cycles 2 and 3 actually serve as teaching devices, parts of this style of teaching. These two cycles enhance the weaning process for both partners and *free the teacher* to reach individuals who most need help or advice.

CYCLE 1 (THE SINGLE TASK)

Anatomy of Cycle 1

	The Role of the Teacher	*The Role of the Student*
Variable No. 1: Pre-class decisions	1. Is involved in making decisions concerning the subject matter to be taught and the tasks involved in this subject matter.	Not involved.
	2. Decides on the organizational pattern of the class. Since this cycle follows the task style, the decision here may favor a random organization or requesting partner to be stationed near a given apparatus or a specific area on the gymnasium floor.	Not involved.
	3. Decides what equipment is needed for the tasks involved. Decisions *must* be made concerning the *quantity* of equipment per task. Enough equipment for *all partners* may not be available—a factor which may affect decisions about subject matter. (For alternatives see section on *range of tasks* in the previous chapter.) The teacher may call upon his students for help in this phase.	May become involved by bringing his own equipment to school. For example, learning volleyball by use of this style will require more balls than the school might have available. Almost every child has some sort of a medium-size ball that can be brought to school. (Make the necessary arrangements through the principal's office.) The learning benefits

The Role of the Teacher	*The Role of the Student*
Other decisions concerning the time dimension, shift of tasks, and the like are treated in a similar manner to that of the previous style.	will be worth the administrative burden and the explanation to parents that might be needed. This has been done successfully in several schools.
	Student reacts to decisions concerning time, shift of tasks, etc. as he does when the task style is used.

Variable No. 2: Execution decisions	4. In this cycle, *only* a single task is explained, demonstrated or both.	*Both* partners listen to the explanation and observe the teacher's demonstration.
	5. Relegates decisions of *when to start* the motion to the students.	Decides who is the *doer* and who is the *observer*. *Doer* begins the motion, and the *observer* watches his partner's performance. (For some students it may be a new function and perhaps a burdensome one.)
	6. *Stops* the action, comments on the *success of the partner* in observation. *It is important* to note *now* the observers who did not perform their function.	
	7. May need to re-explain here *why* one stu-	Unless this simple phase has been ac-

dent observes the other.

complished, the following will not succeed.

8. Repeats the details of the previously taught task and *points out* the things to look for in the performance of that task. It is worthwhile to ask questions about these observable details.

By answering the questions the students will ascertain their comprehension of the necessary details of the task to be performed.

9. May want to execute the task himself with *some incorrect* detail and ask the students to relate the result of their observations.

   Thus, the teacher helps sharpen and reinforce the students' observation abilities.

After the students observe the teacher's performance, they may offer the results of their observations by pointing out the correct and incorrect aspects of the teacher's performance, based on the criteria previously offered by the teacher (adherence to the task).

10. Asks the doers to perform the given task.

Doers perform the tasks; *observers* observe the performances and note the correct and incorrect aspects of their partners' performances.

   Partners *change* roles.

   Teacher may have to remind the partners to *change* roles.

11. Stops the action and asks the observers (in this case the whole class) what *correct* aspects have been seen.

   Now the teacher asks

Students offer their observations of the correct aspects.

   Students offer their

The Role of the Teacher	*The Role of the Student*
for observation of incorrect aspects.	observations.
12. The teacher's response here is a nod: "Good," "Yes," "You saw a great many details." (Use these phrases only if it is really so.)	Students begin to see themselves as observers. They realize that the teacher trusts them in their *new* role.

Comment: The behavioral order in Step 11 is not an arbitrary one. Seeking the correct instances *first* has a dual function: first, it reinforces the doer; and, secondly, it hints to the observer that looking for successful aspects of performance strengthens the doer and may make it easier for him to *accept* corrections, comments, and reinforcements from a peer.

Thus far, the purposes of this cycle have been: (a) to present the observer with a small opportunity to play at his new role, (b) to reinforce the observer, (c) to help develop an *accepting* climate between the partners. This level must be accomplished before any further attempts are made in seeking better success in the doer's performance. The essence of this style is based on the success of the *observer* in his observations and his relationship with his *doer*. *The doer's success is contingent upon the observer's success.*

	13. Introduces the next task and points out the things to look for. The teacher may need to explain that it is all right to point out to a partner the good things about his performance. Many students may think that working with others means only pointing out errors.	*Doers* perform the task, *observers* watch, correct, and reinforce. Students may begin to realize the value of positive statements to the performing partner.
Variable No. 3: *Evaluation*	14. *The most crucial step* in this phase: the teacher has the opportunity now	Both partners realize that the teacher has the *time* to observe

to move about and observe the performance of *both* doers and observers.

The teacher *corrects the observer only*!!!

The teacher *never* corrects the doer. This involvement with the observer develops the proper status for the observer, and the doer is also strengthened in anticipating his role as an observer.

This continuous communication with the observers will help develop the doer's independence of the teacher and will enhance the doer's relationship with his observer-partner.

This process takes time and patience, but it is worthwhile because in the long run the students will be more independent, will develop keen observation ability and a sharper analytic eye.

The teacher may feel that he must evaluate the doer's performance and make corrections. If this is done, the purpose of this style is defeated, and the teacher loses the help of so many helpers in the class.

them *individually* and that the teacher actually does it.

This process of communicating with the observing partner has a profound effect on the self image of *each* partner. It shows the student that the teacher trusts him and that the teacher is willing to carry out the proposed behavior offered when this style was introduced. Some students will develop the observing qualities faster than others, but this is also true in any other facet of the learning situation.

Here, each pair is given the opportunity to move along at their own pace and on their level.

The minute the teacher takes over the corrections of the doer's performance, the observers must retreat; his status as a teacher's helper is revoked, and his trust in his role is diminished.

The Role of the Teacher	*The Role of the Student*
If the teacher *must* make a correction, he should stop the entire class and elaborate on the oversight and then allow the observers a second chance. The results will improve. Thus, the teacher develops a *process* of learning—how to observe and work with a partner.	It is more encouraging for the students to accept a comment to the observers—it will strengthen their role in the partnership. Experiments in schools have shown that most students accept their new role with understanding and responsibility.

Comment: Students *can* and *do* help each other. They are involved in this process in school on many occasions and even more so in activity outside school. This style adopts this behavior within a given subject matter. One realizes that the teacher may find this change difficult and frustrating in the beginning, but the teacher *must* learn to shift to alternative behavior *first.* Any attempt to teach students in a different manner requires first a change in the teacher's behavior, and this requires the teacher to refrain from verbal and social behavior which is more appropriate to another style. It is worthwhile to concentrate for two or three lessons on the understanding and execution of this style at the small temporary expense of skill learning, because once the students accept their new role, progress in skill learning will be rather rapid. Each performer has, virtually, a personal tutor for helping in the single task at hand.

Examples in Various Activities

The following examples will illustrate how this style can be introduced in tumbling, basketball, and track and field.

Example No. 1

Subject matter: Tumbling—a variation in the forward roll.
Task details: Starting position—feet apart. Motion—forward roll with right leg fully extended and left leg bent. End position—stop at a squat position, head tucked between the knees, hands on the floor.

Now, as suggested on page 73, Step 1, the mode of communication for Cycle No. 1 (the single task) is verbal, visual, or both. In the present case it might be useful to demonstrate this different forward roll and explain the various details.

At this point the pairs disperse to their respective mats. (It is obvious that all available mats must be used. The reader is referred to the previous style for an analysis of efficiency of the use of equipment, space and time.) The doers begin to perform, and the observers watch for the details of the roll. When the roll is completed, the observers are asked by the teacher to tell the doers which parts were well performed and which details need to be corrected. This process is repeated several times. The teacher seeks *one* successful pair, stops the class, and points out the success of the observer in teaching the doer to perform well. This reinforcement helps to reassure *both* observer and doer. Ask for other successful instances and let the doers perform. Praise the *observer* and the doer.

The class assured in its new role may continue now until more students are successful in the performance of the roll. Experimentation in this phase of the style (Cycle No. 1) will show an increase in motivation in most students. It is quite clear that in a class of forty students, for example, the teacher alone *cannot* observe all students and identify *all* the errors *when* they occur; but *twenty* helpers *can* observe twenty others and see the details of the bent knee, the straight leg, and the end position.

In a more advanced step, after the new roles are clear to the members of the class, the teacher may suggest a little game of competition among the squads in the class to find out which squad has the largest number of pairs who taught each other a given task during a lesson. Competition, here, must be used with discretion. The main purpose of this style must be kept as the focus of attention of both teacher and students. *An important* achievement of this style is that greater development in the details of the given forward roll will result from the direct and *immediate* observation and reinforcement by the partner.

Example No. 2

Subject matter:	Track and field—the shot put.
Task:	The initial stance.
Task details:	Stand on your stronger leg; shift your weight to the direction of this leg. Twist your body slightly in that direction and hold up your stronger hand over the shoulder as if holding the shot. Raise your elbow

slightly. The foot of your other leg, in a comfortable step, slightly touches the ground. The free hand is relaxed in front of the body.

Mode of communication: Demonstration and explanation.

Things to look for: (1) shift of weight far enough on the supporting leg, (2) body turned in that leg's direction, (3) both arms in their respective positions.

At this point the pairs find their random places on the field and begin to work with each other. The doer assumes the required position, and his partner offers comments and corrections. The teacher is *free* to move about, observe individuals, and offer help to *those observers* who seem to miss some of the details. When the teacher helps the observer, he can ask the following questions:

1. Is the weight in the right place?
2. Will the position of the holding arm permit the shot to fly in the right direction?
3. Is the trunk twisted enough?

These questions will help the partner relate his observations to the task details previously presented by the teacher. In this example, again, more students will assume the correct position faster because the partner offers an *immediate* observation of the positions of the body, the legs, and so on. These immediate comments accomplish two important purposes:

1. Initial errors are reduced.
2. The process of self awareness in performance begins to develop.

When most students have accomplished this single task, the teacher may go on to present the next task in the shot: shift of weight in the direction of the put and the "pushing" of the imaginary shot. The pairs repeat the process of reciprocal teaching of the second task.

Example No. 3

Subject matter: Basketball—bounce pass (against a wall).

Task details: Hold the ball with two hands. Change the distance from the wall every six passes. (See the markers on the floor.)

In the case of the pass it is impossible for one teacher to observe all the details, particularly the subtleties of the fingers' motion. A partner, however, can develop a keen eye and detect the necessary details. The observer can check the bounce-point and the height on the wall and thus help the doer concentrate on the performance. In this kind of task the observer can check the number of good passes (when most or all details were performed well). How many good passes in twenty trials thrown from the first distance? How many good passes in twelve trials hit the blue line on the wall?

CYCLE 2

Once the class has demonstrated the understanding and the ability to be independent for a short span of time in pursuing a *specific target*, it becomes possible to introduce the second cycle. This cycle involves the presentation of several tasks which are part of the same activity and permits the student to experience a longer period of independence in performing and learning a larger quantity of subject matter. (For the analysis of tasks and series of tasks see previous chapter.)

There are two major differences between Cycle 1 and Cycle 2:

1. More tasks must be demonstrated and explained to the class. A reasonable connection among the tasks should exist in the series.
2. The mode of communication must change in order to be as efficient as possible. When a series of tasks is presented to a class verbally and visually, some students will always forget a few of the tasks, and many might forget some of the details.

Task cards are suggested as an excellent means of communication. They serve a triple role: (a) they establish a goal (the task); (b) they offer a reminder of the *sequence* of tasks and the *details* to be performed; (c) they individualize the instruction in classes of varying sizes. Task cards of various sorts are not new to the students. They perform and follow written instructions in every other subject in school, in classrooms and in laboratories. There is no reason why similar procedures cannot be used in the gymnasium or the athletic field during the physical education classes. Many coaches use task cards as instruction reminders to individual athletes on various teams. A variety of task card designs will be presented later in this chapter.

Anatomy of Cycle 2

	The Role of the Teacher	*The Role of the Student*
Variable No. 1: *Pre-class* *Preparation*	1. Is involved in making decisions about the selection of subject matter.	Not involved.

	The Role of the Teacher	*The Role of the Student*
	2. Is involved in designing the *specific* series of tasks: (a) same series for the entire class, (*b*) series based on the concept of range.	
	3. Is involved in preparation of the task cards. These can be handwritten, typed, or Mimeographed. It is important to have at least one task card for each pair of students.	Some students may be involved in the *technical* preparation of the task cards—helping in typing, etc.
	4. See "Anatomy of Cycle 1" for descriptions of organizational decisions and decisions involving equipment.	
Variable No. 2: Execution	5. *First*, the role of the task card must be explained and the values analyzed. Teacher emphasizes the value of knowing the specific objectives to be accomplished, distributes cards, and pauses.	Both partners listen to the presentation and participate in a question-answer period in order to ascertain the *exact* use of the cards. Receives cards. Reads the task cards—either a part or the entire card, depending upon the teacher's suggestions and student's curiosity.
	6. Demonstrates the various tasks (or asks a student to demonstrate) and explains the necessary details.	Follows the tasks on the card and asks questions for maximum clarification of tasks. This will prove

Allows for a few seconds after each demonstration to glance at the cards.

to be very economical; when the students understand the nature of the tasks, their performance will be better.

7. Announces that those who are ready may begin to practice the task.

If some need more time for explanation or an additional demonstration, the teacher is available.

Those who understood the task begin to work with their partners following the task series recorded on the card.

8. Moves about the class observing the involvement of the observers and the doers. Teacher does not intervene until the pairs have performed more than a single task.

If corrections are necessary, offer them to the observers and be specific. Directs his comments in relation to the task card. This will help the students focus on their task at hand.

Due to the *duration* of executing the series of tasks, the teacher is *freer* to observe more students and concentrate more on those who may need immediate advice.

This phase will determine whether the students are capable of persisting in their execution of *several* tasks.

The partners follow through with the performance of their roles of doer and observer.

Students who feel they need advice *may request* the teacher's attention *without* interrupting the teacher's delivery of materials.

When this cycle is well adopted and well performed, it will become evident that the evaluation variable has shifted to the student's column in the anatomy outline. Any pair who reach an operational level will be able to demonstrate a cooperative relationship between the partners, a satisfactory degree of self-acceptance in each role (doer and observer), and an ability to comprehend the tasks at hand; consequently, they will manifest a different kind of physical response, a more meaningful and more individualized response.

Kinds of Task Cards

The simplest form of task card is the card containing only two components: (1) description of the task and (2) a place to check off the completion of the task. The proposed format for such a card is shown below.

Task Card No. ____

Name _____ Partner's Name _____   Grade ____
Activity _____   Date ____

Equipment _____   Completed | Incomplete
                                        Task

Task No. 1 _____
   Details: _____
           _____
   Things to look for: _____
Task No. 2 _____
   Details: _____
   Things to look for: _____
Task No. 3 _____
   Details: _____
   Things to look for: _____

Task Card No. 1

Name _____ Partner's Name _____   Grade ____
Activity   Forward handspring   Date ____

Equipment   Mats   Completed | Incomplete
Task No. 1   Placing the hand and body   Task

   in position.

Details: Try the preliminary step to
the handspring and place the hands
on the floor, width of the shoulders.
Arms in a vertical position, head up.
The rear leg is raised off the floor.
Things to look for: 1. Straight arms,
never bend at elbows. 2. Straight rear
leg.

Task No. 2 Up to momentary handstand.

Details: Using the momentum from Task No. 1, the rear leg serves as a lead leg that swings up to a momentary handstand (may use wall).

Things to look for: 1. Review those in Task No. 1. Don't shift shoulder forward. 3. Smooth and connected motion.

Task Card No. 1 is an example of a simple task card that can be used by both partners. When the doer completes a task to the satisfaction of the observer, the observer can check off the completed task so that the doer will be able to identify his performance status at any time. (These task cards can be used for testing purposes and whenever a written record is needed.) It is important for the teacher to spot check the checked card and to compare it with the doer's performance. This spot check keeps the teacher "in the know," and the students (observer and doer) will realize that the teacher knows what is going on in the class. This technique of spot checking is excellent for awakening those students who lag behind and those who still do not completely see themselves as self-learners. It permits some dependency, which is still needed by some students in every class.

Another kind of task card (No. 2) includes a more refined evaluation

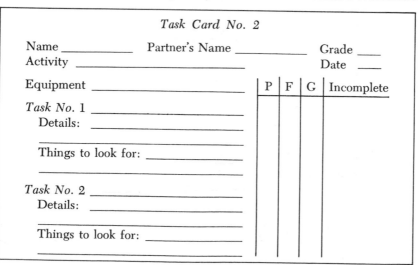

Task Card No. 2

Name _____ Partner's Name _____ Grade ____
Activity _____ Date ____

Equipment _____	P	F	G	Incomplete
Task No. 1 _____				
Details: _____				
Things to look for: _____				
Task No. 2 _____				
Details: _____				
Things to look for: _____				

recording. It offers a differentiation of quality of performance (following the task description) into three levels: poor, fair, good.

A task card like No. 3 may be more useful in certain activities. The teacher could experiment with this idea and try to identify the activities which were most helped by a particular kind of task card. Let us try to design a card (No. 4) for dribbling in basketball.

Task Card No. 3

Name _____   Partner's Name _____   Grade ____
Activity   Straddle Vault   Date ____

	P	F	G	Incomplete
Equipment Side horse and mats—a spotter				
Task No. 1 Run and take off using two feet, placing				
Details: both hands on the horse, and lift your body in pike position. Land back on take-off spot.				
Things to look for: 1. Springy take-off. 2. Body in pike position in the air. 3. Arms must be straight.				
Task No. 2 Review task No. 1 and as you take off				
Details: straddle the legs and land on top of horse.				
Things to look for: 1. Keep legs straight, if possible. 2. Arms must be straight.				
Task No. 3 Following details in No. 1 and No. 2, use a stronger				
Details: approach and clear the horse.				
Things to look for: 1. Spotter stands in front. 2. See Task No. 2. 3. ?				

You will have noticed that the parts included in the card design vary. Sometimes it is necessary to include the detailed description of the task, and often it is sufficient just to identify the task in a brief sen-

Task Card No. 4				
Name _____ Partner's Name _____ Grade ___				
Activity ___Basketball—dribbling___	P	F	G	Incomplete
Task No. 1 Dribble forward 20 steps				
Things to look for: 1. Height of ball— hip level. 2. Elasticity of the palm.				
Task No. 2 Dribble sideways 10 steps				
Things to look for: See Task No. 1.				
Task No. 3 Dribble forward with "weak" hand				
Things to look for: See Task No. 1.				

tence. One can include or omit the recording of equipment, date, etc. If, however, the card's format is pre-typed or Mimeographed, it is advisable to include all the potential components, which can be either used or ignored when the card is filled out.

Another form of task card may include a quantitative record and check. This is very handy when the task is measurable by simple units or counts which do not require measuring devices (twenty push-ups, a jump over the blue line, ten shots to the basket).

Task Card No. 5				
Activity ___Developmental Movement___	Quantity	P	F	G	Incomplete
Task No. 1 Push-ups	20				
Things to look for: Straight body.					
Task No. 2 Sit-ups—bent knees.	25				
Things to look for: Straight trunk hands behind the neck.					
Task No. 3 Hop with slightly bent knees	50				
Things to look for: Hop on the balls of the feet.					
Task No. 4 In wide straddle, shift weight from leg to leg.	15 to each				
Things to look for: Keep trunk straight	side				

This design can be very helpful in a series of tasks in basketball, where the teacher or coach may seek a quality of a particular performance in addition to the score of getting the ball into the basket. It is conceivable that a particular shot is just fair from the standpoint of smoothness of motion or a technical detail but that the ball did go through the hoop. A teacher who is concerned with the improvement of the quality of the motion for the sake of more successful subsequent shots may design a task card (No. 6) which combines the qualitative and quantitative evaluations by the observer.

Task Card No. 6						
Activity Basketball shooting		No.				
	Quantity	Scored	P	F	G	Incomplete
Task No. 1 Set Shots— from foul line.	10					
Task No. 2 Set shots— farther than foul line.	10					
Task No. 3 One-hand shot—foul line.	10					
Task No. 4 One-hand shot—farther than foul line.	10					
Task No. 5 One-hand shot—45° to the left.	10					
Task No. 6 One-hand shot—45° to the right.	10					

The task outlined in Card No. 6 includes very few words but in turn requires relatively more motion than the previous examples. It all depends on the activity, the degree of details needed, and the level of the class. The teacher will have to *make decisions* concerning these facets. This task card is a good example of the objective awareness, the task sequence and the degree of achievement. Once again, this kind of card can be used for tests in basketball—it is simple, clear, and easy to administer in classes of varying size.

Another kind of task card which reflects a higher level of observation by the partner and offers more reinforcement and feed-back value is the one which includes comments by the observer—comments expressed in words and sentences which elaborate on the check mark. This level of detailed observation and analysis can be achieved by conscientious teachers and students. The values of this level are obvious.

Task Card No. 7					
Activity					
Name _____	Partner's Name _____				
			Quality		
	Quantity	P	F	G	Comments & Corrections
Task No. 1 _____					
_____					
_____					
Task No. 2 _____					
_____					
_____					
Task No. 3 _____					
_____					
_____					

The comments and the corrections are not *generalized* according to the teacher's knowledge of the subject matter but are *individualized* according to the specific need of the performing individual. An example of individualized commentary is seen in Task Card No. 8.

Still another level of relationship between observer and doer can be reached when the observer asks the *doer* to describe the rights and wrongs of his performance. The doer's statement is compared by the

Task Card No. 8					
Activity Handstand and forward roll					
Name _____	Partner's Name _____				
			Quality		
	Quantity	P	F	G	Comments & Corrections
Task No. 1 Place hands					Your lead leg was bent
at shoulder width					most of the time.
and swing up—					
both legs straight.	10 times		x		

Task No. 2 Extend both legs upward to a momentary hand- stand.	10 times	x	Keep your shoulders over the base. Do not move them too far forward.
Task No. 3 Lower your- self slowly, tuck your head and roll.	10 times	x	The lowering of the body was not smooth.
Task No. 4 As you roll, pike your body, keep your legs straight.	10 times	x	Don't land on the head. You did not maintain the straight position of the legs in the pike.

observer with his own evaluation. If disagreement occurs, the partners can discuss the details of the performance, or the *doer* may try to perform again. This process may help the doer develop more self-awareness, a better insight into his own precision in performance. Since the observer's comments are written, it is more efficient to conduct the communication concerning self-awareness orally. Ask your partner, "Did you perform all the details well?" If the answer is "No," then you may continue: "What was incorrect [in terms of the given task]?" "Do you know what your left foot did?" "Were your knees together?" "Were your arms above shoulder level?" "What was the position of your head during . . .?" "During the swing, what was the position of your shoulders?" "During the dribble, what did your other hand do?" Ask any question *related* to the given task.

IMPLICATIONS OF THIS STYLE

This style has been successfully used in the elementary and secondary schools and on the college level. It is relatively easy to introduce this style to most classes. This is an excellent opportunity to enhance the social climate in the class by creating this situation where one is actually dependent on the help of the peer. One learns how to receive criticism and evaluation from a peer. This style can probably be used with all activities. Each teacher, however, must find through experimentation which activities in his particular situation are best taught by this style. It is important to permit the partners to take the necessary time in developing their association; it will save time in the long run. Remember that you will have as many helpers in observing, correcting, and reinforcing as there are students in your class. This will *free you* to do whatever is necessary and be wherever you are needed.

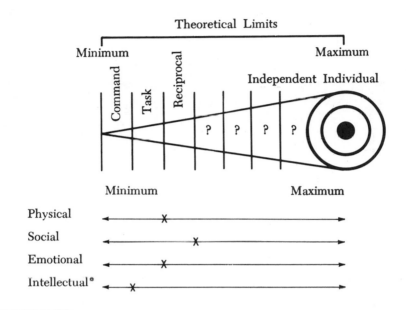

*A discussion of the "intellectual lag" and how to close the gap will be offered in Chapter 7, "Guided Discovery."

Figure 14. *Present Position in the Spectrum of Styles and the Channels of Development*

5

The Use of the Small Group

An important variation on the previous styles is the use of the small group of three or four members. Here again, it is not an organizational issue of having the class in small groups which determines the style; it is rather the process of interaction and communication among the members of the group. This style merely calls for more than *two* people to partake in the process of participation, observation, mutual correction, and reinforcement. The bond, however, is established by the creation of a *focus* for the *whole* group: the participating member.

This style calls for a specific designation of the role of each member in the group. If there are three members in a group, No. 1 is the doer, No. 2 is the observer, and No. 3 is the recorder. If four people participate in the group, roles might be distributed like this: No. 1 is the doer; No. 2 is the observer; No. 3 is the observer; and No. 4 is the recorder.

Let us examine in more detail the role of each member of the group and the process of interaction that evolves.

THE DOER

As when partners are used, once the task or range of tasks has been presented by the teacher, the doer proceeds to execute the tasks. (Mode of communication can be oral, visual, or both.)

THE OBSERVER

In this variation of the style the observer or observers can concentrate on the details to be observed and communicate their comments to the doer. They can also *exchange* views on their observation. This is an excellent way to sharpen the ability to see details and to separate the grain from the chaff. This exchange of observations should be conducted in the presence of the doer, since the discussion is for the benefit and the improvement of the doer. If in doubt, the observers may ask the doer to repeat the performance.

THE RECORDER

This member of the group takes care of the clerical work. He records the numbers involved in the performance (quantitative aspect of performance) and writes down whatever comment or correction is offered by the observers (qualitative aspect).

At the end of a given period, usually decided by the group, the members change roles.

The values of this process of interaction seem to be:

1. A sense of responsibility develops, or its absence is clearly evident. The concept of peer relationships evolves and unfolds in such a situation. The members of the group are forced to make decisions concerning their peers; this requires a degree of responsibility and dignity of behavior. In its absence, the group will deteriorate, and no task will be executed. In this sense this style serves as an *outstanding* diagnostic tool for identifying group climate, individual relationships within the group, and potential leadership abilities.
2. A special kind of discipline develops—a discipline which requires self-control in order to survive in the group. Here again, the keen teacher will be able to tell whether the apparent discipline is a result of subjugation of the group by one strong individual or a result of mutual understanding and ability to exchange points of view amicably. The important dimension is that the weaning process is in progress—the main disciplinary relationship *is not* between the student and the teacher but between the student and his peers.
3. A stronger sense of communication develops. Since each member of the group assumes all the different roles, the ability to communicate with others has an opportunity to develop. When this ability is hampered for whatever reason, the teacher will be able to detect it and provide the student with whatever help he can. It is a most rewarding phase of a lesson to observe and listen to groups of students discuss their common project.

4. An ability to *analyze* seems to emerge in this situation, particularly when there is more than one observer. Inevitably, more than one point of view emerges, and *the need to examine alternatives arises.* This process helps sharpen observation and decision making. It is quite clear that instances of this kind can develop also in the previous style; but they are more likely to occur in a group situation.

This style is particularly useful in large classes and with limited facilities. The division of the class into small groups requires less equipment than the partner style, and yet each member of the class is engaged in the learning process in one capacity or another. It is conceivable that in some activities the small group is advantageous, since it provides the observers and the recorder with a short period of rest from physical activity. In gymnastics, for example, it is impossible to involve the participants on the rings in constant motion. It is a very fatiguing activity. When a group of four participants rotate performances on the rings, each member has a chance to recuperate. At the same time each member is involved *in* the group situation, involved *with* the performing individual and with the subject matter to be learned. It is *this involvement* which makes the *difference* between this style and an arrangement in which the student *is* merely *in* a group awaiting his turn to perform.

The anatomy of this style is very similar to that for the use of a partner, with the exception of additional roles for more than one observer and a recorder.

6

The Individual Program

The essence of teaching is *individual learning*. Learning is always the affair of the individual; no one can learn for somebody else. This style of teaching—the individual program—is a design of subject matter manipulated in such a manner as to provide the learner with full opportunity for self-motivated learning, self-assessment, and decision making over a relatively prolonged period of time.

The assumption is that at this stage of development along the spectrum of styles the student has learned to free himself to more prolonged independence and that following the individual program will help the student free himself still more. Attaining this level of self decision making is one purpose of education for a democratic society.

This style of teaching (and learning) brings students one step closer to the target of independent individuals than does the reciprocal style using partners or small groups. In the reciprocal style the evaluation variable was the one that was transferred to the student's decision-making column. Assessment there was by a peer. This is the very component which *changes* now! We move from peer evaluation to self-evaluation. Thus, two out of three variables in the teaching-learning process are being carried out independently by the student. The anatomy of this style is outlined below.

ANATOMY OF THE INDIVIDUAL PROGRAM

	The Role of the Teacher	*The Role of the Student*
Variable No. 1: *Pre-class* *decisions*	1. Decisions concerning selection and organization of subject matter are in the teacher's hands. Presentation of tasks	Receives and accepts the general scheme of tasks (programs) presented by the teacher.

	The Role of the Teacher	*The Role of the Student*
	(programs) is done by teacher by means of explanation, demonstration, or both, with the use of any mode of communication previously offered.	
Variable No. 2: *Execution* *decisions*	2. Mainly observation, and correction and evaluation if necessary.	The individual program is carried out by *each* student independently. Student makes the decision concerning all the components: when, where, how much, how well, and so on. At *this stage* of individual programming the decisions concerning the *what* are still in the hands of the teacher.
Variable No. 3: *Evaluation* *decisions*	3. Assists *only* if it is necessary. The teacher can decide when it is necessary to intervene, or he may respond to the student's request. The teacher *must* learn to *refrain* from interfering while the student is learning to *become* a self-directed learner.	The *self-evaluation* phase, which is one component of the evaluation process, is performed by the student — an additional dimension in the process of freeing oneself.

DESIGNS FOR INDIVIDUAL PROGRAMS

There are several operational designs of individual programs which have been successfully used on all levels of elementary school, high school and college, in the physical education classes for all, and the coaching of the selected teams.

These designs proceed from the simple to the complex; they are all individualized on different levels and require different kinds of responsibility and responses from different individuals. They do have, however, several important dimensions which are common to all individual programs:

1. They all have a specific purpose, a subject matter objective of accomplishment.
2. They all require and develop a high degree of independent execution of tasks.
3. They all require and develop a *longer range* of independence. This *time* dimension is a critical factor. A successful performer of an individual program has learned to free himself from the control of immediate stimuli emitted by the teacher and has reached the level of prolonged self-responsibility of carrying out a program of multiple tasks.
4. They serve as a continuous motivation for improvement on the individual's level.
5. They provide high *visibility* of progress. Both student and teacher can view the progress of performance by looking at the markings on the individual program.
6. They provide the teacher with an excellent diagnostic tool for differentiating performance levels in an heterogeneous class. It also provides the teacher with instant control (if desired) by spot checking the performance of individuals. This technique is rather helpful in *large classes.*
7. It provides recognition and acceptance of individuals in large and heterogeneous classes.
8. It *frees* the teacher from being constantly tied to the stimuli-emitting chores of teaching.

The operational designs are:

Design 1: The tasks—check list for individual program.
Design 2: The quantitative individual program.
Design 3: The qualitative individual program.
Design 4: The combined individual program (multiple levels of performance differentiation).
Design 5: Programmed instruction (or programmed learning).

Operational Design 1

This design, which involves merely lists of a series of tasks, with a place provided for a self-check mark, can be used as a *preparatory phase* of the individual program style. Even this step may be quite different and perhaps hard for students who are accustomed to learning by other styles.

This design is basically concerned with the individual's ability to follow through with the execution of tasks which are organized and prepared by the teacher. It helps develop a degree of stamina in the performance of a program. This design is applicable to all activities. Let us examine the format of this design in a variety of activities: (*a*) developmental movement, (*b*) basketball, (*c*) track, (*d*) swimming, and (*e*) tumbling.

Individual Program No. ____
(Task Check List—Single Level)

Name _____   Starting Date _____

Subject Matter: Developmental Movement

To the Student: Check the completion of each task in each of the
following developmental categories. Use a different
date column for each lesson.

Dates

Tasks

A. *Agility*
   1. High straddle jumps. 10 consecutive times
   2. High knee raising
      hops.   10 consecutive times
   3. Repeat No. 1 with
      turns of 90° each
      time you land.   10 consecutive times

B. *Strength*
   a. *Legs*
      1. In side lunge shift body weight 20 times.
      2. In wide straddle position, bend both
         knees to half squat position 20 times.

   b. *Abdomen*
      1. In forearm-supine rest position, lift both
         legs to 45° off the floor. Perform scissors
         motion for 25 seconds.

   c. *Shoulders and Arms*
      1. Pull-ups (grip: shoulders' width) 7 times
         (hands supinated).

2. Push-ups—arms a bit wider than shoulders' width, body in inverted **V** position —10 times.

C. *Flexibility*

  a. *Shoulder joint:*

   1. Straight-arm circles backward—20 slow circles at shoulder level.
   2. Repeat No. 1—larger circles—20 times.

  b. *Pelvic joint:*

   1. In a wide straddle position, 20 slow bending movements, hands reaching to the floor.
   2. Repeat No. 1—hands reaching 10 times to left foot and 10 times to right foot.
   3. In straddle seat position—review movement of Nos. 1 and 2.

D. *Balance*

  1. Perform a T scale 5 times on each foot.
  2. Jump up vertically, turn 180°, and land on the same spot. Repeat 10 times. Check yourself if you were *balanced* after landing 5 out of 10 times.

Individual Program No. ____
(Task Check List—Single Level)

Name _____ Starting Date _____

Subject Matter: Basketball Shooting and Dribbling

To the Student: Perform each task as proposed in the program below and place a check next to the completed task.

		Dates
Tasks		
A. *Shooting*		
1. Set shots—foul line.	25 shots	
2. Set shots—45° angle left of basket.	25 shots	
3. Set shots—45° angle right of basket.	25 shots	
4. One-hand shot—foul line.	25 shots	

5. One-hand shot—right side
   of basket.   15 shots
6. One-hand shot—left side
   of basket.   15 shots
7. Jump shot—from center, left, and right.
   15 shots from each side—foul line distance.
8. Repeat No. 7—from greater distance.

B. *Dribbling*
   1. Right hand—width of gym.   6 times
   2. Left hand—width of gym.   6 times
   3. Around obstacle course (chairs). 10 times
   4. Dribbling sideways—width of
      gym.   6 times
   5. Dribbling backward—width of
      gym.   6 times
   6. Zig-zag dribbling.   10 times

Individual Program No. ____
(Task Check List)

Name _____   Starting Date _____

Subject Matter: Track: Start and Short Sprints

To the Student: Perform each task as proposed in the program
below and place a check next to the completed
task.

                                              Dates

Tasks

A. *The sprint start*
   1. 10 starts, as fast as you can, with 3–5 run-
      ning steps.
   2. 10 starts, with 10 running steps.
   3. 10 starts with 10 fast running steps fol-
      lowed by 10 slow steps followed by 10
      fast steps.
   4. 6 fastest starts with 3 fast steps.
   5. 6 starts followed by 60-yard sprint.

B. *Sprints*
   1. Alternate approx. 25 yards fast/slow
      around the track.
   2. Alternate 60 yards fast running and 30
      yards slow running once around the track.

> 3. 60 yards full speed, 15 seconds interval of rest by walking; 60 yards full speed, etc. Repeat 10 times.
> 4. 200 yards sprints with half the speed. 60 seconds rest intervals. Repeat 10 times.

Individual Program No. ____
(Task Check List)

Name _____ Starting Date _____

Subject Matter: Swimming—free style _____

To the Student: Perform each task as proposed in the program below and place a check next to the completed task.

Dates

Tasks						

A. *Complete stroke*
1. 100 yards half the speed.
2. 25 yards, ¾ speed.
3. 50 yards, ¾ speed.
4. 75 yards, ¾ speed.
5. 50 yards, ¾ speed, 20-second interval of rest followed by 50 yards, ¾ speed. Repeat 4 times.

B. *Arms only*
1. 100 yards, slowly (rest for a couple of minutes).
2. 100 yards, ½ speed.
3. 25 yards, full speed. Repeat 6 times with 30-second rest intervals.

C. *Legs only* (with kick board)
1. 200 yards, comfortable speed.
2. 200 yards, ¾ speed.
3. 50 yards, full speed, 15-second interval. Repeat 4 times.

D. *Complete stroke*
1. 100 yards, full speed, 60-second interval, 100 yards. Repeat 4 times.

İndividual Program No. ____
(Task Check List)

Name _____   Starting Date _____

Subject Matter: Tumbling

To the Student: Perform each task as proposed in the program below and place a check next to the completed task.

Tasks	Dates					

A. *Forward roll variations*

    1. 5 compact rolls (all joints bent).
    2. 5 rolls, one leg bent, the other straight.
    3. 5 rolls, both legs together and straight.
    4. 5 rolls, both legs straight and apart.
    5. 5 rolls, both legs straight; one moves before the other.
    6. 5 rolls, the knees at a 90° angle.

B. *Backward roll*

    7. Repeat the details of No. 1—backward.
    8. Repeat the details of No. 2—backward.
    9. Repeat the details of No. 4—backward.
   10. Repeat the details of No. 4 and *end* with feet together.

C. *Combinations*

    1. Combine roll of No. 2 with No. 9. Repeat 3 times.
    2. Compact forward, compact backward, compact forward.
    3. 2 compact forward rolls followed by 2 compact backward rolls.
    4. Alternate forward and backward straight legs rolls (2 to each direction).

In viewing these proposed designs one can observe:

1. There is enough physical activity for the individual. (Obviously, the teacher will vary the quantity depending on the class's minimal ability and the length of time available for the lesson.)
2. All these designs can serve as learning programs for several days. Often, in physical performance, there is a need to review and repeat the same tasks.

3. When these programs have been performed and checked off for several days, the teacher can follow up and present the class with a program which is more advanced.

This design offers a single-level program. This means that the entire class strives to achieve the level proposed in the program. This *is not* complete individualization. If the program is designed cleverly so that most students can perform most tasks, a variety of values will be gained as a result of this preparatory phase toward more complete individualization and independence. The students will learn to assume their new role as self-controlled learners and self-evaluators, although the self-evaluation merely requires the student to indicate that he has performed the task. The student may learn his capacity and pace of performance in the given activity.

Operational Design 2

The next operational design requires more *self evaluation*. This is the quantitative individual program. In this design the student is offered the opportunity to make quantitative decisions about himself. He can either find his *maximum* (which may border on fatigue) or determine his comfortable position on a scale of minimum to maximum in the performance of a given activity. This comfortable amount can be a part of one's maximum and used as a physiological unit of repetition in order to induce development. (Future research in physiology of exercise may supply us with more accurate formulae for manipulating parts of the maximum.)

Let us look at some samples of this operational design, and then we shall analyze its contribution. Suppose we examine this design in (a) developmental movement, (b) a ball game (soccer), (c) track and field (running), (d) volleyball.

Developmental Movement

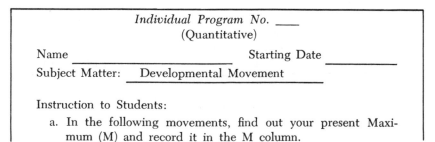

Individual Program No. ____
(Quantitative)

Name _____   Starting Date _____

Subject Matter: Developmental Movement _____

Instruction to Students:
  a. In the following movements, find out your present Maximum (M) and record it in the M column.

b. For the first few days practice with 2 or 3 sets containing $\frac{M}{2}$ as the quantity to be repeated. This procedure will apply to movement in agility, strength and endurance development. It should be used with more discretion with balance and flexibility development since these attributes are not so readily measurable.

c. After a week or two check your *M* again. In all probability your M will increase and your new $\frac{M}{2}$ will become the set to be repeated. So, your training load is: $X\left(\frac{M}{2}\right)$, where X indicates the number of times you do the set which is half your maximum.

d. If after a while you find that $\frac{M}{2}$ is too easy, increase the set to $\frac{2}{3}$ M and so on.

The following are movements in agility and strength which will serve as examples of this design:

Tasks	Present M	$X\left(\frac{M}{2}\right)$	New M
A. *Agility* (and endurance)			
1. Consecutive high-knee-raising hops. (knees raised to hip level.) Let's assume that M is $\frac{M}{2} = 10$. The set is	20		
10 hops. Suppose we start with 3 sets of 10.		3(10)	?
2. Consecutive hops—knees raised to chest level.	12	3(6)	?
3. Step jumps—long steps in the air—consecutive.	30	3(15)	
B. *Strength*			
a. Shoulder Girdle:			
1. Push-ups—straight body—arms at shoulders' width. *Interval* between sets: 15 seconds.	24	3(12)	?
2. Push-ups — straight body — arms wider than the shoulder, at 45° angle between arms and floor. *Interval*: 20 seconds.	16	3(8)	?

   b. Abdominal Region

1. In supine position, legs slightly bent—straight-trunk sit-ups with straight arms raised above the head.	15	3(8)	?
2. Supine — forearm support position: Raise your straight legs to 60° off the floor: "write" numbers in the air, 1, 2, 3, etc.	19	3(1to10)	?

Ball Game—Soccer

Individual Program No. ___
(Quantitative)

Name _____   Starting Date _____

Subject Matter: Soccer—Kicking and Dribbling

Instruction to Students:

In the following tasks determine what your comfortable maximum (M) is today. Then, practice the various tasks by repeating several times (X) the sets with half your maximum $\left(\dfrac{M}{2}\right)$. Use short intervals of rest (15, 20, 25 sec.) between sets. For example—suppose you can run quite fast and dribble the ball two lengths of the soccer field before you feel fatigued. So your M for this task is 2L (two lengths); $\dfrac{M}{2} = 1L$. Practice 3 or 4 of these single lengths while dribbling: 4 (1L). You'll be doing 4 sets of one length with a short interval between sets.

Tasks	Present M	$X\left(\dfrac{M}{2}\right)$	New M
A. *Dribbling* (for endurance)			
1. "Long distance" dribbling—¾ speed of running. (Intervals—? Determine your *need* for rest!)	2L	4(1L)	?
2. Obstacle dribbling—check for number of (W) widths of the field, dribbling around obstacles stationed every 20 feet.	2W	4(1W)	
3. Repeat Nos. 1 and 2 with different kinds of dribbling.			
4. Repeat Nos. 1, 2, 3 and change directions!			

B. *Kicking* (for control of distance)

   Use maximum number of approach steps.

   a. Toe kick.

      1. Determine your maximum distance | 40 yards

         Practice with set of $\frac{M}{2}$. | 10(20)

      2. Repeat $X\left(\frac{M}{2}\right)$ from less number of approach steps. | 10(20)

      3. Repeat $X\left(\frac{M}{2}\right)$ using only 2 approach steps. | 10(20)

   b. Instep kick.

      Repeat *a*. 1, 2, 3 for the instep distance kick.

Comment:

   a. Count only the successful kicks that reach the prescribed distance.

   b. Your objective is to be able to accomplish $X\left(\frac{M}{2}\right)$ without faulty kicks.

   c. If you find $\frac{M}{2}$ too easy, use $\frac{2}{3}M$ in the set.

Track and Field

Individual Program No. ____
(Quantitative)

Name _____   Starting Date _____

Subject Matter: Increase of Speed and Endurance in running (Interval Training)

Instruction to Students:

   In the following task find out what your Maximum is today. Some of the tasks below will be repeated in different quantities. These will be in sets consisting of parts of your M.

Tasks	Present M	$X\left(\dfrac{M}{Y}\right)$	New M
A. *Short sprints*			
1. Find out your maximum speed of 100 yards.	12 sec.		
2. Run the distance several times at ¾ speed. Rest intervals between attempts—30 seconds.		$6\left(\dfrac{3}{4}M\right)$	
3. Run the distance several times at ½ speed. Rest intervals—15–20 seconds.		$6\left(\dfrac{M}{2}\right)$	
4. Find your maximum speed of 50 yards.			
5. Run several 50's at ¾ speed with 15-second intervals.			
B. *"Longer" distances*			
1. Find out what is the maximum *distance* you can run in 60 seconds.	?		
2. Run 6 sets in maximum speed *half* that distance. Intervals: 30 seconds. (Check your time.)		$6\left(\dfrac{M}{2}\right)$	
3. Try the same ½ distance in less time.			
4. Rest for a few minutes.			
5. Check your new maximum distance in 60 seconds.			?

Comments: In this particular subject matter there are several variables that can be used in the design of the program and the use of M and parts of M for sets:

Variable 1: The speed.
Variable 2: The distance covered per unit of time.
Variable 3: Length of the interval.
Variable 4: The number of repetitive times the task is performed at a given speed using an interval of given length.

Manipulating these variables by holding three constant and changing one, or by changing two at a time, the runner will be introduced to a number of different situations which will improve his speed and endurance.

Volleyball

Individual Program No. ____
(Quantitative)

Name _____ Starting Date _____

Subject Matter: Volleyball—Tapping and Serving _____

Instruction to Students:

In order to develop better tapping and serving ability a variety of tasks is offered below. Each task represents a different degree of difficulty of ball control, since the distance and height change from one group of tasks to the next. In each situation check for your maximum (M) and then practice in sets consisting of parts of your M. Check for your new maximum every few days.

Tasks	Present M	$X\left(\dfrac{M}{Y}\right)$	New M
A. *Tapping*			
1. Establish the number of consecutive overhead tappings you can do in a slight straddle position, without moving from that spot.	?		
2. Under the same conditions practice with sets containing ½ your maximum (short rest intervals between sets).		$X\left(\dfrac{M}{2}\right)$	
3. Find out what your maximum is in tapping the ball overhead when you *stand* with feet together—don't move from this spot. (This situation is not usual during a real game situation, but for learning purposes it imposes more demands on the player because of the added balance problem.)	?		
4. Practice several sets of ½ your M under the same conditions.		$X\left(\dfrac{M}{2}\right)$	
5. Now, for the *fun of it*, check your M in overhead tapping without restriction of body position. Check *this M* every few days!	??		
6. Check your M in consecutive number of tappings against a wall—			

standing behind a line *10 feet* away from the wall.   ?

7. Practice with $X\left(\dfrac{M}{2}\right)$.

8. Increase the distance to 15 feet and check your M.   ?

9. Practice with $X\left(\dfrac{M}{2}\right)$.

10. Establish your M of consecutive tapping from 10 feet and hit the wall *above a given line!*

11. Practice with $X\left(\dfrac{M}{2}\right)$.

12. If you feel you can do more, practice with $X\left(\dfrac{2}{3}M\right)$.

13. Repeat the former by increasing the distance.

14. Repeat with increase of *distance* and *height* of the line on the wall.

B. *Serving* (underhand)

1. From 10 feet away from a wall establish your M in serving a ball over a *given line* marked on the wall. M means maximum consecutive balls that hit the wall above the line.   ?

2. Practice with $X\left(\dfrac{M}{2}\right)$.

3. Vary the distance and the height.

Comments and Discussion

An important aspect of this design is the self-testing process. Any activity which can be measured quantitatively can challenge the student to self-evaluation, an evaluation which will have a meaning to the performer.

As mentioned before, this design offers *visible results.* Everyone likes to see something concrete, the results of their efforts and learning. This visible result is *immediate.* The immediacy of the concrete results can help the student recognize the *realities* of his strengths and weaknesses. It does happen sometimes that the awareness of this reality creates a negative behavior response, and in this respect this design of the individual program (or for that matter *all* individual program designs) can serve as a *diagnostic tool* to identify the students who need support and

more encouragement than the rest of the class. The immediacy of results can, on the other hand, serve as immediate reinforcement and
motivation to move on.

From a technical standpoint, this design can furnish a permanent record of where the student began in the activity and the direction and
amount of progress which occurred during the learning process. It also
provides an immediate profile of the student at any moment. The
teacher can identify the place of the student by glancing at the program
or by asking the student to perform the checked item or items. This aspect of spot checking will create a feeling that the teacher *knows* what
is going on in the class. This is an important asset of this technique,
since it is very easy to lose track and get lost in the wide variety of
achievements in the same heterogeneous class.

While one examines the proposed samples of this design, it must be
clear that the designer of an individual program must know the subject
matter well. It requires more than just arbitrary selection of movements
in a given activity. In order to design a measurable task one must have
insight into the subject matter and into the relationship of the specific
task to the entire activity and knowledge of the relative position of the
task in the progress of learning *that* activity.

Operational Design 3

In this design the student is given the opportunity to make qualitative decisions about himself and answer the question: How well? The
process of answering this question requires that the student go through
the following steps:

1. Accept and understand the program presented by the teacher.
2. Understand the *details* of performance as explained or demonstrated.
3. Attempt to look at oneself and *judge* oneself against the offered
   criteria.
4. Be willing to execute the program and Steps 1, 2, and 3.

This design is more difficult to execute, since it requires more insight
into one's performance and more neuromuscular awareness. It is also
more difficult for the teacher to design, since the answer to "How well?"
depends on:

1. One's view of what constitutes good performance.
2. One's knowledge of what is necessary and important for better techniques in the activity.
3. One's knowledge of physiological and kinesiological principles.

4. One's ability to integrate these three requisites into an all-embracing judgment.

Let us examine the designs of the qualitative individual program in the following activities: (*a*) gymnastics (vaulting) and (*b*) track and field (javelin throwing).

Gymnastics

Individual Program No. ____
(Qualitative)

Name _____ Starting Date _____

Subject Matter: Gymnastics—Vaulting Side Horse—Flight Variations _____

To the Students:

Since vaulting requires terrific precision and complete awareness of body position in the air, the following tasks are arranged in a gradual manner, requiring progressively more details and more coordination. As you perform the tasks, "teach yourself" to be alert and be aware of every detail as described in the task. The first tasks will require an awareness of *one* detail only. The subsequent ones will increase in complexity. Place a check at the appropriate column—fair, good, excellent—based on your judgment of your own performance. You may enter in the last column the errors of your performance. The ability to perform what one sets out to perform (exact execution of the predetermined task) is *execution with form!*

(You may execute the particular task several times before you make your judgment and record it on the individual program. You may attempt another judging period after a few days of practicing your program.)

Tasks	F	G	E	Errors

A. *Two-feet take off and flight control*
The variable here is the posture of the body in the air on the way up toward the horse, while on top of it, and after leaving the horse.
a. Two-hand support on the horse—facing it.
   1. Compact body—all joints bent—land on horse.
   2. Compact body—all joints bent except pointed toes.				

3. Repeat No. 2 with head up.
4. Repeat No. 2 with knees apart.
5. Repeat No. 2 with knees and feet apart.
6. Repeat compact trunk, leg half bent, toes "not pointed"—vary the landing.
7. Repeat 1–6 with the center of gravity kept as low as possible during the ascent to the horse.
8. Repeat 1–6 with the center of gravity kept as high as possible during the ascent.
9. Take off and land on the horse with straight legs, feet between the hands.
10. Repeat No. 9 and keep the legs straight during the ascent.
11. Repeat No. 10 and vary the position of the feet during landing.

b. Two-hand support — change direction of landing on horse and change of posture.
1. Take off—fly in compact posture and land in the same posture on the horse—facing 90° to the original direction.
2. Repeat No. 1 with knees and feet apart.
3. Repeat No. 1 with varying feet positions.
4. Take off — fly in "sloppy" pike position.
5. Fly in pike position, straight legs, bent arms, toes "not pointed."
6. Pike position, straight legs, pointed toes, straighten supporting arms as soon as you can.
7. Vary the distance between the feet and the arms at landing on the horse.

c. Still change of posture—toward full body extension.
1. As you take off, pike your body and then straighten it before

Are
   you
      aware
   of
what
   you
      are
doing?

landing on the horse.

2. Take off and fly with straight body sideways and land on horse.
3. Any other variations?
d. Repeat a, b, c to the other side.
e. Raise the height of horse and repeat a, b, c.
f. Review a, b, c and increase the distance between the horse and take off spot (beat board).

Javelin Throw

Individual Program No. ____
(Qualitative)

Name _____   Starting Date _____

Subject Matter: Javelin Throw—the Throwing Motion _____

To the Students:

There are several components which make up the javelin throw: the approach run, the cross steps, the throwing position, the throwing motion and the follow through. This individual program is concerned with the throwing motion. All the mentioned components must operate in perfect harmony in order to translate the body momentum and power into a sequence of throwing motions which will produce a perfectly forward straight flight of the javelin. In order to do so, there is a need to control every part of the motion sequence. The following tasks consist of a minute breakdown of the details involved in the throwing motion. Perform each one several times—becoming aware of the details. Then combine each task with the previous part, two previous parts, and so on. On your program check the degree of performance: fair, good, excellent.

(Distribute your judging time. You may record it after trying each task several times. You could record again after several days of practice.)

Tasks	F	G	E	Errors
A. *The throwing stance (for a right-handed person)*				
1. Stand with your left side toward the throwing direction—feet in a comfortable straddle.				

2. Shift your weight to the rear leg (right leg in this case) and bend it slightly so that you can feel its springy action.
3. The left foot slightly touches the ground.
4. The trunk is slightly bent forward (facing 90° to the throwing direction).
5. The right hand, holding the javelin, is extended to the right side of the body, the javelin across the chest. *Its point* is approximately in front of the face and pointing to the direction of the throw. The javelin's tail is dropped to the ankle's height and is pointed to the opposite direction of the throw.
6. The left arm can be relaxed at the left side of the body or bent in front of the left shoulder at shoulder's height.
7. Review each part of the position *separately* so that you can concentrate on the accuracy of each position and become aware of what each part of the body is doing.
8. Combine 1, 2, and 3 without a javelin.
9. Combine 1, 2, 3, and 4 without a javelin.
10. Repeat 8 and 9 with a javelin.
11. Review 1, 2, 3, 4, and 5 without a javelin. Check the relationship between the body and the throwing arm.
12. Repeat No. 1 with a javelin.
13. Add No. 6.
14. Repeat the *whole* stance *slowly*.
15. Repeat the *whole* stance *fast*.
16. Walk around the field and at different intervals; *stop* and assume the stance *slowly*.
17. Repeat 16 *fast*.
B. *The throwing motion*
The sequence of motion is as follows:

ankle—knee—hip—trunk—shoulder—elbow—wrist.

1. Assume the throwing stance—check every detail.
2. Push off the right foot. The motion is at the ankle and the knee. Repeat several times.
3. As the knee straightens out, begin to rotate the hips to the left and begin to shift your weight in the direction of the throw. Keep the javelin in its plane! Check its point! Check the direction and height of the javelin's tail.
4. Complete the hip rotation so that the chest faces the direction of the throw. At this point your right ankle is raised a bit off the ground, and your right foot is turning toward the direction of the throw. The left foot *is* pointing at the direction of the throw, and the back is slightly arched backward. (Need for great shoulder and upper back flexibility) *keep* the javelin in the direction of the throw. At this point the javelin will move into a new direction if you do not control it!
5. The left arm is bent at shoulder's level and is pulling to the left, aiding the rotation of the body.
6. The right shoulder continues to move forward to complete the trunk's rotation *pulling* the elbow as close to the *ear* as possible.
7. The elbow extends in a forward direction followed by the wrist's whip to release the javelin.
8. The body follows through in a relaxed manner.

Operational Design 4

This design presupposes the intrinsic developmental quality in the structure of the activity. It provides the learner with a *choice* of levels of performance—quantitative, qualitative, or both. It is the job of the individual learner to test his ability and assess the quality of his performance against the proposed levels in the individual program. The levels are designed according to physiological and kinesiological insights into what constitutes *more* and *higher* on the degree of difficulty scale. The beauty of the multi-level individual program is that an individual will identify his varying abilities in different tasks. He may be on a lower level in some tasks and higher in others. The road to progress and improvement is clear and open. Samples are offered in the following activities: (*a*) developmental movement, (*b*) gymnastics—the balance beam, (*c*) basketball—shooting.

Developmental Movement

Individual Program No. ____
(Multi-level)

Name _____   Starting Date _____

Subject Matter: Developmental Movement _____

To the Students:

In the following tasks check your performance and determine where you are *today*. Circle the description or the amount of your *present level*. You can see that the tasks are arranged in a gradual manner. If your present level is your maximum, you may practice for the next few sessions using the tasks below your present maximum level, particularly if you find that the consecutive maximum performances create undue fatigue. After a few days of practicing the present level try the next one.

Developmental Objective	Region of the Body	Level 1	Level 2	Level 3
A. Agility	Whole body	1. Jump off the ground and raise your knees to hip level— 5, 6, 7, 8, ⑨ 10 times.	Same jump: 11, 12, 13, 14, 15, 16, 17, 18, 19, 20 consecutive times.	2(10) (read 2 sets of 10 with a short interval), 3(10), 2(15), 3(15), etc.
		2. Jump off the ground and raise your knee to chest level— 3, 4, 5, 6, 7, 8 times.	Same jump: 9, 10, 11, 12, 13, 14, 15 consecutive jumps.	Same jump: 2(7), 2(10), 2(12), 2(15), 3(10), 3(12), etc.

		3. Jump off the ground sideways from behind one line over another line 3 feet apart 3, 5, 7, 9, 11, 13, 15 times.	Same consecutive jump with raised knees during every jump 3, 5, 7, 9, 11, 13, 15 times.	Same jump, increase the distance to 4 feet (tape on the floor). 3, 7, 9, 11, 13, 15 times.
B. Strength	Shoulder Girdle	1. "Seal walk" in yards 10, 15, ⑳, 25, 30. 2(10), 2(15), 2(20).	"Seal walk" —arms in a wider position. In yards 10, 15, 20, ⑤, 30, 35, 40.	"Seal walk" —wide base and motion backward 10, 15, 20, 25, 30, 35, 40.
		2. Push-ups —"regular" base: hands at shoulders' width 10, ⑫, 14, 16, 18, 20 times.	Same—increase the quantity 21, 22, 23, 24, 25, 26, 27, 28, 29, 30.	Push-ups— wider base: 45° between each arm and the ground 7, 8, 9, 10, 11, ⑫, 13, 14, 15.
(See Comment about degree of difficulty at the end of this individual program.)		3. Push-ups —extended: place your hands ahead of your shoulders. Start with any comfortable distance 3, 4, 5, 6, 7, 8, 9 times.	Move your arms a few inches forward and execute the push-ups 3, 4, 5, 6 times.	Move them forward again 1, 2, 3, 4, 5, 6, 7, 8, 9, 10.
	Abdomen	1. Sit and lean back on your forearms. Lift your legs (straight) to 45° off the ground. In this position "write" your name in the air with your toes. Repeat twice.	Same position: "Write" your first and last name in the air. Repeat twice.	Lower the legs to approximately 30°. "Write" your full name. Repeat twice.
		2. In position similar	"Write": 1–25, 1–30,	Legs at 30° "Write"

Developmental Objective	Region of the Body	Level 1	Level 2	Level 3
		to No. 1, "write" numbers in the air 1–10, 1–15, 1–20.	2(1–15), 2(1–20), 3(1–10), 3(1–15).	2(1–10), 3(1–10), 4(i–10), etc.
	Legs	1. Stand in a wide straddle (example —legs 2 feet apart). Shift weight to one leg, bend the knee and shift to other leg 10, 12, 14, 16, 18, 20 times to each side.	Wider straddle (3 feet)— shift weight 10, 12, 14, 16, 18, 20 times to each side.	Wide straddle (3 feet) 2(10), 2(15), 2(17).
C. Flexibility	Shoulder Joint	1. Stand in a straddle position arms raised sideways above shoulder level. Pull both arms backward *slowly* 10, 15, 20, 25 times.	Same position, arms raised 45° above shoulder level— pull back 10, 15, 20, 25 times.	Same position; arms raised upward (keep abdomen in!); pull back 10, 15, 20, 25 times.
	Hip Joint	1. Stand in a straddle position. Bend down and forward 10 times and reach with fingers to *ankle* level.	Same position and same movement; however, reach with your fingers to the floor in the center of the straddle.	Same position and movement. Reach to the floor with your *palms*.
		2. Sit in a straddle position and bend several times along each *straight*	Same position and movement. Reach with your fingers to the soles	Same position and movement. Reach to the sole and bend your

		leg. Reach with your fingers to the *ankle.*	of your feet.	forehead to the respective knee.	
D. Balance: Stationary		1. Execute a T scale. Hold it for 5, 10, 15, 20, 25 sec. on each leg.	Execute a round-back scale. Hold it for 5, 10, 15, 20, 25 sec. on each leg.	Execute a diagonal scale (head below the heel level) 5, 10, 15, 20, 25 sec.	
Recaptured		1. Jump and turn 180° and land on the *same* spot—2, 4, 6, 8, 10 consecutive times.	Repeat with 270° 2, 4, 6, 8, 10 times.	Repeat with 360° 1, 2, 3, 4, 5, 6, 7.	

Comment: The simplest way to design levels of tasks is, of course, by increasing the number of repetitions and/or sets.

A more sophisticated design of levels calls for keener insight into the structure of the movement involved and knowledge of the concept of degree of difficulty (D. of D.) which is *intrinsic* in any movement and is manipulative by the process of identifying and changing the variables involved in the given movement: place of center of gravity, length of lever, angle of the lever, etc. For a full discussion of this matter the reader is referred to (56).

A careful design of tasks which progress step by step within a given program or within a group of programs will actually lead the student to higher achievement in an independent manner. This arrangement is quite similar to the concept of programmed instruction, since it revolves around the ingredients of step-by-step development, self-motivation through achievement of one's own level of accomplishment, and high visibility of achievement.

The previous example could probably serve as a guide for self-development for a month or so (practicing several times a week). If the design offers sufficient steps in progress in each level and several levels to be achieved, then one program can be used for several weeks. From the practical standpoint, however, it is more desirable to design shorter programs and use several of them consecutively. This procedure will give the student a feeling of completion when he proceeds from Program 1 to Program 2 and so on.

The circular markers on the program indicate the starting position of the student at the beginning of the program. The performance-profile is quite clear. The student's position in each movement and level is well identified. The square marker indicates the position of the student in his program a few days later. The time for self-testing can be determined by the teacher, by the student, or by both. Some students might be better motivated by attempting a higher level each lesson, while others may be content with practicing the "present" level for a while before attempting the next step. The decision making concerning this procedure could also be individualized.

These programs can be used as permanent progress records for each student in the given activity.

Now, let us examine this design in some other activities.

Gymnastics

Individual Program No. ____
(Multi-level)

Name _____   Starting Date _____

Subject Matter: Gymnastics—Balance Beam: Turns, Turns and
One Additional Position

To the Student:

One important aspect of developing good performance on the balance beam is the ability to execute any turn at any place on the beam, following most movements and preceding most movements. It is also very important to be able to perform each turn in different body positions. In the following program which offers you many tasks in a graduated manner, circle the ones you can do presently and keep marking your achievement as you progress in your performance.

Turns in standing position: stand on the beam facing the length on the beam, arms raised sideways for improved balance. In this position turns can be done under the following conditions: (a) with the line of gravity remaining between the legs, (b) with the line of gravity moved to the rear leg, (c) with the line of gravity moved to the front leg, (d) Combinations of a, b, and c.

Tasks	Level 1	Level 2
a. *Line of Gravity in the Center*		
1. Turn 180° in a regular standing position.	1, 2, ③ 4, 5, 6 consecutive times.	7, 8̲ 9, 10.
2. Turn 180° in standing position.	With arms at the sides of the body 1, 2, 3, 4, 5, 6, 7, 8, 9, 10.	With crossed arms 3, 6, 9, 12, 15, 18.

3. Turn 180°, propelled by one-arm swing at shoulder level.	3, 5, 7, 9, 12 consecutive times.	Use two raised arms for intentional momentum: 3, 5, 7, 9, 11, 13, 15.
4. Repeat No. 2.	Drop your chin to your chest 3, 5, 7, 9, 11, 13, 15 times.	Look upward! *Safety!* 3, 5, 7, 9, 11, 13, 15.
5. Repeat No. 3 — use both arms for momentum.	Drop your chin to your chest 3, 5, 7, 9, 11, 13, 15 times.	Look upward! *Safety!*
6. Repeat No. 2 with closed eyes.	Arms at sides of the body: 1, 2, 3, 4, 5, 6.	With slight arm momentum: 1, 2, 3, 4, 5, 6.
7. Repeat the turn.	With arms raised upward: 2, 4, 6, 8, 10.	Raised arms with a ball: 2, 4, 6, 8, 10.
8. Turn with slightly bent knees.	Arms as in 4: 2, 4, 6, 8, 10.	Arms as in 4—increase speed of turns: 2, 4, 6, 8, 10.
9. Turn in half squat position.	As in 8: 2, 4, 6, 8, 10.	As in 8: 2, 4, 6, 8, 10.
10. Turns in full squat position.	Turn 90° at a time: 2, 4, 6, 8.	Turn 180°. 2, 4, 6, 8, 10.
11. Turn in full squat with use of both straight arms to gain momentum.	Eyes focusing ahead 180° turns: ②, 4, 6, 8, 10.	Eyes raised above horizontal line—180° turns: 2, 4, 6, 8, 10.
12. Repeat No. 11 with different arm positions.	One arm raised upward, the other hanging down: 2, 4, 6, 8, 10.	Both arms raised upward: 2, 4, 6, 8, 10.
13. Start in standing position.	Turn 180° and get down to squat position 2, 4, 6, 8, 10.	Get down and immediately get up and turn 180° 2, 4, 6, 8, 10.
b. *Line of Gravity shifts to the rear leg*		
1. As you turn shift your weight to the rear leg.	In regular standing position 2, 4, 6, 8, 10.	Turn 180° with arms raised above the head.
2. Repeat No. 1, bending the rear leg as much as you can.	2, ④, 6, 8, 10, 12.	Turn 180° and use both arms for momentum (increase speed of turn) 2, 4, 6, 8, 10, 12.
3. Repeat No. 2.	As you turn lift the front foot to a slight touch of beam 2, 4, 6, 8, 10.	As you turn lift the front foot and keep it in the air 2, 4, 6, 8, 10.
4. Repeat No. 3.	As you turn bend your head forward 2, 4, 6, 8, 10.	As you turn bend your trunk forward 2, 4, 6, 8.

Tasks	Level 1	Level 2
5. Repeat No. 3.	Bend your head backward 2, 4, 6, 8, 10.	Bend your trunk backward 2, 4, 6, 8, 10.
c. *Line of Gravity shifts to front leg*		
1. Turn 180° and as you turn shift your weight to the front.	Keep your arms at the sides of the body 1, 2, 3, 4, 5, 6, 7, 8, 9, 10.	Swing your arms upward as you turn 2, 5, 8, 11, 15.
2. Turn 180°.	As you turn bend your trunk forward 3, 5, 7, 9.	Bend your trunk backward 3, 5, 7, 9.
3. As you complete the 180°—	Raise your rear leg slightly off the beam 1, 2, 3, 4, 5, 6, 7, 8, 9, 10.	Move into a scale 1, 2, 3, 4, 5.
4. As you complete the 180°—	Bend your trunk sideways hands on hips 1, 2, 3, 4, 5, 6, 7, 8, 9, 10 consecutive turns.	Bend your trunk sideways with arms raised above the head. 1, 2, 3, 4, 5, 6, 7, 8, 9, 10.
5. Repeat No. 3.	Bend the front leg to half squat 2, 4, 6, 8, 10.	Bend front leg and extend arms forward 2, 4, 6, 8, 10.

d. *Combinations*

Here you can design a series of combinations of turns based on the materials presented above. These combinations can be assembled from several different tasks in Level 1 or a mixed arrangement of Level 1 and Level 2.

Basketball

Individual Program No. ____
(Multi-level)

Name _____   Starting Date _____

Subject Matter: Basketball—shooting

To the Student:

In developing better shooting the following are some important aspects:

A. Accuracy from any place around the basket.
B. Accuracy from various body positions.
C. Accuracy from various distances.
D. Accuracy combined with the speed of shooting.

The following program provides you with many specific situations designed in graduation in order to help you improve in these four aspects.

Tasks	Level 1	Level 2
1. Set shot from foul line.	5 out of 10.	8 out of 10.
2. Repeat No. 1 twice.	2 (5/10).	2 (8/10).
3. Set shot from 45° right. (foul line distance)	5/10.	8/10.
4. Set shot from 45° left.	(5/10.)	8/10.
5. Repeat No. 3 and No. 4 twice in a row.	2 (5/10).	2 (8/10).
6. Set shot from right 30°.	5/10.	8/10.
7. Set shot from left 30°.	5/10.	8/10.
8. Set shot from right 10°.	(4/10.)	7/10.
9. Set shot from left 10°.	4/10.	7/10.
10. Combined left and right 10°.	9/20.	12/20.
11. From center — back to the basket.	5/10.	8/10.
12. 45° right—back to the basket.	Can you decide how to determine the level?	?
13. 45° left — back to the basket.		
14. Right 20° right side of basket.		
15. Left 20° left side of basket.		
16. Repeat No. 11 2 yards more than foul line.	?	?
17. Repeat No. 12; *vary* distance from basket.		
18. Repeat No. 15; vary distance from basket.		
19. Try as many shots as you can, in 60 seconds, from the foul line. (The balls are supplied as rapidly as necessary by a partner.)		
20. Try as many lay-ups as you can in 60 seconds.		

It is obvious that this proposal for an individual program in basketball shooting will need to be adjusted according to the length of time per session available for the improvement of shooting. The above program could very readily be divided into three consecutive programs.

Further programs could be designed with the same sequence of shooting tasks by introducing *additional* elements of the game, so that each task in the individual program is performed in *conjunction* with an element or elements drawn from the real game situations. *Examples of additional elements* which may *precede each* specific task in the program are:

1. A short pass from the right.
2. A short pass from the left.
3. A longer pass from the left.
4. A longer pass from the right.
5. A short or a long pass from the back.
6. A short pass from under the basket.
7. Repeat Nos. 1–7, using *various* passes.
8. Two short passes.
9. A partner dribbling from the right—bounces the ball to you.
10. A partner dribbling from the right—bounces the ball to you.
11. *Introduce another game reality:* Place a *player between you and the basket* and execute the entire program with this human obstacle standing there.
12. Repeat No. 11 with the defensive person moving just his body.
13. Repeat No. 11 with the defensive person trying to disturb your shot.
14. Can you introduce other game realities?
15. Can you *vary* these realities in order to challenge and sharpen shooting performance?

Operational Design 5

Thus far, the proposed operational designs serve as freeing agents in individual physical performance and help the performer to develop a new self image. The *subject matter* arrangement offered:

1. Gross tasks which are parts of a given activity
2. A variety of *small innovations* designed to challenge the neuromuscular process and to create a greater psychological motivation, which usually occurs when innovations are introduced
3. *Interrelationship* of the tasks, which were: (*a*) random or (*b*) traditional (in the sense that certain given tasks seem to be a necessary part of a whole activity) or (*c*) inventive—the results of the prolific imagination of the instructor.

All this is fine and important in contributing to the development of a more self-reliant and self-motivating student. Three elements, however, are needed for a program which is growing and reaching a *specified* target. These elements are:

1. The sequential consideration of a given program. There is a need to determine the unique sequence of tasks in every programmed situation.
2. Attention to the size of the interval (the step) between tasks.
3. Immediate built-in reinforcement, which is given to the student by the very fact of succeeding in the performance of the sequential tasks.

These three elements seem to be the essence of Skinner's proposals for programmed instruction (72). The first proposal is for a unique and special *order* of relationships which is *intrinsic* to the structure of the subject matter; this applies to all subject matter. The second is the basis for the reinforcement theory (and reality) which proposes that *all* can learn if subject matter gaps are eliminated; this is individualistic. Therefore, in order to design the most efficient program in a given activity one must develop the most refined insights into the structure of the subject matter and its minute components. One must recruit all available knowledge in order to understand all the possible bonds which may exist among these components. Only then does it become possible to select the most probable universal bond which will lead the learner with optimum success from one step to the next. Since the current discussion is in reference to physical execution of sequential tasks, the term "programmed execution" is offered. This is to differentiate it from "programmed learning" in the cognitive sense, a dimension which is analyzed, discussed, and demonstrated in the chapter on guided discovery.

So, in order to program the execution of a given activity, the following things must be determined:

1. *The final target must be clear and specific.* It is not enough to decide to teach the learner the hook shot, the headstand or the arm movement in the breast stroke; rather, a very definite image of the shot must be determined and indicated in the written program. The specific line of the body and other necessary details must be predetermined for the headstand, and a very accurate and specific arm position must be selected for the given stroke. All this is necessary because the pre-selected target determines the components of the activity and the steps for getting there.
2. A decision has to be made concerning the major variables of *the activity* For example, in a hook shot the major variables can be: (*a*)

Body posture (which includes starting position, body position during the shot, and the release position). (*b*) Relationship between the body and the ball. (This includes components such as: one-hand ball dexterity, two-hand ball manipulation, using one hand or two hands to move the ball through the air.) (*c*) Relationships between the body and the basket. (Including components such as: angles between the body and the basket, distance from the basket, height or closeness to the basket.)

3. Small tasks must be selected and arranged in such a sequence that most learners (perhaps all) will reach the target after executing all the tasks. These small tasks are *always* related to the given *variable* of the activity and are arranged in close intervals—that is, each subsequent task is just a little closer to the target than its predecessor. It is like climbing a tall ladder that has rungs at small intervals to insure the success of the journey upward.

Let us examine an example of programmed execution based on these principles. Suppose we program the headspring over a side horse.

Our first decision concerns the target. Well, here is the description of this vault: after a few steps of an approach run, take off, fly to the horse in pike position, place your hands and head on the horse, shift your weight forward, execute a kip motion, and land on your feet in standing position—then, back to the horse, arms raised sideways above shoulder level. This is a gross description of a vault. Our next step is to decide about the *variables* involved in this activity. The following are the variables in this vault:

> Variable 1: The take-off.
> Variable 2: The posture during flight to the horse.
> Variable 3: The posture while over the horse.
> Variable 4: The landing.

The description of the vault, given above, specifies to some extent the elements in each variable. We must now continue to particularize the description of the vault by looking at the *components* of each variable and selecting a specific component.

In Variable 1, the take-off, it is possible to offer a variety of components, such as the distance between the feet position at take-off or the angle of the knees. Perhaps in this case it would suffice to ask for a comfortable take-off executed from the balls of the feet. (The word "comfortable" is not very specific, but it provides each individual with the opportunity to adjust the take-off to what will come after.)

In Variable 2, many different posture components can be executed here. The body can be in many different postures after taking off. We must *specify* our selected posture. Let it be a pike position so that the angle between the trunk and the legs is a little less than ninety degrees. This is the flight posture. It requires an immediate lift of the hips right after take-off.

Variable 3 calls for a "momentary" angular headstand on the horse (preferably an angle between forty-five and sixty degrees). This position accommodates the kip motion which follows. Note that this variable, too, includes many different components: varying angles between trunk and legs, position of hands in relation to the head, and so on.

Variable 4 includes a specific landing position. After the kip motion, which causes a flight away from the horse, land on two feet, with knees slightly bent, trunk straight, arms raised sideways above shoulder level. This landing position is only one *among many* landing possibilities which depend on components such as direction, number of points of contact with the ground, or compactness or extension of the body.

Now we are ready for the last phase of designing the variety of small tasks or small steps in each variable. The *check list* will do the job here, since the learner concentrates on accurate execution of *sequential tasks*.

Variable 1—The Take-off

1. Run toward the horse from a starting point located a few steps away from the take-off area (or the beat board).

2. Repeat the approach run with a steady speed.

3. Repeat the approach run, at steady speed, and hit the beat board with both feet. That means that your last step must be of the right length *for you*. If your last step interferes with a comfortable and coordinated two-feet bounce off the beat board, move your starting spot sufficiently farther from or closer to the horse to adjust the last step.

Variable 2—Posture during Flight

4. Repeat the approach run from your prescribed distance, hit the beat board with two feet (on the balls of the feet), and bounce into the air. If your momentum is too strong, you may reach to the horse and support yourself on two hands placed on the horse.

5. Now, as you take off the beat board place your hands on the horse and elevate your hips. Fly upward in a pike position.

Variable 3—Posture over the Horse

6. Repeat Step 5 so that you will be in pike-support position for a second or two.

7. Repeat the pike-support position on the horse and tuck your head. (You will find that the tucking of the head will aid the lifting of the hips in the pike position.)

8. Repeat the pike-flight, and as you touch the horse bend your arms gradually until the tucked head will reach the horse. At this point you are in an angular headstand.

9. Repeat Step 8 several times until you are secure in executing this step. (For *safety* reasons it is advisable to have one or two spotters from this step on.)

10. Repeat Step 8, and when you reach the angular headstand position on the horse, slowly move your weight forward up to the instant of *losing balance*. The spotter intervenes at this point and stops you from rolling off the horse.

11. Repeat Step 10 several times until you become *aware* of the exact moment of loss of balance.

12. Repeat Step 10, and as you reach the moment of loss of balance, execute the kip motion.

Variable 4—Landing

13. The kip motion will carry you away from the horse. You will land on your feet, your back to the horse.

14. Repeat Step 12 and keep your legs straight through the entire flight away from the horse. Bend your knees slightly as you land to accommodate the elasticity of the landing.

15. Repeat the entire vault, and as you execute the kip motion, extend your arms in a deliberate manner. This motion occurs at the elbows and at the shoulders. It will help elevate the upper part of the body during the arched flight away from the horse, and will assist a more vertical landing.

16. If you wish to add a few more details concerning the landing variable, you may add here Steps 17, 18, 19 and so on.

Comment:

The sixteen steps above are examples of sequential small tasks within each variable. These steps are based on some degree of insight into the structure of the headspring. If further insights can be developed and more detailed tasks can be isolated, then they should be inserted in their proper order.

If you find that at any point the *interval* between two steps is too large for the student, insert an additional step that will *effect* the connection between the two steps in question. *Reduction of gaps between steps always increases success in execution and learning.*

The example given above, of deciding the variables in a particular activity and designing small steps to accomplish the activity variables, can serve as a guide for designing individual programmed execution in all physical education activities. It is important to realize that the example presented here presumes knowledge of the kip motion. The kip motion, itself, can also be programmed and would be presented to the student before he tried the headspring over a horse.

Several of these *programs* can be arranged sequentially to constitute a *chapter*, a *unit*, or a complete *course* of study in a particular activity or sport.

Let us examine the kinds of things that can be programmed in a particular sport. In basketball, for example, one can program:

1. The learning of a single shot.
2. Series of different shots.
3. Techniques of dribbling.
4. Techniques of passing.
5. The role of each player in given defense situations.
6. The role of each player in given offense situations.
7. The relationships between any two players in common defense or offense situations.
8. The relationships among all members of the team in common defense or offense situations.
9. Proposals 5 through 8 in a single situation.
10. Proposals 5 through 8 in a changing situation leading to better execution of a given strategy.

In gymnastics one can program:

1. The execution of any given single movement (which includes a starting position, one movement, and an end position).
2. The execution of two combined movements.
3. A series of movements (repetitious or different ones).
4. A particular sequence of movements.
5. A particular quantity of movement.
6. A particular quality of movement.
7. A particular rhythm of movement. This will occur when a specific sequence of movements is executed to prescribed *music*.

Can you suggest the kind of things that can be programmed in track, field events, swimming, tennis, soccer, football, softball, baseball, hockey, volleyball, other sports; locker room procedures; taking attendance; distribution of equipment; other physical education activities?

TECHNICAL PROPOSALS

All individual programs should include the following parts:

1. *General information.* Name of student, grade, date, the activity, the specific subject matter.
2. *To the student.* This part includes the necessary instructions to the student. It could contain a statement of purpose, a general statement about the activity, and a statement of how to go about this program and how to treat the evaluation part. This will reduce the need for repetition in case of review or if students are absent.
3. *The actual body of tasks.*
4. *An evaluation section.* Preferably, there will be an evaluation section next to each task. Both student and teacher can identify instantly the present status of the student.

All programs should be numbered. It provides for faster identification, easier filing and Sequential Order of several programs.

All programs should be Mimeographed. This provides the teacher with *mass communication* and *instant control.* Mimeographed individual programs release each student from the need for constant contact with the "central source," the teacher. In large classes the mimeographed program which contains the students' achievement and progress markings provides for instant control by spot checking the present development level of various individuals in the class.

Experiences in high schools have demonstrated successful execution of individual programs in classes of more than 100 students in volleyball, track and field, developmental movement, and other activities. Individual programming has been equally successful in smaller classes in several elementary schools. A major part of the developmental program of the majors in physical education at Rutgers University has been conducted for the last several years through individual programs.

IMPLICATIONS OF THE INDIVIDUAL PROGRAM

Since the individual program is quite far away from the command style on the spectrum of styles and brings the student much nearer the target of individual independence, it would be helpful to study the implications of this style for the following aspects of the teaching-learning situation:

1. *Organizational matters.* (*a*) class organization (space arrangements), (*b*) the time dimension, (*c*) equipment distribution.
2. *The student.* (*a*) his position in the four developmental channels, (*b*) implications for discipline, (*c*) implications for motivation, (*d*) reactions of the students themselves to the individual program .
3. *The teacher.* (*a*) changes in self concept (his own freedom), (*b*) his leadership role.
4. *Curriculum.* (*a*) implications for flexibility and variability (mixed curriculum), (*b*) relationship to the individual student's abilities and interests.

Organizational Matters

Class Organization

This style calls for complete geographic freedom and freedom of mobility on the gymnasium floor or on the field. The student must be free to choose an area in which he can execute his program. His choice may be affected by the activity, by the availability of facilities and equipment, and by the degree of congestion; nevertheless, the choice is his. The overall view of the gymnasium or the field is one of random arrangement of students all occupied with their respective programs. In smaller areas with larger classes, every square foot is utilized; you never see big empty areas and groups congregating around a single piece of equipment.

The Time Dimension

Implications for the use of available time are staggering. Since every individual student has his own program, his own targets to reach, and his own area in which to work, hardly any time is wasted on useless waiting, which is physically unrewarding and psychologically demoralizing. It has been shown that classes which are well educated in the values of the individual program use close to 100 per cent of the available time for learning purposes. These classes are also capable of endurance. Learning can continue on an individual basis for up to two hours and more without any lengthy stops or disturbances. Therefore, coaches, for maximum efficiency, use individual programs for training sessions.

Equipment Distribution

Quite a novel thing happens to the use of equipment. Every piece of equipment seems to be in demand; every available ball is in use. In one case a school managed to produce forty-five balls for a lesson in volleyball. Some balls were the usual ones used in the gymnasium; others seemed to appear from the obscurity of hidden shelves of the equipment room; some were old but usable; some were rubber playground balls, which are quite good for practicing tapping against the wall; some were basketballs, which were used by the stronger boys as a "degree of difficulty" device to strengthen their fingers; and some balls were borrowed—the students brought them to school. No one questioned the amount of learning that took place in the thirty-five or forty minutes available that day for volleyball. The sight may be strange in the beginning, but one can easily and happily get used to the sight of everybody learning.

On another occasion all the mats owned by a school (including those usually piled unused in the corner) were used simultaneously for the first time.

Often one is stimulated to improvise equipment in order to accommodate individual learning. For example, in some schools which had either one regulation balance beam or none, small individual balance beams have been built by the school's shop. All one needs is a few two-by-four planks. Another example is the use of marked targets on the wall for practicing various basketball shots.

A more efficient use of equipment was reached in schools where the *mixed curriculum* was used (see p. 137).

The principle is simple. Equipment is used to the maximum extent; everyone moves; everyone is engaged in learning; every piece of equipment, every inch of floor, every wall is used—to fulfill the concept of *maximum activity per student per unit of time*!

The Student

Now, let us examine what happens to the student who is engaged in the individual program.

Position in the Four Developmental Channels

In the physical channel he is nearly achieving complete independence. All decisions about his physical performance within the given program are in his hands. His position on the social channel is moving toward maximum development, since there are no geographic or association restrictions imposed by the teacher. These two aspects of the freeing process have a profound effect on the emotional status and self concept of the individual student. At this stage of the freeing process he has learned to accept himself as a self-directed learner. In fact, it has been observed that unnecessary intervention by the teacher at this stage can create a disturbance in the students' learning tranquility and continuity. The weaning process is *almost* complete at this stage.

It has also been observed that the high degree of social and emotional freedom and stability has effected improved physical performance. These changes occurred in *all* students. They varied in intensity, frequency, and duration because of a variety of individual and group intervening variables; but they occurred in *all* students.

One channel, though, is still inhibited. The position of the individual on the intellectual channel drags behind. Only a limited number of intellectual activities are required and performed in connection with the physical performance at this stage. An analysis and development of this phase of learning is offered in the chapters that follow.

Implications for Discipline

Discipline problems are sharply reduced. The self-involvement in one's own program and development creates a new focus for the student: himself. He has the opportunity to see himself in a new light, the light of a self-directed learner, a person who has the ability and knowledge to go about the things he wants to do. This new focus on oneself reduces the chances of students' getting involved in activities which are traditionally considered discipline problems. With the reinforcement of the self in this kind of learning and seeking, a new sense of responsibility evolves toward one's role in the creating social climate of the group.

The student finds himself among other people who are engaged in self-development, and a feeling of kinship permeates the learning climate. This can happen to most students within varying lengths of time. Those who demonstrate inability to become self-directed learners are readily identified, and here the teacher has the opportunity to make a direct contribution by association with these students who proclaim by their behavior their need for the teacher's aid. This direct, individual contact with the teacher may be what the student, lost in the anonymity of mass education, has needed.

Implications for Motivation

The result of individual involvement and self-direction is increased motivation. The high visibility quality of the individual program, which offers the student the realization of his progress supported by the accepting attitude of the teacher, creates a unique chain reaction of motivation–achievement–strengthened self concept, which in turn enhances motivation; and the reaction continues. The teacher's observation, correction and encouragement given at the right time can develop an enduring motivation.

The Teacher

As in all previous styles, the teacher who uses individual programs learns to make behavioral adjustments. The most spectacular adjustment, however, occurs during the development of the individual program. The teacher needs to learn to accept the drastic degree of weaning which occurs. He needs to adjust to his new role, which requires him to send out stimuli at a much reduced rate. This, in the beginning, as teachers themselves have stated, meant to them loss of class control; and loss of class control is the most potent and eternal fear of all teachers. Teachers who have tried individual programming state that a degree of anxiety developed at first, until they realized that a new control system was being formed, a stronger and more lasting one.

Another anxiety promoter was the change (reduction) in verbal behavior. During the execution of the individual program there are many moments of silence; there is no need for the teacher to say anything, at least not in the usual mode of class communication—broadcasting statements for the mass. This opportunity to observe individual students and communicate with individuals while the rest of the group is engaged in learning is perhaps a unique experience for some teachers, but this style of teaching provides the teacher with that unique luxury.

The teacher's concept of his own leadership role, his role in the hierarchy of decision makers, standards producers, and evaluators, is in the process of adjustment.

Curriculum

Perhaps the most dramatic and far-reaching implications within the school walls are the implications for curriculum development and curriculum structure. Any teacher who is actually carrying out the individual program style on a sustained basis must be provided with adjustments and changes in several important facets of the curriculum. The teacher might find that these affected facets are stated in the curriculum but are usually under the headings of philosophy, objectives, or general statements—all of which connote remoteness. The needs for adjustment during the execution of this style are *real* and *present*.

Some of these facets of the curriculum which need to be looked at anew are:

1. The selection of subject matter—that is, what to teach?
2. The sequence of activities within the year.
3. The sequence of activities over a period of several years.
4. The relationship of the seasonal sports to the school program and to the students' needs, abilities, and interests.
5. The role of the developmental activities (developmental movement, gymnastics, wrestling) to the school program and to the students' developmental needs and interests.
6. The design of so called "units".
7. The issue of the cluttered curriculum, which attempts to "cover" everything in one year.
8. The issue of the repeated curriculum, which offers virtually no change or progress from year to year.
9. The need for a *mixed curriculum*.

A word of explanation about the need for a mixed curriculum is in order here. Most curriculums in physical education seem to be single-minded, pre-determined, and rigidly fixed in their distribution over the year. Thus, the school offers so many weeks of this activity and so many weeks of that one. Obviously, this kind of a curricular arrangement is based on only one principle—that is, X number of activities must be covered during the year. There is no relationship at all between this structure and the performance status of so many varying students. Either all students are requested to learn all the presented activities— an impossible feat because of the heterogeneity of classes in physical education—or there is *no* demand for learning, accomplishment, and developing in any meaningful way, since the activity changes, not when the student has reached a desirable level, but when the number of prescribed weeks are over, usually in the middle of the progress of most students.

Another grievous flaw which needs to be corrected is our single-minded approach to curriculum. "Six weeks for wrestling" says the course of study, "eight weeks of basketball," and so on. Let us assume for a minute that this length of time is sufficient for learning some aspects of the activity for most students; then, one must realize that this is possible only under good learning conditions where the student-equipment-space-teacher ratio is reasonable. The reality in most schools, however, presents an unreasonable ratio of these components of the teaching-learning process; and what one observes in many schools is the familiar picture of large masses of students crowding the basket, the volleyball net, the few available mats, and so on, depending upon the unit at play. This situation produces minimal physical development because there is infrequent active participation, and it results in educational demoralization because there is a lack of continuity in learning. When a wrestling unit is taught and executed, it means in many cases that forty, fifty, or sixty students are gathered around a small collection of mats and take turns in learning the activity. This kind of situation offers insufficient opportunity for physical development and learning. At the same time, though, one observes that all the basketballs, the baskets, the walls, and good parts of the gymnasium floor are *idle, unused.* What an absurdity! There we have students who sit and waste time in waiting (just multiply the number of minutes between turns on the mats, parallel bars, or any other equipment by the number of school days, and the results will astound you); and on the other hand we have equipment, space, and a teaching-learning device called *the individual program!* With a slight adjustment in scheduling the classes' group rotation from wrestling to basketball during each week, we can approach a much more efficient use of time and facilities, and much greater learning. While some groups (a part of the class) are involved with the teacher in wrestling (using any of the styles), the rest of the class is involved in learning basketball by means of the individual program. There is really nothing new in a mixed program. It is done in other areas of the school curriculum both in elementary and secondary schools. Some students of the class read, others write, some eat lunch while others are at the library, and so on. All it takes is a slight concept-adjustment. Instead of having a large class in which individuals learn a little about one activity, we'll have a large class in which each individual learns *more* about *two* activities as a result of better use of time, space, equipment, and greater responsibility in self-directed learning. (The reader is referred to the analysis of time-space-equipment in the chapter on teaching by task). Another interesting result of this adjustment is that in terms of *real* time both wrestling and basketball will have fourteen weeks, a rather respectable amount of time to achieve more learning continuity and more proficiency in performance in both sports. Under the present structure inadequate achievement occurs during the first year of school (let us say first year of high school); a similar inadequacy repeats itself in the second year and is multiplied in the third and fourth years. All this occurs because of a rigid curricular structure and a failure to realize the contributions of alternative styles of teaching. These two deficiencies short change the individual student as well as the group and do not help students to approach the educational goals agreed on by educators. The use of the individual program has strikingly far-reaching implications for curricular adjustments, for the individual's progress along the four developmental channels, and for attainment of the educational goals of a democratic society.

MORE IDEAS FOR THE INDIVIDUAL PROGRAM

An interesting, amusing, imaginative, and useful idea for the design of the individual program is the *theme*. For the necessary purpose of developing a particular aspect in a sport, or just for fun, you can develop an entire individual program which *focuses* on a particular theme. A theme would be a single idea which links all the tasks in the program. The theme does not need to be large and earth shaking; on the contrary—a small idea which is the center of the whole program will add spice and interest to learning. In fact, the theme idea adds a game-like quality to the program and increases the fun of execution.

Examples of Themes for Various Activities

Developmental Movement

All movements in the program will include or demonstrate the following:

1. Slow motion.
2. Very fast motion.
3. All joints bent.
4. All joints extended.
5. The body is never vertical.
6. All movement is backward.
7. All movement is sideways.
8. The entire body in motion.
9. All movements while body is in minimum balance.
10. All movements while body is in maximum balance.
11. Lowering the center of gravity.

12. Elevating the center of gravity.
13. Circular motion (whole body and/or segments).
14. Wave motion.
15. Appendages are moved in opposite directions.

There are many more. Can you think of a theme that will permeate an entire individual program?

Vaulting

1. End all vaults with a turn.
2. All vaults with all joints bent.

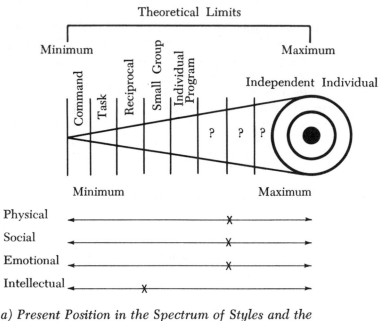

a) Present Position in the Spectrum of Styles and the Channels of Development

b) Teacher's Present Position on the Freedom Scale

Figure 15.

3. All joints extended.
4. End all vaults facing north!
5. Shake your head at some point.
6. Clap hands at some point.
7. Do everything as slowly as you can.
8. Courage! (Include only vaults which require courage.)
9. Two consecutive obstacles (horse and Swedish box, buck and rolled-up mat).

Can you think of any theme?

Basketball

1. Motion backward.
2. Motion sideways.
3. With the weak hand.
4. Hopping on one foot (dribbling, passing, shooting).
5. Head down! (Look at the floor all the time.)
6. Overhead ball handling.
7. Ball below knee level.
8. Stiff body!
9. Limp body!

Do you have any suggestions?

7

Guided Discovery

The styles already discussed have offered the learner very limited intellectual activity. In order to assess this assumption we need to define in more specific terms the meaning of the phrase "intellectual activity" or at least suggest some of the components which make up this unique human activity. Psychologists and researchers in cognition who offer operational explanations of mental activities speak in terms of "the ability of the intellect to. . . ." The following are some of these abilities of the intellect:

1. Ability to inquire.
2. Ability to compare.
3. Ability to draw conclusions based on the comparison.
4. Ability to make decisions.
5. Ability to use different strategies in approaching a problem.
6. Ability to invent.
7. Ability to discover.
8. Ability to reflect.

As we view the behavioral details (variables and components) of both teacher and student in all previous styles of teaching, it becomes apparent that, in fact, *the student* is not engaged in most of these operations. *They are not required and not induced; neither do they develop spontaneously.* Therefore, the intellectual capacities of the learner are inhibited. They remain dormant, unchallenged, and unused. Even those abilities which are partially evoked—such as memory, recall, and some sort of understanding—are in most cases passive and unrelated.

In effect, all the previous styles which made significant contributions
to the growth of the individual in three important freedoms have curtailed the fourth. Thus far the learner has been in a condition of *cognitive acquiescence.* In order to develop potent intellectual behavior
which uses and demonstrates the varieties of cognitive operation, the
learner must cross the *cognitive barrier* which exists at this point on the
spectrum of styles. Figure 16 illustrates this condition.

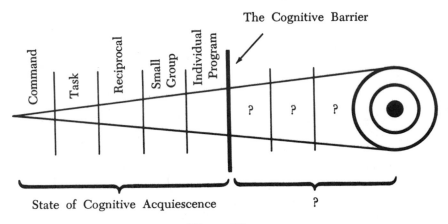

Figure 16.

Our next question must be: How does the learner cross the cognitive
barrier? What should the teacher *do* and *say* and what should he *not*
do or *say* in order to *initiate* and *develop* that new kind of learning
process?

Festinger's *Theory of Cognitive Dissonance* (31) proposes that a
cognitive disturbance, an irritation, creates the need to seek a solution
and that only the act of finding a solution will remove the disturbance,
the dissonance. Peace and tranquility, consequently, can be restored.
This theory has great implication for teaching behavior and learning
processes. The state of *cognitive acquiescence* ceases to exist when
cognitive dissonance occurs. New dimensions of the thinking process
are aroused. The dissonance induces *the process of inquiry*, which reflects the need to seek an answer, a solution. The process of inquiry
leads in turn to *discovery*. The act of discovery (Bruner [14]) occurs
as a result of the cognitive dissonance. Let us examine these three steps:

Cognitive Dissonance ⟶ Inquiry ⟶ Discovery

This schema proposes that discovery comes about as a result of a
previous operation—inquiry. One does not begin to inquire unless one

needs to find out something. This need to find out is created, aroused, and stimulated by that little mental dissatisfaction which forces the mind to focus on the problem at hand and awakens the possibility of discovery.

Bruner in his statement on the act of discovery values small discoveries. He does not refer to great discoveries of things unknown to civilization; on the contrary, he expounds on the merit of this act to any person who discovers that which has been unknown *to him*. When these three phases of the cognitive process operate in integrated succession, the learner crosses the cognitive barrier. If any one of the phases stands alone, the cognitive process is either incomplete or fruitless.

It is proposed, then, that the prevalent term "exploration," which is currently used in the literature (Halsey [42], Andrews [6], and others), serves only to identify one phase of the cognitive process and needs to be supplemented by the others' terms. In the theoretical construct of the spectrum of styles the phase of exploration or inquiry must be preceded by a motivating force—the cognitive dissonance—and must come to fruition by the act of discovery itself.

Before we discuss the anatomy of the styles which translate these theoretical proposals into operational designs for teaching behavior, it is important to answer the following question: What kind of things can people discover? Here are some possible answers:

1. Facts (in any subject matter).
2. Ideas, concepts.
3. Relationships (similarities, dissimilarities).
4. Principles (governing rules).
5. Order or system.
6. A particular physical activity—a movement.
7. How?
8. Why?
9. Limits (the dimension of "how much," "how fast," etc.).
10. *How to* discover.
11. Other elements! Can you suggest any?

Any of these categories can become the *focus* of discovery and of the subject matter itself. When you use any of the discovery styles of teaching, you may focus on the *concept of the limits* as the "what" of your teaching. For example, you might want your students to discover the varieties of body postures which may exist during the flight in a given kind of vault. Let us take the side swivel vault (sometimes known as the front vault). Now, in this vault the place of the two hands on the vaulting horse, the direction of flight, and the landing posture are specified. If you ask your class what are the limits of the body posture in the air, they will respond that a compact body (all joints bent) will represent minimum posture and a fully extended body will represent maximum posture. In response to your next question—"Are these the only two possibilities of body posture?"—they will say, "No, these are the *limits*; but there are many other postures in between." Thus, by using vaulting as the physical activity and by your specific verbal behavior, you induced in your students a small discovery. They know now not only a few unrelated vaults, but they also understand the role of each posture in this vault within a specific concept—the limits!

I have used many times in schools, demonstrations in conventions, and on the C.B.S. educational television program "Shape Up," a classic illustration of how children can discover *a concept*. The concept sought is: the realization of individual differences in physical ability and the design of opportunity for all in the same activity. The activity chosen is the high jump.

Step 1: Ask two children to hold a rope for high jumping; invariably they will hold the rope horizontally at a given height (for example at hip level).

Step 2: Ask the group to jump over. Before they do so, you might want to ask the rope holders to decrease the height so that everybody can be successful.

Step 3: After everyone has cleared the height, you ask, "What shall we do now?" "Raise it!" "Raise it!" is the answer—always! (The success of the first jump motivates all to continue.)

Step 4: Ask the rope holders to raise the rope just a bit. The jumping is resumed.

Step 5: "Now what?" "Raise it!" the children will respond.

Step 6: Raising the rope two or three more times will create a new situation, a new reality. Some children *will not* be able to clear the height. In traditional situations these children will be *eliminated* from the jumping, and only the better ones will continue; there will be a constantly diminishing number of active participants. The realization of individual differences becomes real; the *design* for opportunity for all has not yet come about.

Step 7: Stop the jumping and ask the group, "What can we do with the rope so that nobody will be eliminated?" Usually one or two of the following solutions are proposed by the children: (*a*) Hold the rope higher at the two ends and let the rope dip in the center. (*b*) Slant the rope! Hold the rope high at one end and low at the other.

These solutions provide the democratic high jump. Both solutions provide all jumpers with the opportunity to be successful. Each can pick his height and progress to the next level. No one need be eliminated.

This kind of high jump has implications for the self concept of each jumper; for his role and place in the group; and, moreover, for a whole new set of values in physical education. The *focus*, however, of this example is on the discovery process—discovery of *a concept expressed in motion*. Similar examples can be designed with the focus on the categories mentioned above: fact, principles, relationships, and so on.

The bond of cognition and motion must be carefully defined, and styles of teaching must be designed to accomplish the purpose of teaching students to learn by the heuristic process.

> A great discovery solves a great problem but there is a grain of discovery in the solution of any problem. Your problem may be modest, but if it challenges your curiosity and brings into play your inventive faculties, and if you solve it by your own means, you may experience the tension and enjoy the triumph of discovery. Such experiences at a susceptible age may create a taste for mental work and leave their imprint on mind and character for a lifetime. [Polya (65) from the preface to the first printing.]

How does one behave to reach this level of teaching? What can a teacher of physical education do to create this kind of heuristic climate in the class and lead the students to and through the paths of discovery?

The first style of teaching which embodies the discovery concept is identified as *guided discovery* (Katona [47]). A very modest example of this process was presented in the beginning of this chapter (the democratic high jump). Several more examples will be offered in various activities and sports after the discussion of what is involved in this kind of teaching behavior and the description of the anatomy of guided discovery.

The most *fundamental* difference between guided discovery and all the previous styles is that in guided discovery *the teacher never tells the answer!* The instant an answer is given to a student the process of cognitive dissonance ⟶ inquiry ⟶ discovery ceases to exist.

If this principle is understood, then several behavioral adjustments are necessary in order to implement this style of teaching. First, the teacher needs to make *linguistic adjustments*. Instead of using exclamation words, one uses question words. There is an enormous difference between an exclamation and a question, particularly when used by a teacher. An exclamation connotes authority, something to accept, perhaps without questioning. To many young students the teacher represents the omnipotent and omniscient being. It must be obvious that when this kind of behavior is manifested, other styles of teaching, not guided discovery, are operating. A question, on the other hand, may have a completely different set of connotations for the student, and a different set of action may occur:

1. The student learns that the teacher is interested in what he has to say.
2. He learns that he is *expected* to give an answer.
3. The expectation to give an answer requires an understanding of the question. One must pay attention in order to hear and understand the question.
4. If the question is relevant (we shall return later to the issue of relevancy), then the student is *beginning* to be *actively* involved with the teacher.
5. This involvement is usually a result of the cognitive dissonance created by the question.
6. The cognitive process has begun. The student now *must* pursue the answer.

All this and much more occurs as a result of the adjustment in the linguistic behavior of the teacher.

The next adjustment, equally important in preference and impact, is an emotional one. The teacher *must wait for the answer* to come from the student. One needs unfathomed patience and tranquility in order to create the aura of accepting what the student says or does. An affirmative word, a head nod instead of "yes," any sound of approval coupled with a relaxed manner are the most important ingredients in the actual behavior of the teacher who uses guided discovery. The *student* is the *focus*, and he must remain so if this process is to continue and succeed. Therefore, the decision by the teacher to attempt these two behavioral adjustments represents the moment of truth in teaching. Perhaps the teacher needs to cross an emotional barrier in order to help the student cross the cognitive barrier.

It has been observed that many teachers cannot behave like this. With some it is the philosophy of the roles in the teaching-learning process which prevents them from making the necessary adjustment. With others it is a matter of a self image which dictates the need to assert oneself at all times and *be* the focus of the process. In either case guided discovery cannot be used, and the students will not benefit from this style of teaching.

This behavior of waiting for the response (a verbal answer or a movement response), manifesting an accepting climate, and offering an approval is compatible with the reinforcement theory of learning which is founded on the principle of stimulus-response-reinforcement (Skinner [72], Harlow [43]). It has a tremendous impact on success in learning because the stimuli are so directed and so designed as to produce *particular* responses—hence, success! When the success is rewarded, the learner is reinforced and is motivated to continue to receive the next stimulus (a question, a problem, or a statement to do a particular thing). This next stimulus is also designed to elicit a particular response which is rewarded when produced. Thus begins the cycle of a particular kind of learning: meticulous, economical (in terms of cognitive efficiency), and channelled to a specific purpose. In guided discovery, in its pure and perfect form, there is *no failure!* The assets and power of this style of teaching are recognizable to anyone who has used it.

The cognitive economy in leading a student to comprehend a phenomenon, to see relationships, to engulf systems is spectacular and overwhelming. The fact that the student by himself evolved the answer, by himself discovered the response, reflects a special dimension of internalizing data (Piaget [46]), which creates a more intimate relationship between the student and the subject matter.

Now then, on the basis of these theories and assumptions, what should be the structure of the teaching behavior which produces this kind of learning? What is the anatomy of guided discovery? Since this style represents a departure from those discussed earlier, the anatomy is presented below in detailed, rather than outline, form.

ANATOMY OF GUIDED DISCOVERY

Variable 1

Pre-class decisions in guided discovery consist of determining the specific subject matter to be taught and learned. The next and most important step in the operation of guided discovery is to determine the *sequence* of steps. These steps consist of questions or clues arranged in a manner which slowly, gradually, and securely leads the student to the end result (a fact, a concept, a particular movement, etc.). *Each step is based on the response given in the previous step.* This means that each step must be carefully weighed, judged, tried out, and then established as most efficient at this particular location in the sequence. It also means that there will be an internal connection between steps, related to the *structure* of the subject matter. In order to design related steps the teacher needs to anticipate the possible responses which the students may offer to a given stimulus (step). If these possible responses seem to be too diverse or tangential, then the teacher needs to design another step, perhaps a smaller one, closer to the previous step, and thus narrow down the number of diverse responses. In fact, the pure and perfect form of guided discovery is structured in such a way that a minimum number of alternative responses is possible—perhaps even one response per clue. Whenever more than one response is possible and available, then the teacher must be ready with a clue which guides the student to select only one (the most appropriate for the present end in view) and abandon the other. This happens frequently in guided discovery. It is also understandable. People's minds are different, and they do not always respond to the same clue (carefully as it may have been selected) in the same expected way. Often the learner will approximate the "correct" response, and then there is the need to guide him to the desired response by an additional clue or question.

Variable 2

The execution phase in guided discovery is the test of the sequence-design. It is also a test of the extent to which the teacher made the necessary adjustments mentioned above: (*a*) Never tell the answer. (*b*) Always wait for the student's response. (*c*) Always reinforce the response.

Even if the student's response is incorrect or inadequate, you can behave in an accepting manner by saying, "Would you like to think some more?" or "Have you checked your answer?" There are many more ways of saying it. A very special cognitive process is being developed, integrated with an emotional process of learning to be accepted and a willingness to speak up, to risk solutions, and so on. This process must not be killed by a harsh response from the teacher. Any such response not only interrupts the developing process in the verbally or physically responding student but also curtails the flow of thoughts and movements in the rest of the class. In addition, any harsh or frequent negative responses from the teacher will create a suspicion about the genuine intentions of the teacher. If failure is met with hostility, then there is no sense in responding or being involved. The emotional and cognitive streams are quite visibly intertwined during the process of learning by guided discovery.

Any serious failure among the students to respond indicates *inadequate* design of the individual clue or the sequence as a whole.

So, the execution phase in guided discovery is a process of the most delicate interplay of cognitive and emotional dimensions between teacher and student—both bound most intimately and intricately to the subject matter. The tension that develops with the anticipation at each step is relieved only when the *final discovery* has occurred. The student, by himself, without being given the answer, has accomplished the purpose, has found the unknown—has learned!

In the execution phase, then, the teacher must be aware of the following factors:

1. The direction of the sequence of steps.
2. The "size" of each step.
3. The interrelationship of the steps.
4. The speed of the sequence.

Variable 3.

The nature of the evaluation phase in guided discovery is unique to this style. In a sense evaluation is built into every step of the process. The reinforcing behavior, the success of the student at each step, indicates a positive evaluation of his learning and accomplishments. A total evaluation is exercised by the very fact that the process is completed, purpose is achieved, and the subject matter is learned.

The approval of the response at each step constitutes the evaluation process which is most immediate, precise, and personal. In turn, this immediacy of positive evaluation and reinforcement serves as a continuous motivating force to seek more solutions, to investigate more, to learn more.

This kind of evaluation, consisting of the teacher's accepting behavior in conjunction with approval of "correct" responses, has been observed to have a potent social effect in a group situation. When this process begins to develop in a class, the willingness to participate and offer overt responses (verbal or physical) becomes contagious. It seems as if more and more students acquire the feeling of security and are less and less afraid to respond. Although this process is more efficient and promising in classes of "regular" size, it is possible with the aid of experience and energy to make it succeed also with large classes. With large classes it is difficult to ascertain that each individual student is at or near the current step; nevertheless, the general climate of excitement of learning does seem to permeate even a large group and helps recruit more active participants in the cognitive and physical processes.

Well executed guided discovery can lead anyone from development level A to development level B (see Figure 17). Relevant, small steps will get the learner to the objective. Too large a step, at any point, creates a gap and stops the fluent process of guided discovery.

Occasionally the learner will present a tangential response (Figure 18). An additional clue is needed to bring him back to the directed sequence of clues and responses.

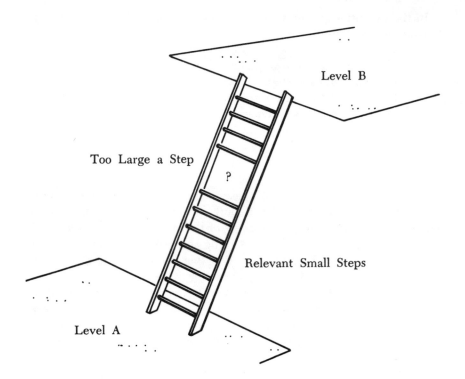

Figure 17. *The Ladder of Guided Discovery*

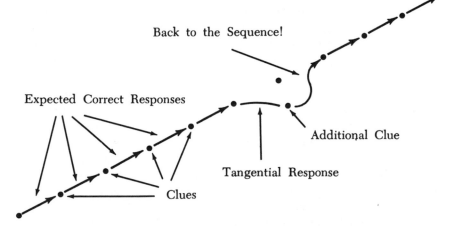

Figure 18. *The Process of Guided Discovery*

EXAMPLES OF GUIDED DISCOVERY IN PHYSICAL EDUCATION AND RELATED AREAS

Example 1

Subject matter:	Soccer.
Specific purpose:	To discover the use of the toe-kick in long and high-flying kicks.
Question 1:	"What kind of kick is needed when you want to pass the ball to a player who is far from you?"
Anticipated answer:	"A long kick!" (Response: "Good!")
Question 2:	"Suppose there is a player from the opposing team between you and your teammate."
Anticipated answer:	"Then the ball must fly high!" ("Right!" says the teacher.)
Question 3:	"Where should the force produced by the foot be applied on the ball in order to raise it off the ground?"
Anticipated answer:	"As low as possible!" ("Yes!" responds the teacher.)
Question 4:	"Which part of the foot can comfortably get to the lowest part of the ball without interference with direction of the run and its momentum?"
Anticipated answer:	"The toes!" ("Very good!" proclaims the teacher.)
Question 5:	"Would you like to try it?"

Let us analyze this process. This short process of interaction between the questions and the responses produces results which are inevitable and universal. It will always work because there is an intrinsic (logical, if you wish) relationship between the question and the answer in terms of the stated purpose—the toe-high-kick. Every so often it might be necessary to inject an additional question due to the age of the learner, level of word comprehension, and the like. The basic structure of the sequence, however, remains the same. The teacher will find that after several experiences in using a given sequence it becomes quite refined and more successful.

Perhaps it is superfluous to repeat here, but one can see why the two behavioral adjustments proposed at the beginning of this chapter are necessary in order to achieve the development of this cognition-motion bond. The same *physical objective* of using the toes for the high flying kick could have been accomplished by *showing* and *telling.* The student would have learned the high kick as demonstrated and told by the teacher. The student would observe and repeat in action; but the comprehension of relationships, the understanding of the "why," so essential to high-quality learning, would be missing from the whole experience.

Now, let us try to understand the technical aspect of the sequence design. Which question comes first? What is the second? As a rule of thumb, proceed from the *general to the specific* and relate each question to the *specific purpose* of the movement. The purpose of the long high kick is to get the ball to a faraway player. So, by presenting the learner with the situation of two players far apart, the *obvious* need is for a long kick. Now, it is true that one could produce two kinds of long kicks—one rolling on the ground and the other the high flying kick. In a real game situation the high flying kick will be used to get over the heads of the opponents, so you introduce this condition in the form of question No. 2, which suggests the need to raise the ball into the air. Now to simple mechanics of forces (which is within the realm of every child's experence)—If you want to raise the ball into the air, you must, in most cases, apply the force to the bottom of the ball in an upward direction—hence question No. 3 and its appropriate, inevitable answer. The next question practically follows by itself; you need to apply a particular part of the foot to meet the conditions which were established in the previous response. This is where the toes come in handy.

It is suggested that the following *benefits* are derived from this process:

1. The student has learned the physical response as planned by the teacher in the lesson in soccer.
2. The student has learned the relationship between the flight of the ball and *his foot,* the rudimentary mechanics involved, and the place of this kick in the tactics of soccer.
3. The student has learned that he *can* discover these things by himself.
4. Learning psychologists believe that when this process is employed frequently and purposefully, the learner will reach the point of *asking* the questions by himself whenever a new situation arises; the learner will be able to transfer this thinking and discovery process.

The beauty of guided discovery is most patent while teaching novice students. It is most interesting to use this style with students who do not know anything about the subject matter at hand. They respond almost uninterruptedly to the sequence of clues and responses. They are not pulled astray by partial knowledge or dim memories of some movement detail. Learning is fresh, clear, and flowing.

Example 2

Subject matter:	Shot put.
Specific purpose:	To discover the stance for putting the shot.
Question 1:	"What is the main purpose of putting the shot in competition?"
Anticipated answer:	"To put it as far as possible."
Question 2:	"What is needed to achieve distance?"
Anticipated answer:	"Strength—power!" (Teacher's response, "Correct!")
Question 3:	"What else?"
Anticipated answer:	"Speed!" ("Good," says the teacher.)
Question 4:	"In the total motion of putting the shot *where* should the power and speed reach their maximum?"
Anticipated answer:	"At the point of release!" ("Excellent!" responds the teacher.)
Question 5:	"Where would be the point of minimum strength and speed?"
Anticipated answer:	"At the stationary starting position!" ("Very good," says the teacher.)
Question 6:	"In order to achieve the maximum strength and speed at the point of release, how far from this point should the starting position be?"
Anticipated answer:	"As far as possible!" ("Good answer!")

Comments: This is the rationale behind the present starting position used by the top shot putters. If the answer to question No. 6 is not readily given, an additional step must be taken—"In order to gain maximum momentum should the body and the shot travel a short or a long distance?"—then, "How long?" From this point on, physical responses are called for.

Question 7:	"If the point of release is at this line in front of your body, what would be *your* starting position which fulfills the requirements of response No. 6?"
Anticipated answer:	Here some students might stand in a wide stance (the balance requirement becomes clear immedi-

ately, and some sort of straddle position is usually offered. If this is not apparent you may ask, "Are you well balanced?" and wait for the new physical response) with the shot resting someplace on the shoulder. However, others may take the concept of "maximum distance" from the point of release quite literally and attempt to stretch out the arm holding the shot; here you intervene with another question.

Question 8:	"Since the shot is quite heavy, can the arm do the job alone, or could the body help?"
Anticipated answer:	"The body could help!" (The student already felt the weight of the shot and the awkwardness of holding it in the outstretched hand.)
Question 9:	"Where could you place the shot in order to get maximum push from the body?"
Anticipated answer:	"On the shoulder!" ("Good!")
Question 10:	"In order to gain maximum momentum, do you place your body weight equally on both legs?"
Anticipated answer:	"No. On the rear leg!" ("Good!")
Question 11:	"What should the position of this leg be to gain maximum thrust from the ground?"
Anticipated answer:	"Slightly bent!" ("Very good!")
Question 12:	"Now, what would be the position of the trunk to fulfill the conditions discovered above?"
Anticipated answer:	"Slightly bent (and twisted) toward the rear leg!" ("Excellent!")
Teacher:	"Good! Does this position seem to be the starting position we were looking for?"

This painstaking procedure may frighten the uninitiated teacher; but one gets used to it. Since the accomplishments in learning outweigh by far the initial difficulties and apprehension, the teacher will be motivated to try it whenever the situation merits this style.

The sequence developed here follows the same principles as in the previous example. As always, the biggest obstacle is "What is my first question?" Once the purpose of putting the shot becomes clear, the steps toward the accomplishment of the purpose became rather clear and interrelated. In fact, the *intrinsic structure* of the shot put becomes clearer to student and teacher alike. Actually we progressed in the teaching-learning process by moving backward, by retracing the movements and positions from the end result (the put) to the starting position (the stance).

It reminds one of the technique used for discovering the road between point A and point B in a maze. Often one starts from the target and traces the road back to the starting point.

It seems that together we have discovered the technique of how to structure the process of guided discovery.

Polya ([65], p. 230) sums it up in the following way:

> There is certainly something in the method that is not superficial. There is a certain psychological difficulty in turning around, in going away from the goal, in working backwards, in not following the direct path to the desired end. When we discover the sequence of appropriate operations, our mind has to proceed in an order which is exactly the reverse of the actual performance. There is sort of psychological repugnance to this reverse order which may prevent a quite able student from understanding the method if it is not presented carefully.
>
> Yet it does not take a genius to solve a concrete problem working backward; anybody can do it with a little common sense. We concentrate upon the desired end, we visualize the final position in which we would like to be. From what foregoing position could we get there? It is natural to ask this question, and in so asking we work backwards.

Example 3

Subject matter:	Developmental movement, dance, gymnastics.
Specific purpose:	To discover the effect of the base of support and place of center of gravity on balance. (This lesson has been taught successfully many times to Grades 3–5.)
Question 1:	"Do you know what balance is?"
Anticipated answer:	(Answer is given in motion; there is no need here for a verbal response.) Some children will place themselves in a variety of balance *positions*, and some will *move* sideways, which requires a degree of balance other than "normal." The chances are that *all* children will have a response which illustrates the issue of balance.

Question 2:	"Could you *be* in maximum balance?" Sometimes it is necessary to use the word *most* instead of maximum.)
Anticipated answer:	Usually the responses here vary. Some will assume a variety of erect positions, and some will assume lower positions they have seen in football, wrestling or in various gymnastics stunts. It becomes necessary to repeat this question.
Question 3:	"Is this your most balanced position?" (It is worthwhile checking the solutions by pushing each child slightly and thus upsetting the position of balance.) Within a relatively short period of time several children will get close to the ground in several very low balance positions. Some may even lie flat on the floor. (These will be the hardest positions to upset by a slight push.)
Question 4:	"Could you, now, be in a position which is in a little bit *less* balance?"
Anticipated answer:	Most or all children will assume a *new* position by reducing the size of the base. This is often accomplished by the removal of a hand as a support, raising the head in supine position or rolling over to one side from supine position.
Question 5:	"Now, could you move to a new position which is still *less* balanced?"
Anticipated answer:	Now the process is in motion. All children will assume a position which has less area of contact between the body and the floor. *Some* will start rising off the floor. Within two or three more steps to reduce the balance, most of the class will be in rather high positions with close to minimum point of contact between the body and the floor (Questions 6, 7, 8).
Question 9:	"Could you be now in the *least* balanced position?"
Anticipated answer:	Most children stand on the toes of one foot; some raise their arms. Occasionally somebody will suggest standing on one hand or even on one finger.

So in a sense, by use of motion, they offered the correct answers and discovered some of the factors affecting balance. They discovered that a low, wide-based position is more balanced than a high, small-based position.

This is really sufficient. The concept is understood through the use of motion. Verbalizing the principles is really not necessary. However, if the teacher feels that a verbal summation is needed, he can ask, "What is the difference between the most balanced and least balanced position?" "What made it so?" The correct answers will be readily available to the children. Children can learn to discover not only new movements and a variety of these but also the principle which organizes them into a concept.

Example 4

Subject Matter: Basketball

Specific purpose: To discover the principles of the fast break. (This lesson was designed and executed by Prof. Rudolph Mueller at Rutgers, the State University of New Jersey.)

The following is a planned learning experience on the theoretical basis of a specific concept of attacking in basketball. This concept is known as *pattern or controlled fast-break basketball.* In reaching this object, the lesson is structured in such a manner that the student will develop an understanding of the factors which are the very essence of the concept, fast-break basketball.

The physical education majors at Rutgers University are exposed to a total learning situation on fast-break basketball which includes several theoretical sessions and actual participation during the laboratory sessions. There is also a student assignment which is given in conjunction with this experience; this assignment encourages the students to seek alternative concepts of the fast break and to make a comparative analysis of the strengths and limitations of their proposals. The following lesson is in reality an isolated fragmented experience; but it does illustrate how specific subject matter can be taught by guided discovery.

The actual design presents the question, the desired answer, and some clues which may be needed for further clarification or to re-direct the students toward the desired answer. This particular lesson does, on several occasions, require students to draw on previous experiences; the experiences, however, were not left to chance, but were planned learning experiences in previous classes.

Questions	*Clues*	*Desired Answers*
1. What factors concerning fundamentals, shooting, did we find will influence the success of the shot?	*a*) What can we say about the player shooting and the possibility of the shot going in?	*a*) Will depend on the ability of the shooter to put the ball in the basket.
	b) In what way might the defense influence the success of the shot?	*b*) Defensive man's position in relation to the shooter.
	c) What relationship is there regarding actual execution of the shot and possible success?	*c*) Kind of shot which is being executed.
		d) The shooter's distance from the basket.
2. Holding all the shooting variables constant, except the distance from the basket, what relationship did we observe between the shooting percentage and the distance factor?		*a*) In most cases, the closer to the basket, the greater the possibility of being successful.
3. Then, if this assumption—the closer to the basket, the greater possible success—is valid, what kind of shot should offer us the greatest probability of success?		*a*) The layup.
4. The layup seems ideal; yet haven't we all observed teams during warm-ups rarely missing, and yet	*a*) What is the basic environmental difference between the warm-ups and the game situation?	*a*) Pressures of the game situation evoke certain adjustments by the shooter.

they miss more fre- *b*) All the factors you
quently in the actual have identified create
game situation? Why? stresses to which a
shooter must make ex-
ecution adjustments—
they might all be clas-
sified as environmen-
tal or game stresses.

5. Let's list some of *a*) What is the primary *a*) Awareness of the
the factors which con- purpose of the de- defensive purpose
tribute to creating fense? which is to gain pos-
"game pressures." session of the ball.

b) What kind of offen- *b*) Offensive errors
sive errors can be such as: poor passes,
committed which will muffed dribbles,
create pressures on shooting without ball
the shooter? control, shooting before gaining body
control, etc.

c) Besides the offen- *c*) Real or imagined
sive errors concerning pressures which affect
fundamentals, what the emotions and the
pressures might affect mental process of
the shooter? concentrating on flaw-
less execution.

Let's take a moment to summarize the important material (concepts)
which has been developed thus far.

1. We have a premise—based on observation—that, all things being
   equal, the closer the shooter is to the basket, the greater the probability of success.
2. There is likelihood of more offensive mistakes because of the intensity of defensive pressures.
3. There is possibility of offensive mistakes because of lack of offensive
   control.

Problem: Can we design an offense which would increase the number
of opportunities for layups and yet decrease defensive and offensive
pressures?

Questions	*Clues*	*Desired Answers*
6. What would be a very simple solution to the stated problem?	*a)* What factors must be present in order to have the ideal situation: the layup with no defensive or offensive pressure?	*a)* The shooter at layup distance from the basket.
	b) If answer is "baskethanger," then give a description of a baskethanger.	*b)* In possession of the ball.
	c) What factors must be present in order for this baskethanger to be successful at his role?	*c)* Before defense can pick him up.
7. This baskethanger who actually stations his physical self at his basket has found one way of getting to that particular floor location. How else might he get there?	*a)* This method will place additional offensive game pressures on the shooter.	*a)* Single man—break as the other team shoots.
	b) This method of offense is less crippling than the baskethanger method.	
	c) At what moment during defensive action can this man break and have a minimum weakening effect on the defense?	
8. What are the limitations of the aforementioned offensive tactics?	*a)* What can we say about the defensive limitation of the team using the baskethanger?	*a)* Makes four-man defense five-man.
	b) What can the defense do to prevent	*b)* Easily stopped by dropping one man

the advantage gained by the baskethanger or one man early release?

back when shot goes up.

9. Do you think it is necessary to have at least one man behind all the defensive players in order to have a "fast break"?

a) No.

10. What other ratios of offensive players vs. defensive players might still constitute a "fast break"?

a) Two on one, three on one, three on two, four on three.

11. What could occur while attacking two on two, or three on three, which might still give a team a "fast break" situation?

a) In order to prevent the offensive team from getting in on the basket, what should the defensive man do?

a) The defense might not fully gain or maintain good defensive position.

12. Can we now identify the factors which are important in order to increase the chances of a successful "fast break"?

a) How can the offense put manpower pressure on defense?

a) Having more offensive men on attack than defense has defending the basket.

b) In general terms, describe the shot we would like to get at the end of the break.

b) Getting as close to the basket as possible and shooting before defensive pressure develops.

c) What offensive techniques are important in order to reduce pressures created during actual execution?

c) Ball control, body control, gaining and maintaining floor position.

13. Other than perfecting the execution

a) Because of the dependent action of one

a) Being aware of our role and being able to

Questions	*Clues*	*Desired Answers*
of fundamentals and techniques, how else might we reduce offensive pressure?	teammate on the other, what would be helpful to know concerning the other person?	anticipate the actions of our teammates.
14. What observations did we make about the usual defensive recovery of the teams we observed?	*a*) What can we say about the direction of the defensive recovery?	*a*) Defensive recovery was back and toward middle of court.
	b) What can we say about locomotion of the defensive player?	*b*) Because of backward locomotion, defense moved at slower rate of speed.
	c) What can we say about defensive manpower and recovery?	*c*) Usually because of offensive position and rebounding, defense's initial manpower was one or two, with other players making long defensive recovery.
15. Therefore, what floor weakness might we exploit?		*a*) Because of defensive recovery patterns, sideline lanes are weak.
16. What directions or lines of locomotion will discourage or hinder defensive "ball hawking"?		*a*) Lines of locomotion away from recovering defense and toward man passing the ball.

Teacher: Now that we've identified some factors which should be considered while designing a fast break, let's see if we can develop a controlled pattern fast break from a 2-1-2 zone defense. We'll actually start the design from rebound position, although it could remain constant in most backcourt situations where there has been a change of ball possession. In order to simplify communications we'll number the players in the following manner:

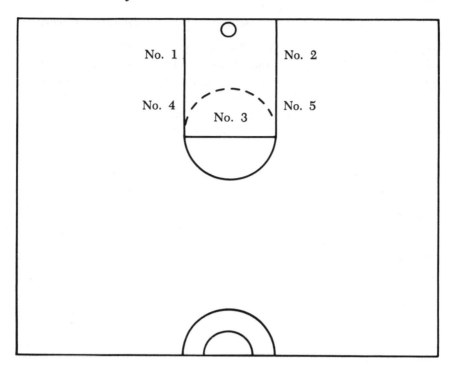

Questions	*Clues*	*Desired Answers*
17. On the rebound, player No. 1 gets ball; which way and to whom would he make his clearing pass? Why?	*a)* Remember the area of court we wish to exploit.	*a)* To No. 4 man moving toward near side line and slightly back toward passer.
	b) What constitutes a good line of direction for a man who is trying to receive the ball? Why not clear ball to opposite lane?	*b)* Why? To prevent cross-court pass. To take advantage of defensive recovery weakness.
18. Still exploiting the recovery defense and yet remembering which offensive man had to hold longest for rebounding, what	*a)* Which of the three remaining rebounders can begin to release once the length and direction of the rebound is determined?	*a)* Player No. 5 will get the second pass from player No. 4.

Questions	*Clues*	*Desired Answers*
player will receive second pass and where?	*b*) At what locations on the floor could player No. 5 get the ball? Why can we eliminate the left lane, and why can we eliminate the center lane?	*b*) Player No. 5 will receive the pass in the right lane at or near the mid-court line.
19. At what point of the process that we've covered so far would it be safe for players No. 3 and No. 2 to become involved?		*a*) Once the clearing pass has been executed.
20. Once players No. 2 and No. 3 can be involved, what advantage will they have over the defense?	*a*) Describe the locomotion possibilities of players No. 2 and No. 3.	*a*) Because of lesser degree of ball involvement the two offensive players can run as quickly as they are able.
	b) What things must the defense be conscious of during their recovery?	*b*) Defense must concern themselves with ball floor position and man.
21. Knowing how we utilized the other three players, how can we best use players No. 2 and No. 3 in our pattern?	*a*) One way to make the defense's job more difficult is to spread them by spreading the attack. How can we best spread three men on attack?	*a*) Use them to fill up the front line, No. 3 in the middle, No. 2 in left lane.
22. The third pass from player No. 5 will go to whom? When?	*a*) Keeping the ball progressing forward and never throwing it cross court, who is the only choice to get the pass?	*a*) To player No. 3 in the center lane as quickly as possible.

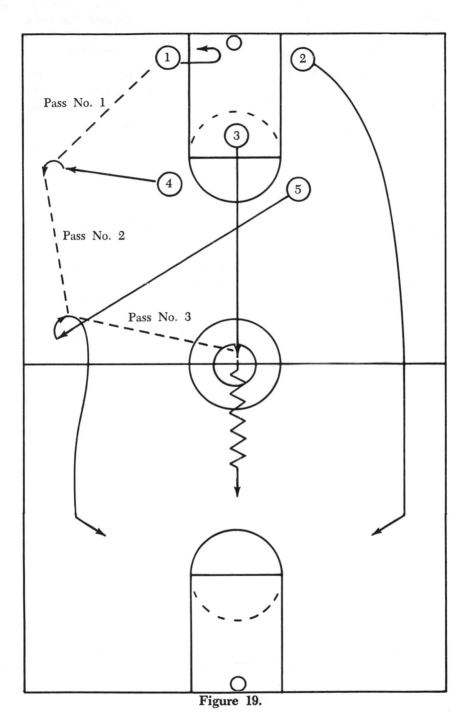

Figure 19.

Questions	*Clues*	*Desired Answers*
23. Why would it be advantageous for the middle man to have possession of the ball during the last phase of the attack?		*a*) He is in the best position to make the defense commit themselves.
		b) Could pass to all players without violating cross-court pass.
24. Who are the fourth and fifth offensive men up the court, and what are their responsibilities?	*a*) After initial involvement, who should be free to move up the floor at controlled rate of speed?	*a*) Player No. 1 and No. 4 are fourth and fifth men up the court after executing the initial responsibilities of the fast-break pattern.
	b) What factor will dictate their next course of action?	*b*) They should be conscious of ball location, pattern, development, and defensive formation and exploit recognized weaknesses.
25. In order to be consistent with our design, what will happen if the ball control occurs on the other side of the court?	*a*) What is the only difference regarding the pattern?	*a*) Same pattern, only to other side with player No. 5 getting clearing pass from No. 2, No. 4 getting the second pass in the alley, and players No. 3 and No. 1 making free runs to fill up the lanes in front line.
	b) Exactly what is the expected role of each player with the ball being cleared to the left side?	

26. It would be extremely helpful if we were able to develop rules for each situation. Is there a key to which way the patterns will flow?

a) If the rebound goes right, pattern is run right—if rebound goes left, the pattern goes left. But what if rebound is middle man?

a) For rebounding purposes, the court is divided in half. If the rebound is gained on the left of center—pattern goes left; if rebound is gained right of center—pattern goes right.

b) What can we say about the rebounder's floor position?

In order to cover the entire situation, it may be necessary to develop rules in two categories—primary and secondary, based on where a team gains possession of the ball.

Questions	*Clues*	*Desired Answers*
27. What rules would you say are necessary for player No. 1?	*a)* What can be said if No. 1 gains possession of the ball?	*a)* If I gain posession on my side of court: primary—clear ball to near sideline; secondary—trail fast break up court.
	b) What can be said if ball possession is gained on opposite side of court?	
28. What rules would you develop for No. 2 player?		*a)* Same as No. 1.
29. What rules would you develop for No. 3 man?		*a)* I gain possession of ball: primary — clear ball to short side; secondary—run up middle and take middle lane of front line attack.

Questions	*Clues*	*Desired Answers*
		b) If rebound possession goes elsewhere: primary—run up middle and take middle lane of front line attack.
30. What rules would you develop for No. 4 man?		*a*) If rebound possession is gained on my side: primary—go to sideline to take clearing pass; secondary—trail fast break up court.
		b) If rebound possession is gained on opposite side: primary—cut diagonally across court to mid-court lane for second pass; secondary — pass to middle man and be part of front line attack in that side lane (left).
31. What rules would you develop for No. 5 man?		*a*) Same as for No. 4 man.
32. Now that we developed a pattern for the fast break from a 2-1-2 defense, how adaptable is it to other defenses?	*a*) Let's examine the 1-2-2 zone, 3-2 zone, 2-3 zone, etc.	*a*) It is adaptable to other forms of defense in various degrees of difficulty.
	b) Let's examine the man-for-man defense.	*b*) The degrees of difficulty may be based on the degree of rule involvement.

33. Is running a pattern break in basketball a rigid or flexible (adjusting) situation? Why?

a) What effect will the defense have on a rigid pattern?

b) What effect will the offense have on a rigid pattern?

a) Flexible.

b) Because of the ever-changing situation created by defense.

c) Because of the element of human error by the offense.

Teacher: Are there any questions which you might have concerning fast-break basketball?

Example 5

A classic lesson in guided discovery in a related area is the following process of teaching students to discover the three classes of levers and the roles of the axis, the force arm, and the resistance arm in the operation of the lever in each class.

This lesson has been used many times in kinesiology classes. In order to understand the relationship between the three classes of levers and muscular action the student must see clearly the components of each class and their integration into a system of levers. The rote method and sheer memory rarely produce the ability to develop insight into a new condition and apply to it the proper level analysis. The use of guided discovery has proven most successful with most students. The success in understanding and application also make kinesiology a bit sweeter pill to swallow.

The equipment needed for this lesson is the standard meter-stick and a balancing stand used in physics classes. Two equal weights (50–100 grams), two weight hangers, and a string will complete the set.

Step 1:   Place the meter-stick on the balancing stand in a balanced position.

Step 2:   Ask, "How can we upset the equilibrium?"

Anticipated answer: "Push one side down or up!" ("Correct!")

Step 3:   Ask, "Can we do the same by use of weights?"

One of the students usually places one of the weights on one side of the meter-stick. ("Good!")

Step 4:   Ask, "Can you balance the seesaw now?"

Anticipated answer: Another student will place the other weight on the other side of the meter-stick and will move it around until it balances.

Step 5:   Ask, "What factors are involved in the maintenance of the equilibrium?"

Anticipated answer: Equal weights at equal distances from the axis A.

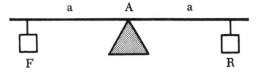

Step 6:   Ask, "Which factor can we change now to upset the balance?"

Anticipated answer: "The distance of either weight from the axis." (One of the students is asked to do it by moving one of the weights.)

Step 7:   Ask, "How far can you move it?"

Anticipated answer: "Until the end of the meter stick."

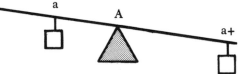

Step 8:   Ask "Is this the maximum distance possible between the end-stick-weight and the axis (A)?"

Anticipated answer: "No. It is possible to move farther the place of A."

Step 9:   Ask, "Would you do it, please?"

Anticipated answer: Action:

Step 10:   "Now could you do anything, using the present equipment, to balance the stick?"

Anticipated answer: More often than not students discover the following solution: they put the string around the stick between the weight (F) and the axis (A) and slowly pull the stick up until it is balanced in the horizontal position.

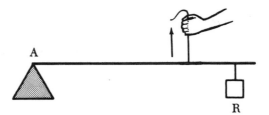

Step 11:   "In terms of A, F, and R, what kind of balanced arrangement have we had thus far?"

Anticipated answer:

Arrangement 1

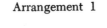

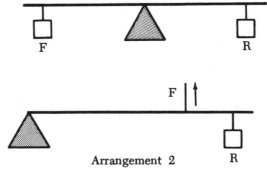

Arrangement 2   R

Step 12:	"Look at the second arrangement. Is it possible to change any factors and have a new balanced arrangement?"
Anticipated answer:	After a possible short pause the following will be offered:

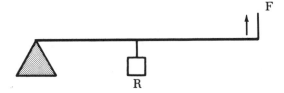

Step 13:	Indeed, these are the three and the only three possible arrangements of levers. They are called:

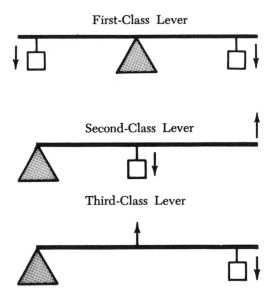

The next step is to relate this to muscular action by identifying the skeletal joint as the axis, the weight of the limb as the resistance (R), and the pulling muscle as the force (F); this makes it relatively easy for the student to relate the lever principle to a particular part of the body which is involved in a particular movement. This, too, is taught by guided discovery.

Bruner (14) in analyzing the assets of the discovery process proposes that memory is greatly enhanced when the student discovers things by himself. Indeed, learning the lever by guided discovery commits this phenomenon to memory and application for a long period of time.

In fact, this lesson has been taught to eight and a half–year–old children, who understood the required relationships and were able, after a year, to reproduce the accurate three arrangements discovered in the seesaw game a year earlier.

Before we conclude the chapter on guided discovery, let us attempt to develop a list of "topics" or phases in various activities which may merit being taught by guided discovery. Select one topic at a time and develop a lesson in guided discovery. It does not have to be a long lesson, not even one that will occupy a complete period. In crucial issues when comprehension is needed for successful learning of the physical activity, fifteen minutes of guided discovery (if done with some frequency) will develop a new learning climate in the class—a cognitive climate!

As suggested earlier in the chapter, in order to invoke full learning participation it is necessary to move the student from the "state of cognitive acquiescence" to the state of cognitive dissonance and thus cross the cognitive barrier. This in turn will precipitate the process of inquiry and lead to discovery.

After you have taught the lesson, try to identify and isolate the obstacles that came up during the lesson. If you can identify these awkward moments, then you can go back to your sequence of clues or questions and make adjustments. Check to see whether your step is relevant to the development of the subject matter at hand. Try to analyze the response or responses you received from the class to that particular clue; try to see *why* the students *did not* produce the anticipated response. Was the step unclear? Did you use words which connoted different things to your students? Did your clue lead to two or more choices, other than your own? Was the step too large? Did you need too many "additional" clues?

After answering all these questions you will be able to introduce the necessary modifications in the awkward *single* clue as in a *group* of clues in the sequence.

Now go back to the gymnasium and try again by teaching another class. Experience and observations of teachers who use guided discovery have indicated that after several attempts followed by analysis of the process one can become quite proficient in the use of this style. Start small. First succeed in one short lesson in one phase of one activity. Then you can proceed to teach another lesson by guided discovery. Eventually, you may find yourself quite adept at this style. It may even interfere with the use of other styles. You will need to decide when to use guided discovery and identify your strengths in this style in relationship to various areas in your subject matter.

SUGGESTED TOPICS TO BE TAUGHT BY GUIDED DISCOVERY

Gymnastics

1. The role of the center of gravity in the performance of the turns on the balance beam.
2. The role of momentum in maintenance of balance on the balance beam.
3. The relationship between the trunk and the appendages in developing balance.
4. The factors affecting stability in positions on the balance beam.
5. The factors affecting stability in motion on the balance beam.
6. The factors affecting the "smoothness" of connecting elements on the balance beam to a continuous sequence of movements.
7. Can you suggest a phase concerning the mounts on the balance beam that you would like to teach by guided discovery?
8. Can you suggest a phase concerning the dismounts?
9. Can *you* suggest any topic in any phase of teaching balance which could be taught by guided discovery?

It must be obvious that all these topics involve more than just the learning of a particular movement; they involve a principle, *a concept.* Principles and concepts are the building blocks of any activity. These principles and concepts have been developed over the years by master teachers, coaches, and supreme performers. The discovery of these principles and concepts by the learner creates a more complete understanding of the activity, and this understanding provides the learner with the tools and motivation for further search, for broader learning and better performance.

This level of insight and comprehension can be reached only through cognitive involvement, and a fuller cognitive involvement can be invoked only by styles of teaching which by their structure and opera-

tional procedures evoke the heuristic process and do not allow the cognitive faculties to take even a small nap during a lesson.

Let us continue with some more examples in gymnastics:

10. A lesson to discover the possibilities which exist in the variety of
    rolls in tumbling.
11. A lesson to discover the principles which relate the variety of rolls
    to one another.

By the way, the novice in guided discovery and other discovery styles
will be amazed to find a new wealth of subject matter materials suggested and found by the students as the discovery process develops and
blooms.

12. The relationship between *directions* and *postures* in movements in
    tumbling.
13. In teaching the kip principle, the relationship between the length
    of the lever, produced by the legs, and success in performing the
    kip.
14. The relationship between the kip principle learned on the mat and
    the kip used for various mounts on the parallel bars.
15. The role of the lever (the whole body) in producing various degrees
    of momentum in swinging on the parallel bars.
16. Do you have any suggestions for other aspects of the parallel bars
    performance?
17. Are your suggestions specific to the parallel bars, or can they lead
    to discovering the application to other apparatus?
18. In vaulting, the various phases involved in a vault.
19. The assets and liabilities in each phase of a vault. Discovery of a
    generalization!
20. Application of the generalization to a *specific* vault.
21. The *variables* affecting changes in the form of a given vault.
22. Any suggestions for other aspects of vaulting?
23. Can you suggest two consecutive aspects to be taught by guided
    discovery?
24. Three consecutive aspects?
25. *Any* other proposals?

In the area of gymnastics, with all its variety, there are dozens of
phases that can be taught by guided discovery, creating a deeper
understanding of gymnastics.

Developmental Movement

An area in physical education which is most readily taught by guided discovery is developmental movement.

1. The physical attributes which exist as prerequisites for movement (agility, balance, flexibility, strength, endurance, and so on).
2. The kind of movements which seem to belong to each attribute.
3. Specific movements which contribute to the development of a specific attribute.
4. Movements which overlap two physical attributes.
5. Movements which develop a particular attribute by use of a specific part or region of the body.
6. The involvement of a particular part or region of the body in a specific movement.
7. The *limits* of involvement of a particular part or region of the body in a specific movement.
8. The variables affecting the degree of difficulty in strength (amount of resistance, duration of resistance, repetition of resistance, intervals of resistance).
9. Specific movements and patterns which will cause the change in degree of difficulty in strength development by manipulating one or more of the mentioned variables.
10. Can you suggest similar topics for discovery in the area of flexibility, agility, balance, other?

Comment: The guided discovery lessons in developmental movement can be integrated with kinesiology in a most satisfying and contributory way. Can you think of some ties?

11. The relationship between a particular physical attribute, a phase of a given sport, and a specific developmental movement.
12. The relationship between the need for flexibility of the shoulder for a javelin thrower and specific developmental movements.
13. The relationship between the need for flexibility at the hip joint for a hurdler and specific developmental movements.
14. The relationship between the need for leg strength in the shot put and specific developmental movements.
15. The relationship between the need for abdominal strength in a performer on the uneven parallel bars and specific developmental movements.

16. Can you suggest other aspects of developmental movement that can be taught by guided discovery?

Basketball

1. The need for a variety of passes.
2. The relationship between various game situations and the variety of passes available.
3. The possible *connection* between two consecutive passes. Three passes. A series of passes.
4. The "logic" (or reason) behind a particular arrangement of players on the court.
5. The feasibility of this arrangement in a *variety* of situations.
6. The best positioning in zone defense against a given strategy of offense.
7. The efficiency factors of a given offense strategy against a particular defense arrangement.
8. Can you teach by guided discovery *all* the techniques of basketball? Some? In which ones would you prefer not to use guided discovery? Why?
9. Can you teach all aspects of strategy in basketball by guided discovery? Would it be helpful if your players understood well each aspect of the strategy as gained by this style?
10. Can you suggest other aspects and topics in basketball to be taught by guided discovery?

Swimming

1. The buoyancy principles.
2. Specific postures for specific purposes (dead man's posture for best floating, for example).
3. The principle of propulsion in the water.
4. The role of breathing during propulsion.
5. The role of each specific part of the body in propulsion.
6. The role of each specific part of the body in propulsion in a specific direction.
7. The relationship between a particular phase in a stroke and the physical attribute needed.
8. Can you teach other technical aspects of swimming by guided discovery?
9. Can you discover which are the preferred aspects of swimming to be taught by this style?

Other Sports

1. Can you think of any phases in football, hockey, volleyball, archery, wrestling, soccer, modern dance, track and field that can be taught by guided discovery?
2. Can you discover which aspects of the techniques of these sports will be desirable to teach by this style?
3. Can you discover which aspects of the strategy of these sports will be desirable to teach by guided discovery?

IMPLICATIONS OF GUIDED DISCOVERY

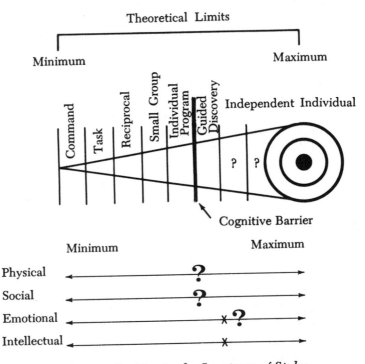

Figure 20. *Present Position in the Spectrum of Styles and the Channels of Development*

Something interesting can be observed at this stage. The students' most obvious progress has occurred in the intellectual channel. Although tightly guided and directed, the cognitive dimension has been released from its quiescence and has become actively and dynamically involved in the responses and decision making. The self has become intricately involved. It is assumed that as a result of this cognitive process, carefully guarded by frequent reinforcements, the students' emotional development reaches a higher level. Continuous success in "correct" and acceptable responses helps strengthen confidence in oneself and enhances one's self image.

It is proposed that the physical and social states along the channels need to be further studied and observed. The very nature and structure of guided discovery *prevents* the student from producing alternative movements in most cases; thus, the physical freedom seems to be restricted by being guided to a specific pre-determined response. Perhaps the social dimension suffers from the same harnessing effect. It is necessary, however, to realize that guided discovery is the most potent and

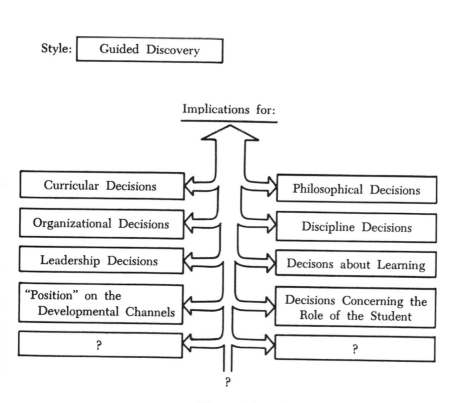

Figure 21.

rigorous style of teaching which teaches the learner the heuristic *process*. This style embodies a *process* of systematically getting to a target. It is actually a process of *training* students to use selection procedures in making small decisions in a definite sequence. As Dr. Richard Anderson once suggested, guided discovery is a *process-centered* teaching procedure (also see [18], chap. 4). So, although physical freedom is sacrificed, there is an enormous gain in a very clear and efficient cognitive involvement and achievement.

Is there a way of involving cognitive processes which will also permit individual choices—cognitive and physical? The style of teaching presented in the next chapter proposes a combination of both.

Just before leaving the discussion of this style, one might want to discover the implications of guided discovery for the various aspects of the teaching-learning process. Compare Figure 21 with Figure 3 (p. 16) and see what adjustments have occurred in the pattern of implications.

8

Problem Solving

Problem solving is the next level of the discovery process. Whereas in guided discovery the dependency of the student's expected responses upon the teacher's clues is the essence of the style, in problem solving the student is expected to seek out the answer or answers completely on his own.

In this style of teaching a single problem often may have several solutions; in fact, many problems are designed to elicit multiple solutions. This small change in structure of the style elicits a greater number of cognitive operations and encourages a greater number of experiments in physical responses. The degree of freedom and self-involvement independent of the teacher's control is almost complete. The word "almost" is used here because the series of problems is still designed and presented by the teacher. But the processes of inquiry, exploration, discovery and judging the merit of the discoveries are fully conducted and executed by the learner. Thus, contrary to the single-mindedness of guided discovery, the teaching behavior which induces and produces discoveries by presenting problems seeks to develop the ability to find *alternatives*, explore them, and select the appropriate ones.

This kind of process puts the student on his own and requires him to learn to cope with the problem individually. The student soon learns that his responses and alternatives are acceptable and valid. He learns that the criteria for "correct" responses are not necessarily the matching of his solutions to pre-determined solutions of the teacher or peer but his act of having solved the problems offered.

It is perhaps superfluous to mention that practically all problems and issues in all areas of learning have more than one correct answer. Physical responses do not constitute an exception. The very fact of the variability of human motion should encourage teachers and students to seek the alternative, the new, the different, the *unknown!*

Teaching by consensus only restricts the possibilities of new discoveries, new ideas in sports, new ways of executing a movement. The history of sports is full of examples of athletes, coaches, and teachers who sought new ways in order to improve the technique, the strategy, the performance.

This process is not a luxury which belongs in the domain of a few; it is rather a necessity, a daily diet needed to develop students who are something other than responding robots. Seeking solutions to problems, large and small, in physical or other activities, is a daily occurrence in every child's life. Why, then, not develop and enhance the ability to do so in a deliberate manner? (See [19], chap. 1.) In every physical activity and sport there is a place to identify and present problems which will evoke cognitive dissonance and create the need to seek solutions and thus, through self-discovery, subject the mind and body to movement possibilities and game variations previously unknown to the learner.

ANATOMY OF TEACHING BY PROBLEM SOLVING

Variables	*The Role of the Teacher*	*The Role of the Student*
Variable No. 1: Pre-class Decisions	1. Decisions about what subject matter to teach.	Not involved.
	2. Decisions concerning the *series* of problems to be presented to the class.	Not involved.
	3. Anticipation of solutions.	Not involved.
	4. Decision concerning anticipated solutions which are more appropriate than others.	Not involved.
	5. Decisions concerning the distribution of equipment to effect individualization.	Not involved yet.

6. Decision concerning the organization of the class: the need for *complete* individualized random organization.

Not involved yet.

Variable No. 2: Execution Decisions

7. Introduce the problem or problems to the class. The mode of communication can be oral or written. In order to complete the individualized process it is *better* to present the problems on a card or a Mimeographed sheet. This will enable each student to perform according to his own pace and ability and sometimes to select the order of problems to be solved.

Receives the problems.

8. Permits time for reading and clarifying the problems.

9. Ascertains the distribution of space and equipment with the aid of students.

Reads the problems—asks questions about the problems. Selects the area in the gymnasium and piece of equipment for the selected problems.

10. *Waits*—just waits and observes!

It takes different lengths of time before different students settle down and get ready to go to work. Wait! Do not interfere with these precious preparatory moments. These are private moments, moments of making decisions. Let the student make the *first*

The individualized process begins, first on a *cognitive level* and then on a physical level. The student may stand in front of the equipment and hesitate, look at the printed problem, hesitate again, think—trying to find a solution—and then act. He produces his first

The Role of the Teacher	*The Role of the Student*

step toward individualized response. You will find that some students are reluctant to try a new physical response which is alien to their experiences.

11. In order to help those who are reluctant, the teacher can use accepting words: "Your solution solved the problem." "It is a good throw!" "This is a very interesting new backward roll!"

At the beginning of the process never offer negative criticism. *This is a time for encouraging the process of self-inquiry and discovery and not for rejecting a response which does not coincide with your aesthetic values or preferred movement.* Novice teachers in this style very often reject a solution which is *new* to *them,* a solution which they did not anticipate or cannot readily accept because of their own limitations. It has also been observed that teachers feel *guilty* having so much extra time available while

physical attempt at offering a solution. A moment of self-evaluation may follow, and then the student repeats the response or discards it and seeks another solution.

Will generally respond well to reinforcement, to an accepting word by the teacher — more so a student who is not accustomed to seek and offer his *own solutions* in a new situation.

Once the student feels relatively secure in producing ideas in movement alternatives, he will continue to do so; periodical reinforcement from the teacher will serve as an additional source of motivation. Thus evolves the process of *cognitive solutions tested by physical responses.* While the problem solving is in progress, more and more students begin to feel and act more independently. They are more capable of the students are engaged in the process of seeking and testing solutions. It seems that this availability of time only indicates the reciprocal relationships of roles in this style. It is not only the student who becomes freer to behave, to think, to be—it is *the teacher, too,* who is freer to perform a variety of functions from which he was previously restricted.

exhibiting responsibilities previously assumed to be impossible.

Variable No. 3: Evaluation Decisions

12. It is quite difficult and perhaps unnecessary to identify the exact moment of evaluation. The evaluating behavior manifests itself all along, from the first reinforcing statement to the last suggestion of modification offered by the teacher to an individual.

Most students will welcome the opportunity for a one-to-one relationship with the teacher. Sometimes, even a glance from the teacher while the student is engaged in trying out an idea will please the student and strengthen the bond between the two.

Comment: Two important aspects of evaluation occur during the process of problem solving: *First,* the evaluation is done individually—the teacher concentrates on the solution of an individual involved in a specific situation (a new way to mount the parallel bars at the side of one bar, another way of stopping a bouncing ball in soccer, etc.) *Second,* the individual student has the opportunity to react to the teacher's comments. This situation of individualized problem solving creates the opportunity for *each* student to seek the teacher's advice when needed. The student also has the opportunity to ask that *extra* question that has been bothering him for a while. He could not do so in a group situation.

This interplay of teaching-learning behavior which weaves individualization of problem solving through cognitive activity expressed in physical responses is a most meaningful way of teaching and learning. The intimacy between the student and the subject matter mentioned in the discussion of guided discovery is even greater in problem solving. *The element of choice*—the availability of a variety of solutions, the possibility of finding still another way, and the climate of encouragement to seek a new response—creates a particular kind of motivation, a special excitement in learning, both based on a new developing ingredient in learning: endurance!

Teaching and learning by problem solving create a higher level of endurance, which is self-motivated. The knowledge that there is still another way keeps the cognitive process kindled, which, as previously formulated, leads to inquiry, which in turn brings about discovery. This behavioral chain of cognitive dissonance ⟶ inquiry ⟶ discovery as represented in the process of problem solving has a dimension which occurs *only* in problem solving in the spectrum of styles.

Problem solving is an *open-end* process! and it is open ended in two avenues: *First*, the *subject matter itself* is open ended because there is always the possibility of another solution, another movement, another way to pass the ball, another way to break through the opponent's defense. Thus, the subject matter becomes dynamic, constantly renewed—alive! *Second*, the *process* of discovery is self-perpetuating. The act of finding a new solution tests the validity of the discovery. The joy of discovery is so powerful that the act of discovery itself becomes the reinforcing, motivating agent. This propels the student to continue to seek more solutions, alternatives and ideas.

All previous styles on the spectrum are different in this respect. All have the dimension of *finality*. Their very definitions, descriptions of their anatomies, and their implications for the emerging individual connote *finality*—finality in the structure and content of subject matter and finality in the learning process. This realization clarifies, in part, the *dependency* upon the teacher in all previous styles in relating to the subject matter, in need for external motivation, and in involvement in the process of learning itself. The problem-solving process proposes to develop greater *independence* in both cognition and physical responses, and it is the *only* process which actually demonstrates the cognitive-physical relation in its various dimensions.

RELEVANCY OF PROBLEMS

How do we design, then, the kind of problems which will induce and develop these processes?

The foremost prerequisite for good problem design is *relevancy*. All problems presented to students must be relevant. *There are three levels of relevancy:*

1. Problems relevant to the subject matter.
2. Problems relevant to the readiness and experience of the group.
3. Problems relevant to the readiness and experience ot the individual.

What makes a problem relevant to the subject matter? Is there an *order* or preference of relevancies in the relationship between the problem and the subject matter? Is it enough to ask a student, "How do you move the ball from point A to point B?" or "What is the best body posture in landing from a leap?" or "Can you suggest two ways of clearing the horse using only one hand for support?" Is there some logic in the design of problems which leads to the process of solving them? First, let us examine the categories of things that can be discovered by solving a problem or a series of problems.

1. *Facts* can be discovered. Facts in physical education will be those things that are usually *told* to students in the gymnasium. For example:

    a) A way or ways of passing the ball from player A to player B. It does not make any difference right now which pass we are talking about or which teacher is *telling* the student how to execute the pass. Categorically, *passes* in basketball can be discovered by people who *never* saw basketball by seeking solutions to problems *designed* to elicit a response or responses which are the *facts*, in this instance—the passes.

    b) In tumbling three different forward rolls can be discovered by *any* student in response to a particularly designed problem. In fact, there is no need to confine oneself to three rolls; any number of rolls can be discovered by a performer or student who seeks a particular number of rolls (that otherwise would be shown and explained to the student).

    c) In vaulting over a horse a posture or a group of postures which reflect a way of manipulating the center of gravity can be discovered through solving certain problems. This is finding out about a fact.

    d) The placement of the take-off foot in the broad jump can be discovered.

    e) The role of body surface in aquatic propulsion can be discovered.

All these, categorically, are facts that ordinarily are either told or demonstrated to students. They can, however, be discovered and, hence, understood better and internalized by the student.

2. *Relationships* can be discovered. Most or perhaps all movements are performed in some relationship to their antecedents and their consequences. There is hardly a movement in work, dance, sports, or any other area which stands alone, isolated! In other styles of teaching the teacher might choose to explain or demonstrate the kind of relationship which exists among two or more movements. In this style, problems can be designed to bring about the discovery of the relationship. Examples of the kinds of relationships that can be discovered:

a) Relationships between the various parts of the body and the soccer ball for the purpose of *stopping* the ball—or the relationships which might exist between the body and the soccer ball for the purpose of having the ball travel under various conditions.

b) In gymnastics one can discover the relationships between the body and the apparatus in a particular condition—i.e., side motion. One can discover the relationship between the position of the extremities and the balance beam under various conditions of speed, height, and rhythm.

c) One can discover the relationship between the head and the body in various situations in the variety of sports.

d) One can discover the relationship between a sporting instrument (club, racket, oar, etc.) to the body in conjunction with various media (water, air, etc.).

e) One can discover the relationship which exists between two participants in a game.

f) One can discover the relationship between himself (as a member of a team) and the other team.

g) One can discover the relationship between one's team and the opponent in reference to various aspects of the game's strategy.

3. *Preferences and validity* can be discovered. This is a category which requires even more cognitive involvement than the previous ones because decisions have to be made about questions such as: which is better? which is best? which are the best two possibilities? which is the worst? Is this solution appropriate? Is this jump more efficient?

It is quite obvious that answers or solutions to these questions can be derived only when the *criteria* are known. If the teacher gives the criterion (a given rule in kinesiology to support a choice in an efficiency problem) then all the student has to do is to use this information for further discovery of the answer. It is possible, however, even to discover the criterion. A skillful teacher can design such problems which will help the student discover that he *needs* a particular kind of information (a criterion for judgment).

a) Preferences can be discovered in a strategy of a game.

b) Preference can be discovered in a hold in wrestling.

c) Preferences can be discovered in synchronized swimming (with a given aesthetic code as criteria).

d) Preferences can be discovered in body positions either in a game or on the apparatus. (In the game the criteria will be the positions of the opposing team, while on the apparatus the criteria will be based on either kinesiological rules or the aesthetic values of the observers).

4. *Limits* can be discovered. This category deals with minimum and maximum, slowest and fastest, lowest and highest, and so on. It is actually a quantitative preference, while the previous examples were mostly qualitative preferences.

5. *Concepts.* Each activity reflects a concept or is built on several concepts. For example, the developmental movement construct is a concept which explains a particular approach to the developments of agility, balance, flexibility, and strength.

   Basketball, football, and other games are based on concepts of particular sets of relationships between offense and defense.

   These concepts and others can be discovered by students. The process of discovery may reveal new concepts yet unknown to coaches and teachers.

6. *Variations* (quantitative and qualitative) can be discovered in practically every movement, game, and sport.

These six categories of *what* can be discovered are offered as a guide for problem design in any activity. Operationally this means that problems must be designed so that solutions to them uncover:

   1. Facts
   2. Relationships
   3. Preferences and validity
   4. Limits
   5. Concepts
   6. Variations

Indeed, seeking to develop relevant problems for each category requires a keen insight into the structure of the subject matter at hand.

Let us examine an example in *one* activity and see how the structure of this activity leads into inquiry and discovery in these six categories.

Soccer

The need for kicking, passing, dribbling, heading, and so on will constitute the facts of soccer. Discovering what to do in dribbling when an opponent stands in front of you, what to do with the ball when somebody intercepts you (advancing) will constitute examples in the category of *relationships*—in this case, discovering the relationships among player-ball-opponent.

At times, when an opponent confronts a player, the player may have several possibilities of avoiding the opponent. A *choice* may have to be made between an on-the-ground kick sideways or an overhead kick forward. It *is* a problem of *preference*. The player can discover *the* preferred kick in the given situation.

In soccer a player can discover the *limits* of different kinds of kicks, speed in dribbling, distance of heading, and the like. These are performance limits; there are also other limits—limits in all the previous categories. One can also discover the limits of the solutions which are bound by a set of rules.

The W arrangement in soccer illustrates a *concept*—a concept of an arrangement of players that permits given strategies to be carried out.

In soccer, just as in all other games, *variations* are born every minute. In fact, this is one of the virtues of a game, any game—the inevitability of unknown variations. A new movement, a different combination of passes, a new idea—one can be engaged in an endless process of discovering variations in the game of soccer.

This was an example of how *one activity* lends itself to all these categories of things that can be discovered through solving a series of relevant problems. (Detailed proposed problems will follow shortly.)

Tumbling

It might be helpful to look into another activity and see how it fits into the six categories for discovery. In tumbling, a student can discover that there are positions, rolls, springs, turns, handstands and so on. These belong to the *facts* category.

Relationships can be discovered in tumbling—the relationship between two parts of the body in the particular roll; the relationship of the body to the ground, to the air, and so on.

Which roll is better before a dive roll? Which handstand is more attractive according to the aesthetic view of the class? Of your friend? Of your teacher? Why? Did they all explain why? Preferences and validity can be discovered in tumbling.

The *limits* of posture possibilities for the execution of a stunt can be discovered. What are the limits of the body compactness or extension for a safe execution of a dive roll? (Here the criterion for judgment is not necessarily a standard-aesthetic one; rather, it is a kinesiological consideration of the body position which will yield maximum safety. The uninhibited tumbler will invariably land on his back when performing a compact dive roll.)

Rotary motion can represent a *concept* in tumbling. Problems can be designed to stimulate the discovery of this concept of rotary motion and, indeed, the various kinds of rotary motion.

Discovering *variations* in tumbling is most stimulating, and there are endless variation possibilities in the many aspects of tumbling.

The solutions to a series of problems, in each activity and sport, in each one of the six categories listed on pp. 189-191 can create cognitive involvement high in quantity and quality.

During this kind of involvement the student is not only immersed completely in the process of learning through discovery; he also develops fresh insights into the structure of the subject matter.

So, operationally, if you wish to develop problems to solve in a given subject matter, you can analyze the activity according to the suggested six categories and then develop series of problems in each category.

How does one go about developing and designing the problems themselves? How does one connect several problems into meaningful series? (A reminder is presented here that we are still investigating that level of relevancy which was identified as problems relevant to the subject matter.)

A quite comfortable and logical way of starting to design a relevant problem is to decide which component of the subject matter to choose first. In most cases the structure of subject matter of an activity or sport appears to be quite logical and orderly. You can simply ask yourself, "What do we need to know first while teaching the use of the parallel bars in gymnastics?" Whenever one asks a group of students, "What is our first question?" invariably the answer is, "How do we get on?" Indeed, how to get on the parallel bars is the first problem area. It is quite *relevant* to the subject matter. One could not really learn to perform on the parallel bars without, first, being on them.

So this question of how to get on actually becomes the first problem. The open-end nature of problem solving is illustrated here by the many possible solutions to this problem. In fact, there is a possibility of having too many solutions. All solve the problem of how to get on, but there is a need to *organize* their many possible solutions. This guides us to our next step in problem design. Right now, we are confronted with the problem of controlling the possibility of endless solutions. We need to narrow it down. This is done by analyzing this part of the subject matter—the mount—into its variables. The variables of the mount are readily identified:

1. Selection of various *parts* of the apparatus as an aid to mounting.
2. Selecting various *body positions* from which (and to which) one can move in executing a mount on the parallel bars.
3. Selecting the *kind of movement* to be used in the mount.

In variable A, one can mount at the end of the bars, at the center, or anywhere in between. One can use one bar, two bars, the supporting uprights, and so on. In variable B one can start from standing straight facing any of the mentioned parts of the parallel bars. One can stand with the back to a given part of the apparatus, and so on.

In variable C one can jump on, one can swing on, one can slowly climb on, or one can pull himself up. Now, problems can be designed in each one of these variables and thus narrow the area to be discovered and the number of possible solutions. For example, you can ask your students to suggest two alternative ways of getting on the bars—starting in the middle, standing between the bars, and facing the length of the bars. These problems focus on the first two variables: the part of the apparatus and the position of the body. It is possible to add the third variable. Thus, you present the above problem and add "And restrict yourself only to the kip motion."

Any student (more so the novice) who attempts a solution will have to think a little bit, then discover a solution, try it out physically, check out some details, and assess his solution. All are important mental and physical operations necessary to the learning process. One can ask for three different solutions, four, any number—keeping one or two variables *constant* and *changing* the third. For example, "Can you design and perform two different mounts starting from standing position, facing the length of the bars, at the middle *but this time* stand outside the bars?" This creates a slightly new situation with a slightly different problem, does it not? Consequently, different solutions will result; and thus *evolves a dynamic approach* to subject matter, discovered by the student himself.

The next aspect of the subject matter on the parallel bars is all those things which answer the question, "What can we do while we are *on* the parallel bars?" Here again, one analyzes the variables:

Variable 1—positions: *a*) On top of bars, (*b*) below the bars, (*c*) between the bars, (*d*) other?

Variable 2—motion along the bars: *a*) On top; (*b*) below; (*c*) between; (*d*) combinations of *a*, *b*, and *c*; (*e*) motion in one direction; (*f*) changing direction; (*g*) other?

The next step is to design problems in each one of these components of each variable. The problems in Variable 1, component *a*, will induce discoveries of possible positions on top of the bars. Very often the novice discovers many of the conventional positions, which is fine. It means that he has learned what we want him to learn—several accepted positions on top of the bars. *But*, in addition, the student often discovers positions which are *new* even to the teacher, positions which open up possibilities for new combinations and sequences. This is a phenomenon which can be used by coaches, who constantly seek new ideas for competitive performance.

Examples of problem design for Variable 1, component *a:*

1. Can you find two *vertical* positions in support position?
2. Can you design and perform positions on top of the bars which illustrate three different *angles* between the trunk and the legs? (Here is where you will get the L support positions, the V support positions, and many others!)
3. Can you suggest two support positions which are *non-vertical* while the entire body is straight?
4. Can you perform a support position with a bent position at *all* joints?
5. What would be your minimum posture (compact body) and your maximum posture (complete stretch) in the support position?
6. Can you find the support position which is *not symmetrical* (referring to the relationship between the body and the parallel bars)?
7. Can you (the reader) design more problems for Variable 1, component *a?*

You must have noticed that the problems here revolve around the *possibilities* of Variable 1, component a, which is "position on top of the bars." When one thinks about positions, the straight line comes to mind (Problem 1); various body angles seem rather obvious (Problem 2); then the opposite possibilities come quite naturally (Problem 3);

and so on until, temporarily, you feel you have exhausted the possibilities.

The guide line then is to determine the *variables* in the activity, then identify the *components* in each variable, and then seek out the possibilities of each component (the sub-components). Ask yourself, "What *else* is changeable? Have I changed the line, the direction, the posture, the angles, the height, the width, the speed, the base, the stability, the mobility, the rhythm, the duration, the amount, the . . . , the . . . ?" Can *you* think of anything else that can be changed? Then what problems will be relevant to this dimension or sub-component?

What is the next aspect of the subject matter used in teaching gymnastics on parallel bars? Can you determine what it is? Can you analyze it and identify its variables? Components? If your answer is "yes," then you are ready to design problems for the next phase of parallel bars activities.

THE STRUCTURE OF SUBJECT MATTER

In order to encompass a broader view and approach to the design of problems which are relevant to the subject matter it becomes pertinent to attempt an analysis of the concept of the structure of subject matter. Any body of knowledge has its own structure: a special arrangement of its components, a special way in which these components relate to one another, a generalized form which makes it possible to identify the body of knowledge for what it is and comprehend its function and operation. The subject matter in physical education is composed of families of activities (ball games, aquatics, track and field, etc.) which are based on some similar characteristics. In turn, *each* activity (football, tennis, shot put, broad jump, backstroke, vaulting, etc.) has its own characteristics, its own requirements, its own structure. This structure determines the uniqueness of the activity and gives it its identity.

Our problem, then, is to find out what *must exist* in order to make a given subject matter (activity X) readily identifiable. What makes activity X what it is? What, if reduced or changed, will make it *not be* what it is?

Figure 22 presents the concept of the *hierarchy of the structure of subject matter*, any subject matter. This concept relates the given conditions (Level 1) which must exist as a premise of an activity to the product, to the result—the activity itself as we know it (Level 4). Levels 2 and 3 are manipulative levels which include the body and its possibilities through any matrix of movement (Level 2) to produce the six categories of what can be discovered in the activity: facts, relationships, preferences and validity, limits, concepts and variations (Level 3).

Levels 1, 2, and 3 interact in a very particular way, which is guided and modified by imposed limitations—physiological, psychological, and cultural—in order to produce the unique thing which we identify as activity X.

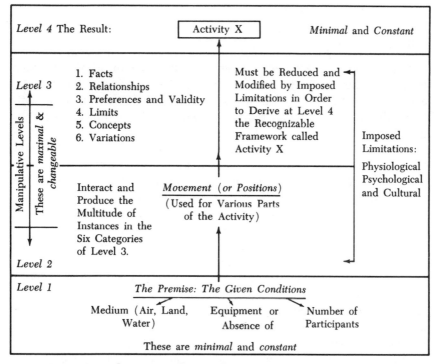

Figure 22. *The Hierarchy of the Structure of Subject Matter*

The premise for the existence of any activity is the given conditions. These include three kinds of conditions:

1. Medium (air, land, water)
2. Equipment (or absence of it)
3. Number of participants (one to infinity)

These conditions constitute the first level of the structure of subject matter. Each one can consist of only a minimal level of being and is constant. Any change in any one of these conditions will create a different premise for a *different* structure of a *different* activity. For example, in order to have an activity known as swimming, one must have these conditions:

1. Water as the medium
2. No equipment
3. At least one participant

In the activity known as fencing, the premise consists of:

1. Land as the medium
2. Swords (as well as masks and protective jackets) as the equipment
3. At least two people

These conditions are *minimal* and *constant*; they must exist in order to achieve the result: the specific activity of swimming or fencing. All activities can be analyzed in a similar manner. Could you do it with football? Javelin throwing? Sailing? Mountain climbing? Diving? Others?

Now, to the next level. No matter what the premise may be, use of the body, in part or as a whole, is involved in the structure of the subject matter. Moreover, different manipulations of different parts of the body produce a great variety of different movements, which constitute the second level of the structure of subject matter. This is the *manipulative level*. This level is also identified as *maximal* and *changeable* because both the use of the body and the movements which are produced by the body are never constant; on the contrary, they are ever-changing and unlimited, and they can theoretically approach maximum in terms of possibilities. This means that in a game of basketball, the structure of which depends upon a defined premise, the body can be used in many changing ways and thus can theoretically produce an infinite number of movements.

The interactions between the *body possibilities* and the *movements actually produced* create in Level 3 the categories of fact (Figure 14) which constitute the *essence* of the structure of basketball.

This level is also identified as manipulative, because of its changeable character. Any of the six categories can be changed by the discovery and presentation of many different instances, perhaps an infinite number of them. This is true in basketball in the categories of relationships, perferences, and others.

In order, however, to cause the manipulative, maximal, and changeable levels to culminate in a *defined* and *identifiable* activity, it becomes necessary to impose limitations on the wealth of possibilities which stem from the body movements (Level 2) and the six manipulative categories. These limitations are grounded in the physiological limitations of the individual; the psychological (emotional and cognitive) limitations of the individual; and the cultural limitations, limitations determined by society, limitations which produce preferences of activities or parts of activities; and limitations imposed by sets of rules, curbing and defining the structure of the activity.

That means that in basketball, for example, you are required to dribble with only one hand at a time (rule limitation), although the manipulative levels suggest that there are many other ways to transport the ball. If you employ certain other ways of transport, the game will cease to be basketball as we know it and will become something else. Similarly, you can apply this structure analysis to other activities. Ask yourself, "What can be produced on Levels 2 and 3 in the activity under analysis" and then "What are the kinds of limitations imposed in order to hold the known activity?"

Now, how does all this relate to the style of teaching by problem solving?

We are engaged in analyzing the need to present problems which are relevant to the subject matter. One cannot establish relevancy to subject matter unless he understands what subject matter is. It is proposed that *every statement* in every field of knowledge is *an answer* to a question! Therefore, the process of teaching by seeking answers (problem solving) necessitates asking relevant questions, the answers to which will constitute the subject matter. *Thus, the total sum of solutions to the total sum of relevant problems constitutes the subject matter!!* Hence, if we know the structure of subject matter we can design relevant problems.

Essentially, one can develop questions and problems pertaining to *any part of any level* of the structure of the subject matter. One can also design problems pertaining to *relationships* between different parts or different levels of the structure.

For example, in activities which develop balance, if the premise consists of land (the medium), one balance beam (the equipment), and one participant, then questions can be asked about the *possible* parts of the *body* (Level 2) which can interact with the balance beam (Level 1) to produce one or more balance positions. Other kinds of questions and problems can be offered in exploring the possibilities of the use of a specific movement (standing tall on the toes, for example) in a given dimension (concept) in balance: change of direction. To illustrate this point:

1. Can you turn right ninety degrees, standing tall on your toes?
2. Can you turn ninety degrees in other directions?

3. Can you turn less than ninety degrees?
4. Can you turn more than ninety degrees?
5. What is your maximum turn in one motion?

Solving these problems, in motion, *is* the discovery of part of the structure of the subject matter of learning balance on a balance beam —the part that involves turns in a position of high center of gravity.

PROBLEM DESIGN

The operational order and sequence of problem design can be described as motion forward from level to level, from one part to the next. This is the exact opposite of the order and sequence of the design of guided discovery, which is motion backward.

The other operational feature of problem solving which is different from guided discovery is the existence of *alternative solutions*. The open-end nature of the problems elicits the variety of solutions which are offered by different individuals. Problem solving creates *independence* of solutions (guided discovery, on the other hand, is based on the *interdependency* of solutions). When you present a problem which requires exploring the possibilities of upsetting the balance of the wrestler who is in the referee position, different novice students will explore and *discover* a variety of *different independent* ways of doing so. *All* these answers or solutions are *right!* They are right because they solve the problem. This realization of the rightness of the solution serves as a powerful reinforcing agent. The *fact* of solving the problem constitutes an intrinsic reinforcement and motivation to solve more problems. The cognitive process is active, is productive, and is rewarded.

Only after alternative solutions are offered by the students can the next step, *preferences*, be approached. Certainly one can recognize that some of the discovered solutions are not appropriate (some teachers prefer this phrase to the word "wrong") to the structure of the activity. They are not appropriate because of the limiting factors previously discussed. At this point the teacher can tell the students that two of his five solutions are not valid or appropriate under the delimiting rules of the game or that his proposed movement is not efficient according to a given kinesiological law. *However*, even *this* can be discovered by the student himself if a problem (or problems) is presented to him which will reveal the *relationship* (Level 3, Category 2, in Figure 14) between his solutions and the established rules of a game or the known kinesiological law.

Now, in order to individualize the process even more, we need to examine the second level of relevancy; this is the relevancy of the designed problems to the experience, readiness, and interest of the group.

If a group of students have been taught an activity previously by other styles of teaching, there is no sense in presenting them with a set of problems which are designed to elicit the material which they already know; these problems will be irrelevant to the group. This is not to say that *other* aspects or categories (Level 3) of the *same* activity cannot be taught by problem solving; it is merely a reminder that the process of problem solving has as its purpose developing individual cognitive involvement and eliciting new responses. *It is not the purpose of problem solving to repeat known responses.* The act of repeating a known movement negates the essence of problem solving. This may be done for purposes of review and pattern development and must be taught by other styles. We have been discussing the teacher's presenting the *same* set of problems in a given activity to the *entire* group.

The next level of relevancy is the most important one. Problems must be relevant to the experience, readiness, and interest of the individual student. A teacher must know the student before he can determine whether or not a particular set of problems will be relevant for him.

Experienced performers in tumbling may not be interested in the following problem: Can you roll forward in two extremely different body positions—most compact and most extended? To the experienced tumbler, this problem is irrelevant. He has performed these rolls before. However, ask him to try this one: Can you roll in three different directions keeping segments of the body of two joints at ninety degrees while you roll? This problem might be quite relevant even to the more experienced tumbler. It evokes cognitive activity and challenges his physical ability.

This aspect of cognitive relevancy is only one element of relevancy and cannot be viewed in isolation. Assumed cognitive dissonance does not always kindle the process of inquiry. If the cultural climate in which the individual has been reared has erected a maze of barriers around his ability to respond, a problem that seems to be relevant to the teacher may not necessarily create the expected excitement in the student. There must exist an emotional relevancy. The student must see himself and accept himself as being ready and willing to face the presented problem.

EXAMPLES OF PROBLEM DESIGN

The remaining pages of this chapter contain an example of a series of problem designs in several different activities. They are designed with the relevancy to the structure of subject matter in mind. Whenever they are presented to individuals or groups, you will have to decide whether the problems are relevant for your students.

When a series of problems in a given activity is presented to individuals in a group, each individual can discard those problems which do not intrigue or challenge him and select only those which *do* create cognitive dissonance and need to be solved. This, in teaching, is attaining a new height in individualization.

Problems to Solve on the Balance Beam

Let us begin with problems involving movements on the balance beam. This activity was selected because of its pliability of content; despite some fundamental common arrangements of movements, the entire experience of learning to use the balance beam for the development of balance, grace, and beauty of movement is composed of endless alternatives. Alternatives in practically every balance beam position, movement, or sequence.

To follow the previously proposed hierarchy of structure of subject matter, one can assume that the given conditions (Level 1) consist of: the medium—land and air; equipment—the balance beam; number of participants—one. Certainly, alternatives *do* exist in the latter two conditions; therefore, problems can be designed to stimulate changes in the equipment. Example: Must the balance beam be always horizontal? The answer can be "No!" (By raising one side, one creates intensified conditions for higher degree of difficulty in balance development.)

The next problems can be: What would be a comfortable angle? What would be the steepest slope? and so on. Similarly, one can design problems which will probe the possibility of change in the number of participants performing on the same beam in a particular fashion of movement.

Once the minimal and constant conditions (Level 1) have been decided upon, it becomes possible and necessary to move to the next level, the design of problems which focus on the relations which exist between the body, the movement possibilities, and the beam.

Phase 1—Getting On (Mounts)

1. Can all the parts of the body be used for getting on?
2. Which parts cannot be used?
3. What is the maximum number of body parts that can be used for the mount (which mounts?) at the same time?
4. For the same mount (which one?) what is the minimum number of parts needed?

5. One part of the body less than maximum?
6. Two parts less than maximum?
7. Other number of parts less?
8. One part of the body more than minimum?
9. Can you get on the beam with maximum area of the body touching the beam?
10. Can you get on with minimum area of the body touching the beam?

Note: Any ten solutions by any one student will constitute ten mounts on the balance beam. It is safe to assume that when two or more students present solutions, the number of different solutions will increase considerably. We achieve several purposes:

1. The quantity of subject matter increases.
2. Quality of mounts is being observed, since the student will see *different* solutions that *do* solve the problems.
3. The cognitive process is in action.
4. Individualization is in progress.
5. Reinforcement (acceptance of solutions) is in process.

Can you think of other ways of asking questions about the mounts? What would you vary in your questions? The speed? Other questions could be: "What is the fastest mount? Can you mount the beam in slow motion?

What else can you use as a different dimension for alternative mounts? Try to design problems with the following as a focus (with the previous mounts).

1. Angle of approaching the beam.
2. Ways of approach (walk, run, hop, etc.).
3. Different body postures (head to toes).
4. Direction of body motion (forward, sideways, backward, other).
5. Combination of the above.
6. Other?
7. Still, one more!
8. Can you arrange the problems designed for 1–7 in a *particular order*? Which order? What is the principle governing the order?
9. Can you scramble your problems? Does it help systematic solving? Do you want systematic solving? Why?
10. Is there still another way of looking at the mount?

Do you realize how many solutions which reflect the *actual* number of different mounts you have now?

Now, what would be the next phase on the balance beam? Once we are on the beam, let us explore the possibilities of positions on the beam.

Phase 2—Positions on the Beam

1. Can you be in a vertical position on the beam?
2. Other than vertical?
3. Three different positions other than vertical? (What is common and what is different in these positions?)
4. Three other positions?
5. Can you balance in a horizontal position?
6. Can you balance when the entire body is horizontal except one part, which is vertical?
7. Can you balance with two body parts vertical? With three parts vertical?
8. Can you balance on one point of contact between the body and the beam? Two? Three?
9. Can you balance on more than three points of contact? How many?
10. Can you repeat 8 and 9 and keep the trunk vertical?
11. Can you repeat 8 and 9 and keep the trunk horizontal?
12. Can you repeat 8 and 9 without using one of the "twin parts" (legs, arms) of the body?
13. Can you repeat 1–12 and have your sagital plane perpendicular to the length of the beam?
14. Can you repeat 1–12 and face in other directions? Can you repeat 1–12 with various angles between your feet and the beam?
15. Can you perform some of the above on the other foot or on the other side?
16. Can you review the above positions and *change* the position of your free arm? Your head? Any other part of the body?
17. Can you design three different *curved* body positions on the balance beam?
18. Can any of these three apply to any of the positions in 1–16?
19. Can you review some of the previous positions and have some of the joints bent? All? None?
20. Can you think of other areas to focus on in designing problems which will elicit more and different positions on the balance beam?

Note: Can you imagine the surge of dissonance-inquiry-discovery if you asked:

1. Can you find out which one of the mounts can *directly* lead to any of the positions?
2. Which mounts lead to the maximum number of positions? Which ones?

3. Which mounts lead to the minimum number of positions? Which ones?
4. Which mounts lead more readily to the vertical positions?
5. Which mounts lead more readily to the horizontal positions?
6. Which mounts lead to the kind of position not mentioned yet? Can you identify the position(s)?
7. Can you identify the mounts which will *need* one additional connecting movement to reach the vertical positions? Horizontal positions? Other?
8. Which mount connects *the fastest* to which position? The slowest? In between the slowest and fastest?
9. Which mount connects to which position facing the opposite direction?
10. Can you think of other ways to focus the connection of a mount to a position?

Well, now we are on the beam, and presumably we are ready to move. Obviously it is possible to move in several directions. We can also perform from minimum to maximum motion. Let us focus on minimum motion and explore it.

Phase 3—One Movement

1. Select one of the previous positions. Which parts of the body in this position can make only a tiny movement? A larger movement? The largest movement without upsetting the balance? (Can you identify the relationship to the limit component in Level 3 of the structure of subject matter?)
2. Which part of the body, in the selected position, will upset the balance if moved along its maximum range?
3. Which direction of maximum motion by a part of the body can be tolerated by total body balance?
4. In the selected position, try out this idea of maximum range and find out which part of the body will cause imbalance by slow motion? Fast motion? Fastest motion?
5. Any other possibility by trying another one of the previous positions?
6. Can you think of any other ways to explore minimal motion in a given position?

It seems appropriate now to find out the possibilities which exist in combining the first phase—the mounts—with the position phase and the one-movement phase. There must be hundreds if not thousands of movement possibilities in this arrangement—all legitimate subject matter content, all discovered by the student, and all discovered by the process of problem solving.

It is possible to create more problems in relation to this single-movement phase by focusing on various other possibilities:

1. Change of direction (up, down, circular, other)
2. Change of size (small, large, other)
3. Change of speed
4. Change of intensity (soft, hard)
5. Other?

Phase 4—Other Movements on the Beam

1. Select *one* position that you discovered before, and find out what movement *can be initiated* from that position.
2. Can you do the same from another position?
3. Can you use any of the initiated movements to move from point A to point B on the beam?
4. Can you group these movements under some common headings?
5. Can you perform these movements with a slight change in the position of the center of gravity (higher, lower, other)?
6. Can you move forward along the beam using the *same* movement repeatedly?
7. Can you repeat 6 while moving backward?
8. Can you perform it moving sideways?
9. Can you move along the beam (in any direction) using *two* different alternating movements?
10. Can you add one of the previous positions after the two alternating movements?
11. Can you add a turn at the end of each of these movements? Which turn? Can you try another one?
12. Can you do the turn from a higher center of gravity and immediately move on?
13. Can you do it with a lower center of gravity?
14. Can you add a movement of any part of the body while you turn?
15. Can you find out the minimum base you need while moving along the beam? (Check different directions.)
16. What is the maximum base (maximum points of contact between the body and the beam) you can evolve and still move along the beam?
17. Can you move along the beam with two points of contact other than two feet? Three points of contact? Four? Five? More?

18. Can you *stop* in any of the positions with the varying number of points of contact?
19. Can you stop and go?
20. While you are moving with various points of contact, can you change your posture?
21. Can you become longer? Shorter? Taller? Round? Straight?
22. Can you review some of the previous discoveries and try them while the free arm(s) and leg(s) stay very close to the body?
23. While the arm(s) and leg(s) move as far as possible from the body?
24. Can you try 23 in various directions? How many?

It is possible to continue perhaps endlessly in the design of problems involving performance on the balance beam.

Problems to Solve in Soccer

Let us examine this process in one of the ball games—soccer. Following the structure of subject matter, let us begin with the possible relationships between the body and the ball (excluding the use of the arms, as decreed by the rules, the limiting factor of the structure).

Some problems pertaining to body-ball relationships (in motion) are:

1. What are the parts of the upper body that can be used to move the ball from point A to point B?
2. Which parts of the lower body can accomplish similar results?
3. Which parts can move the ball from point A to point B, keeping the ball rolling on the ground?
4. Which parts can move the ball from point A to point B, getting the ball slightly off the ground?
5. Which parts can move the ball, getting the ball to fly above your own height?
6. Is there another part of the body that can accomplish what you did in 4, 5, and 6?
7. Are there still other alternatives?
8. Which of the above parts of the body moved the ball the farthest? The shortest distance? The highest? Do you know why those things happened?
9. Which parts can move the ball in a straight line?
10. Which can move the ball along a curved line?

Let us concentrate now on the foot!

1. Which parts of the foot can be used for moving the ball from point A to point B?

2. Can you suggest three ways of kicking and keeping the ball rolling on the ground?
3. Can you suggest two ways of kicking which will raise the ball slightly off the ground? Into higher flight?
4. Which part of the foot is best used for an accurate short kick?
5. Which part of the foot is best used for an accurate long kick?
6. Can you design three different short kicks? Three different long kicks?
7. Can you examine all previous kicks when a change of direction (of the ball) is necessary?
8. Which kicks are suitable for side kicking? Left? Right?
9. Which kicks are suitable for kicking backward?
10. Which kick is best for a "soft" kick?
11. Which kick is best for a hard kick?
12. What happens to each previous kick when it is performed after *one* preliminary step?
13. After two preliminary steps? After three?
14. After a few running steps?
15. Can you tell what will happen if you use each one of the previous kicks after a few running steps when *the ball* is in motion:
    a) Moving on the ground toward you (rolled by a partner)?
    b) Moving on the ground away from you?
    c) Moving on the ground from left to right?
    d) Moving on the ground from right to left?
    e) Review *a–d* when the ball is slightly off the ground (bounced by a partner).
16. Can you repeat each of the previous kicks using your weaker leg?
17. Which kick can you perform well with your weaker leg?
18. Are there any other dimensions that can serve as a focus for problem design?
19. Try this one—can you design problems which will focus on the speed of the ball?
20. Can you design alternative problems to those mentioned in Items 1–17?
21. Can you design problems which will focus on the role of the head in moving the ball from point A to point B? How would you begin?
22. Can you design problems which will focus on other parts of the body as the movers of the ball?
23. Which part of the body can *stop* a ball which is moving toward you:
    a) On the ground?

  b) Slightly off the ground?

  c) High off the ground?

24. What are three ways of stopping dead the ball which is rolling toward you on the ground?

25. Are there more ways than three?

26. What are three ways of stopping a flying ball?

27. Are there more than three ways?

28. Is there a *best* way? Why? How do you judge how good each kick is?

29. Can you stop the ball in all the previous ways and get it ready for a kick forward as fast as possible?

30. Can you repeat 29 and set up the ball for a kick to the left? Right? Other directions?

31. Can you find three ways of stopping a ball rolling toward you, using only the foot?

32. A ball rolling from the right—can you stop it using the foot in three different ways?

33. Can you find ways of stopping a flying ball using only the feet?

34. Are there any other possibilities for problems with a focus on this phase of soccer?

  Similarly, other techniques of soccer can be taught by discovery through solving problems. The teacher needs to decide which techniques of soccer are to be taught, and then he proceeds to design problems relevant to the particular phase or technique of soccer. This has been tried for the following phases of the game: (*a*) heading techniques, (*b*) dribbling techniques, (*c*) techniques for use of chest and thighs in various game situations. Can you think of any other phases for which this can be tried?

  A variety of tactical issues of the game can be taught by discovery. The essence of a tactical issue is *its being a problem.* In analyzing the structure of soccer, one can conceive of a great many tactical situations which call for solutions—moreover, alternative solutions to the same problems. A fundamental example of the *need* to learn to solve a problem and the *existence* of multiple solutions is in the following situation: Player A is in possession of the ball, moving toward the opponent's territory; player B from the opposing team appears in front of player A. The question is: What can player A do? Obviously there are many answers to this question, and each answer depends on the specific circumstances.

  So, the focus here is on the relationship between A and B within a set of possible circumstances as they relate to the rest of the team and the present purpose of manipulating the ball. Let us examine the kinds of relationships that could exist, which in turn determine the nature of the problems to be designed.

The first relationship to be considered is *the distance between players A and B*. This can stimulate the following problem (assume that player A has the ball and that player B is two to three feet away):

1. What are two ways player A can avoid player B without touching him and still have possession of the ball?
2. What are two ways of accomplishing it with touching player B within the limitations of the rules?
3. Can you accomplish 1–2 facing player B?
4. Can you accomplish it with your side to player B?
5. With your back to player B?
6. Other directions in relation to player B?
7. Can you accomplish it moving slowly? Fast? Which speed is preferable? Why?
8. Which one of the above solutions would you select if player A remained stationary? Why?
9. Which one would you select if player B indicated by his body position the intention to move to the left? To the right? Forward? Backward? Do you know why you selected your solution?
10. What can you do if player B charges at you?
11. What else can player B do against you?
    a) _____
    b) _____
    c) _____
12. What can *you* do if he does *a* and still remain in possession of the ball. If he does *b*? If he does *c*?
13. Review 1–12 when the *distance* between A and B is different.

These are *real* game problems. All players face these problems during a game. They focus on a specific phase; and being able to solve them efficiently, accurately, and frequently will create a player who can adjust better to the sequence of game events, a player who is more imaginative—a better player!

Another kind of relationship between A and B could focus on *the size of the players:*

1. What can you do if player B is much taller?
2. What can you do if player B is much faster?

3. What can you do if player B is as fast as you and as tall as you but is considerably heavier?
4. How would you determine the preferences of your solutions to 1–3?

The next kind of relationship can focus on the *location of player B:*

1. He could be between you and the goal.
2. He could be between you and *your* teammate, who is:
    a) Behind player B
    b) On either side of player B
    c) Other places?
3. He could be between you and *his* teammate, who is:
    a) Behind player B
    b) On his side
    c) Other places?
4. Player B could be between you and two other players; one is your teammate and the other his teammate.
5. He could be between you and two of his teammates.
6. He could be between you and two of your teammates.
7. Where else could he be?
8. What can *you* do in each situation?
9. Which of your previous solutions will apply in each one of these situations?
10. Is there only one solution for each situation? Any alternatives?

Organizationally, this process of problem solving requires pairs and sometimes small groups of three or four. You divide your class accordingly; each group either is assigned to an area of the field or selects its area. Then each group receives a ball and set problems (cards or Mimeographed sheets do the job quite efficiently). You do not need special soccer balls for this purpose; any ball (including rubber or plastic playground balls) will be adequate. The students are not playing the game in its full zest and power. They are engaged in *learning* how to think and how to execute the variety of elements which constitute the structure of soccer. This, in turn, will lead to better performance during a full-scale game situation.

A most interesting aspect of soccer which can serve as a focus for problem design is *kicking to the goal.* Here you can design marvelous sets of problems which will elicit discoveries in relationships, preferences, limitations, variations, or any other dimension that you can discover or invent.

Some situations in front of the goal which require a decision and a solution can involve *you alone against the goalie.* Elements of this situation will be:

1. Distance between you and the goal.
2. The angle between your sagital plane and the goal.
3. The location of the goalie in relation to 1 and 2.
4. The relationship between your body postures and the goal.
5. The relationship between your body and the ball.
6. Any other?

If the teacher can identify several variations in each of the above kinds of relationships, then he can convert them into problems. It becomes more and more obvious that in order to design meaningful and relevant problems one must know the subject matter rather well, that one must be able to analyze the structure of the subject matter into its individual components and relationships, and that only then can problems become sequential and purposeful. The solutions to these problems will bring about the synthesis of scattered elements into one complete structure—the activity at hand.

Kicking to the goal can also serve as a focus for problems involving *you, the goalie, and a back.* This new situation may have the following dimensions:

1. Distance—between each two participants in the situation.
2. Location—of each participant. (Example: What are two things you can do when the goalie is close to the near corner of the goal and the back is farther away?)
3. Direction of motion—of each participant in the given situation.
4. Speed of motion of each participant.
5. Posture of each participant at a given moment. (Example: What can you do if the back is half bent in front of the center of the goal and the goalie is kneeling behind him?)
6. Any other dimensions?

Another game situation could involve *you, your teammate, one back, and the goalie.* This lends itself to multiple problems.

You can design problems in *all* these situations by following the formula: *if* so and so occurs, *then* what can you do? It *is* actually possible to continue this chain of additional players—each addition creating new circumstances with new problems, which demand new solutions—until the entire team is on the field exercising thinking processes by solving problems in action—problems relevant to soccer, relevant to them as individual members of a team, and relevant to the total purpose of the team.

We have touched upon some techniques of soccer and some tactics. Now the teacher or coach is ready to tackle the big one—*strategy!* The same process applies. Analyze your strategy into its components and requirements, and present them to your player converted into problems. Your players will inquire, will try out, will examine, and will *learn* the strategy and will be able to execute it better mentally and physically.

Problems to Solve in Movements on the Parallel Bars

The first area of problem design is the initial relationship between the body and the parallel bars. How do we get on? In relating the body to the given equipment (Level 1 in the structure of subject matter), one can observe that several possibilities exist in terms of *where* to mount the parallel bars. Thus, there is a need to develop problems, the solutions of which will establish the possible relationships between the position of the body, the movement, and the position on the equipment.

Mounts onto the parallel bars are possible at the following locations:

1. At the end of both bars, outside the bars.
2. At the end of both bars, inside the bars.
3. In the middle of both bars, inside the bars.
4. At *any* point of both bars, inside the bars.
5. At the above proposals, entry can be performed above, below, and between the bars.
6. 1–4 can be done from under or over the bars.
7. Some of the above can be done using only *one* bar. Which ones?
8. Some of the above can be done alternating one and two bars. Which ones?
9. Are there other locations?
10. Are there other possible bar combinations (excluding for a moment various slope arrangements)?

Let us examine some problems to solve in mounting *at the end of both bars (from the outside), facing the bars:*

1. Design two mounts from a standing position which will land you in support position.
2. Using each one of the solutions of the previous problems, *end* in three different support positions.
3. Design four different mounts from four starting positions *other than* standing, ending in each of the suggested supporting positions of 2.
4. Are there still other alternative starting positions from which you

can execute four discovered mounts? How many? Are they all good? How do you determine that?

5. Using the new alternative starting positions, can you still find another mount to a support position?
6. Is it possible to end the previously discovered mounts in positions other than the front support positions?
7. Can you end *any* of the previously discovered mounts with a turn? What kind of a turn?
8. Can you end any of the mounts on top of both bars?
9. Can you find three different end-mount positions on top of both bars?
10. On top of one bar?
11. Could you end the mount on no bars? Would this constitute a mount?
12. Can you perform any of the previous mounts and shift the position of *one* hand during the mount?
13. Can you shift both hands during the mount?
14. Can you change the position of both legs in relation to the rest of the body (is there another relation?) during the mount? How?
15. Can the legs remain in full extension at all joints?
16. Can you move the legs so that flexion will occur at all joints (connected with the legs) during the mount?
17. Which mounts make it possible for the solutions found in 15 and 16? Which make it impossible? Why?

Comment: The last several problems with their multitude of potential solutions only point out the inappropriateness of the "official" view of what is correct or incorrect in parallel bars performance. The "official" view only reflects one of the limiting factors presented in the structure of subject matter—the cultural limiting factor, limits which reflect aesthetic decisions made by a small group of people. (See the discussion on the "assigned value" of movement in [56], chap. 1.)

18. Are there any other postural changes or adjustments possible during these mounts?
19. Can you introduce changes in:
    a) Rhythm?
    b) Speed (from slowest to fastest)?
    c) Fluency of motion? (Try the range from legato to staccato.)
    d) Other dimensions?
20. Can you think of any other possibility not explored in the previous nineteen problems?

21. Can you adapt these problems to a situation in which your back faces the end of the bars? Which problems (1–9) are applicable here? Which solutions?
22. Can you develop a series of problems relevant to the following phases of performance on the parallel bars:
    a) Mounts performed at the middle of the bars; inside the bars?
    b) Mounts performed at the middle-outside of the bars (using both bars)?
    c) Mounting at the middle of the bars using only one bar?
    d) Other location on the bars?
    e) Movement on top of the bars in relation to various postures?
    f) Motion of the whole body along the bar—in various postures?
    g) Change of direction—while remaining between the bars? Under the bars? Over the bars?
    h) Various principles of motion: kip, circular, etc.?
    i) Possible combinations of any of the movement solutions found in the previous problems.
    j) Problems relevant to combinations of two elements? Three? More—until an entire sequence of movement can be discovered and developed by the student?
    k) Dismounts? First, dismounts at the end of the bars? Dismounts at the middle of the bars?
    l) Other locations for dismounts? What are the relevant problems?
    m) Are there any other phases of performance on the parallel bars that merit the development of problems?

The cumulative solutions to all these problems (and many others that you can design) will reflect subject matter beyond any present conventional course of study in gymnastics. Furthermore, some of the new ideas and movements which usually evolve as a result of multiple solutions may serve as refreshing possibilities for coaches and performers at various competitive levels.

In fact, Olympic performers go through this process constantly, while in search of new ideas. Why wait for the few who reach Olympic standards? Why not start earlier with search for ideas and with examination of new movement possibilities and sequence designs?

Problems to Solve in Football

As was suggested in the section on soccer, all ball games can be taught by the style of problem solving. The three areas of techniques, tactics, and strategy are all amenable to this style of teaching. Some ball games, due to their structure, may be more or less adapted to this style; but some parts in all ball games can be explored through this process. One of the purposes in ball games is to develop players who are more independent in their thinking and thus *contribute more* to the team effort when unexpected events occur. In facing incidents which spring up in every game and destroy any pattern that the team has prepared, those players who are ready to make quick decisions and demonstrate adjustment in performance are the ones who usually save the situation. This ability to make a decision can be sharpened by teaching the players to solve problems and be ready to demonstrate a variety of responses when a new situation confronts them.

In the area of football a phase in techniques has been selected to illustrate the process of designing relevant problems. The technique selected is blocking. Since the purpose of blocking is to prevent the opponent from making a tackle, this becomes the focus for problem design. Solutions to these problems should, of course, be tried out in motion.

1. How can you make contact with your opponent?
2. Can you find a way to block him out only momentarily?
3. Can you design a way to block him through sustained contact?
4. Can you examine 1, 2, and 3 and keep your opponent in place?
5. Can you examine 1, 2, and 3 and move your opponent back? To the left? To the right?
6. Which game situation will call for each kind of blocking?
7. Which part of your body (within the framework of the rules—the limiting factor in Level 3 in the structure of subject matter) can be used to block the player and hold him in place?
8. Which part of your body can be used to block your opponent and move him to the left? To the right?
9. Which part is most efficient for each one of the purposes in blocking?
10. Which part of your body should *not* be used when you block an opponent? Why?
11. What kind of block can be best performed using the head?
12. What kind of block can be best performed using the shoulders? When would you use the left one? The right?
13. What kind of block can be best performed by using the side of the body?
14. What kind of block can be best performed by using the arms and the chest?
15. Can you block your opponent using your shoulder (which one?) to create minimum contact with him? Why?

16. Can you block your opponent using your shoulder to create maximum surface of contact? Why?
17. Can you try 16 while your opponent moves in different directions?
18. In which circumstances would you prefer the solution in 15 to those in 16?
19. Are there any other phases in blocking which could be converted into problems?
20. Can you offer alternative problems to the already suggested ones so that they will elicit more responses appropriate to blocking?

Since the game of football is so rich in alternative possibilities in techniques, tactical decisions, and strategy planning, the teacher or coach might find it very rewarding to convert the situations, relationships, limitations, and preferences (Level 3 in the structure of subject matter) into relevant series of problems.

The relative quantity and intensity of training in problem solving will vary with the relative need of each player to be involved in making series of decisions (small decisions as well as big ones).

Problems to Solve in Wrestling

The phase of wrestling selected for the example of problem design is the breakdown in the referee position.

1. What do you need to do in order to upset the balance of your opponent?
2. Which parts of your opponent's body are supporting the body and keeping it in balance?
3. Can you remove only *one* of the supporting parts?
4. How many of these single supports can you remove in order to upset the balance?
5. Select one of the supporting parts. Can any movement be made to keep this part from being a support?
6. Can you perform a movement forward that will remove the particular support?
7. Can you perform a movement backward that will accomplish the same?
8. Movement sideways? In any other direction?
9. Can you use all these directions of movement to remove all other supporting parts?
10. Which movements work with which supporting parts? Why?
11. Which movements do not work with which parts?
12. Any common elements in the solutions of 10? 11? Can you draw a general rule? Can you try it and see if it works?

13. Are there any uncommon elements in the solutions?
14. Which parts of your own body are involved in the performance of the previous solutions?
15. Can you accomplish the same objective by using fewer parts of your body? One less? Two less?
16. What is the minimum in the use of *your* body that is needed to accomplish the above solutions?
17. What kinds of movement will upset your opponent's balance if you manipulate only his head and neck?
18. Which movements will accomplish it by manipulating the arm and the shoulder?
19. Both arms and shoulders?
20. One arm and trunk?
21. One arm and one leg?
22. Are there any other combinations of parts of the body which will effect the same purpose?
23. Can you examine all previous solutions and see if a *pushing* movement will work in *each* solution?
24. Will a *pulling* movement work?
25. Will *pressure* on any of the parts of the body be helpful?
26. Will *turning* movements be effective.
27. Does shift of weight (yours and/or your opponent's) affect any of the solutions? Shift in what direction?
28. Can you draw a general conclusion about the shift of weight?
29. Are there any other dimensions that can serve as a focus for problem design in the breakdown?
30. Do the rules permit all your solutions?

Similarly, other aspects of wrestling can be converted into series of problems. The wrestler who discovers by himself the role of the base, the role of the supporting arms, the role of weight, and so on has a good opportunity to become a superior wrestler because he has learned to judge alternatives, weigh the possibilities, and select a preferred response. This is exactly what clever wrestlers do during a match. One can teach this to all wrestlers so that each one becomes a bit better as a result of the cognitive dimension added to the physical one.

Problems to Solve in Vaulting

Since this area of activity involves a manipulative piece of equipment, it is also possible to develop a series of problems which will elicit discoveries of the possibilities inherent in the equipment itself (Level 1 in the structure of subject matter—the given conditions). Let us examine some of these possibilities:

1. How can we place the horse or Swedish box? The vaulting apparatus always has the dimensions of length, width, height.
2. Which of these dimensions are changeable?
3. Does the surface have to be horizontal? Why? Can you vault when the surface is at a different angle? Which angle is optional? Which one prevents one from vaulting?
4. How do you determine the height of the vaulting apparatus? What factors will affect the need to change the height?

Now, let us assume that the placement of the apparatus has been decided upon (by the teacher, the students, or both); the problem-design process can move on to the second level—the involvement of the body parts and the possible movements produced. Soon enough it becomes obvious that the legs and the feet are involved in the first phase of vaulting—the approach to the vaulting apparatus. Some problems here can be presented as follows:

1. Can you approach the vaulting apparatus from various directions?

Note: Although the affirmative answer is almost inevitable, it is quite curious to observe that most, or all, vaulting is done with a forward-run approach done perpendicular to the apparatus. Some vaults are performed from an approach at a forty-five-degree angle. These traditional vaults only indicate that somebody in the past has selected these as the preferred ones. Indeed, these vaults do not encompass a fraction of possible vaults when all variables, components, and dimensions are permitted to interact in the endless number of possibilities.

Designing problems and finding solutions for them in vaulting can enrich the subject matter of vaulting to a high degree while the process of discovery through cognitive activity develops.

2. What are the *limitations* of each approach (Level 3 in the structure of subject matter)?
3. What are the limitations in view of the purpose of vaulting—which is—to clear the obstacle.
4. Is there another criterion to aid in checking the limitations of each approach? Is it not the *kind* of movement desired in the clearing of the obstacle? Certainly one can clear the horse by jumping or vaulting over after approaching it forward (running) and backward (walking), but one could not quite use both approaches and perform a flank vault. Or could one do that?

After one has explored and discovered the variety of possibilities in the approach (which could include variations in speed, distance, direction, rhythm, posture, and other factors), it becomes necessary to examine the take-off:

1. Can you take off on two feet? One foot?
2. Can you take off on two feet and "fly" upward? Sideways? On an angle?
3. Can you take off on two feet while facing any direction? Preferred directions?
4. Can you take off on two feet and face the obstacle? Can you start with your back to it? Your side? Facing in other directions?
5. Can you accomplish the same with a one-foot take-off?
6. Could there be reasons for preferring a certain kind of take-off?
7. How does the two-feet take-off affect the direction of the flight? Height? Distance? Balance in the air?
8. Can you try the effect of one-foot take-off on these dimensions?
9. Is there anything else we need to know about the take-off?
10. What is the angle at the knee at take-off?
11. What would happen if the angle gets smaller? Larger? Can you take off when the knee angle is close to 180 degrees? Close to zero degrees?
12. Which part of the foot is mainly involved in the take-off? Why?
13. Can you vary the position of the arms in relation to the body during take-off?
14. What would happen if they remained close to the body?
15. Can you take off and vary the *position* of the arms during take-off?
16. Can you vary the *movements* of the arms during take-off?
17. Can you determine the preferred arms' movement during take-off?
18. Can you vary the position of the head during take-off?
19. What about the shoulders? What can they do?
20. Can you focus your eyes on different targets during take-off?

The next phase of vaulting which needs to be explored is the contact of the body with the obstacle:

1. Can you fly to the vaulting apparatus and come in maximum contact with it?
2. Can you clear the obstacle with minimum contact between the body and the apparatus? (One student offered a unique solution to this problem—he cleared the Swedish box, touching it only with his big toe. The vault became known as the Rutgers Big Toe Vault.)

3. Can you find all the points on the periphery of the body that can come in contact with the obstacle? (Solutions here will vary according to the top surface of the obstacle.)
4. Which points or parts of the body can serve as support for the body during contact?
5. Which parts can serve as duration support?
6. Which parts can serve only as momentary support?
7. Which parts are *unsafe* to use? Why?
8. Which parts constitute a narrow base of support?
9. Which parts constitute a wide base of support?
10. Is there any preference between a narrow or a wide base of support? What are the criteria?
11. Can you clear the obstacle and touch it with only two points of contact? Three? Four? Five? Other?
12. Can you perform three different ways of two points of contact?
13. Can you perform three different ways of three points of contact? Four points of contact? More?
14. Are there other issues or ideas in the "contact with obstacle" phase of vaulting?
15. Can you design problems for these issues?

Now comes the most spectacular phase of vaulting—the manipulation of posture in flight (toward the obstacle, over it, and after clearing it). The endless combinations of the approach phase and the take-off phase with the contact possibilities can create a practically limitless number of vaults which can illustrate a variety of qualities possessed by the vaulter—agility, speed, coordination, strength, precision, and courage. Any one of these and others can serve as a focus for problem designs in the phase of manipulation of posture in flight:

1. Can you review all the previous problems and include the tuck position in every possible solution? Which solutions do not permit this position in flight?
2. Can you repeat the review and include the extended body position whenever possible?
3. Can you do it with any body position between tuck and full extension? Which body positions are possible?
4. Select one of the take-off solutions and one kind of contact with the obstacle. Can you clear the obstacle with the body in compact position facing the obstacle?
5. Same take-off and kind of contact. Can you clear the obstacle in

compact position facing the ceiling? The direction of flight? The direction of your starting position?

6. Can you repeat 4 and 5 with a change in the kind of contact between the body and the obstacle?
7. With a change of take-off?
8. Can you review 4–5 with a fully extended body?
9. Can you repeat 8 with extension at all joints and flexion only at one joint? Flexion at two joints? Three?
10. Can you control the angle between the trunk and the straight legs?
11. What is the smallest angle between the trunk and the straight legs you can maintain during the flight over the obstacle?
12. Can you apply the idea in 11 to the vaults performed when the body flies between the two supporting arms?
13. Can you apply it to vaults performed "outside" the supporting arms?
14. Can you maintain a constant angle between the trunk and the thighs and change the angle betwen the thighs and the calves?
15. Can you review 11–13 and change the direction your chest faces during the flight?
16. Can you review some of the solutions and perform it with an upside-down posture?
17. Are there variations in the upside-down posture?
18. Can you maintain the direction of the upside-down posture through the entire vault? You decide the meaning of the term entire vault.
19. Can you change directions of the body by introducing turns? Twists? Shift of weight? Other?
20. Can you think of other dimensions of the posture in flight that can be changed?

You can continue to explore the possibilities in vaulting by focusing on:

1. Landing variations (there are many dimensions here!).
2. Combinations of various flights and landing possibilities.
3. Combinations of contact, flight, landing.
4. Combinations of take-off, flight, landing.
5. Can you think of any other combination that can serve as a focus for problems?
6. Changes in position of various parts of the body.
7. Changes in speed.
8. Changes in rhythm.
9. Changes in height.
10. Any other changes?

The new result of offering solutions to these and other problems will be the discovery of hundreds of new and different vaults—vaults which represent a challenge to high-level physical performance and reflect depth in understanding the make-up of this exciting subject matter.

Problems to Solve in Games of Low Organization

Games of low organization are most readily adaptable to the creation of thousands of problems and the discovery of many thousands of solutions, creating a wealth of new games for any occasion, any environment, and any purpose. Our majors in physical education, in the course "Theory of Play," are constantly engaged in seeking new ideas, new relationships, new possibilities, new games—all done through discoveries elicited by relevant problem designs. The excitement in such lessons is high, the motivation even higher, and the results are most gratifying.

Our majors never run out of materials in games, nor do they need to memorize someone else's game proposals.

When one analyzes the structure of games, one realizes that it corresponds to the structure (of subject matter) previously proposed. All simple games (games of low organization) have the same prerequisites that must be identified and fulfilled. These prerequisites are the necessary components that make up the game. The interacting components are:

1. The number of participants in the active unit.
2. An organizational arrangement.
3. The equipment used.
4. The movement used.
5. The purpose (stated, implied, or understood).
6. The limits (rules, geography, time, etc.).

By presenting specific instances in each one of these components the teacher creates a game situation and framework within which students have great latitude in proposing a game design. Some examples follow:

1. Can you design a running game for one person using three paper cups as marks on the floor? This kind of design problem is very simple and can serve as an introductory step. It involves the *minimum* number of participants and a known movement, running. The only decisions that have to be made concern the *use* of the paper cups, which in turn will determine the organizational pattern and the geographical limitations of the game. The other decision concerns *something* about running around the cups (simple rules or requirements). Many different students will discover many different solutions and

ideas for the conduct of this game, and all can be within the framework of the given conditions of the proposed game's components.
2. Can you design a game for two, using a rope on the floor for the development of balance? Again these are rather simple conditions which can elicit many discoveries in how to balance oneself on the rope and how to relate to the partner who is also balancing. Two major possibilities come to mind—balance in competition or cooperation? The decision of purpose here will determine the rest—the movement, the organization, the rules, and so on.

Instead of using long sentences it is possible to present to the class Mimeographed sheets that look like the one on p. 225.

After a while it becomes obvious to students (of all ages) that when inventing a game one relates some of the possibilities of the body's movements with what the equipment can do or be. Thus develops the special interaction between the individual and the environment. When you ask, "What can a ball do?" the answers could include the following:

> 1. A ball can bounce.
> 2. A ball can roll.
> 3. A ball can stay put.
> 4. A ball can be thrown.
> 5. A ball can be kicked.
> 6. A ball can . . . ?

Now: "What can the hand do?"

> 1. A hand can touch.
> 2. A hand can hold.
> 3. A hand can push.
> 4. A hand can pull.
> 5. A hand can . . . ?

How would you connect what the ball can do or be with what the hand can do? There must be many ways.

We can ask many such questions:

> 1. What can a stick do or be?
> 2. What can a tire do or be?
> 3. What can a rope do or be?
> 4. What can a can do?
> 5. What can a tree be?
> 6. What can a rock be?
> 7. What can a stream be?
> 8. What can a log be?

Can you invent a game which will be built on the following conditions?				
Number of Participants in the Unit	*Organization*	*Equipment*	*Movement*	*Purpose & Limits*
1	Random	Tire	Hopping	To develop agility
2	Any	Tire	Pulling	To develop strength
2	Face to face	A line on floor	Pushing	To develop balance
2	Random	Medicine ball	Throwing	To develop strength
2	Random	1 paper cup	Any	Speed!
3	?	Tire	?	To develop strength
4	2 lines	One rope	?	State your purpose!
4	Random	4 broomsticks	Crawling	Speed
4	?	2 paper cups & Ping-pong balls	?	Precision
6	2 lines parallel	2 tennis balls	Any, backward	Relay race
4-8	?	2 empty juice cans. Any small ball	?	?
?	?	Many sticks Several tires	?	?
10-20	Circle	A variety of objects	?	Speed and precision
2	Random	A wall, a tire	?	?
4	Connected circle	One soccer ball	?	? No kicking
1	Random	A stick, paper cup	?	Balance
2	Back to back	Short rope	?	?
4	Square	Thin sticks Paper cups	?	Accuracy
3	Random	Round log	Sliding	?
4	Random	2 hoops	Jumping	?

9. What can other things do or be?
10. What can you do with all these things?
11. Many others.

Must we not stimulate, develop, and unleash the hidden energy, the locked imagination? Should we not seek to discover and create new knowledge, new dimensions? We can find answers—as long as we devise questions.

IMPLICATIONS OF TEACHING AND LEARNING
BY PROBLEM SOLVING

When this process is in progress, the learner is approaching a high level of individualization in all facets of development. Any student in any area of subject matter who can accept and understand a set of relevant problems and is willing to exhibit the physical responses which emerge after a cognitive process of discovery and decision making demonstrates a high degree of independence—emotional independence in the ability to seek out and tackle new situations.

Being successfully involved in this process strengthens one's feeling about his ability to meet new situations and solve problems that arise during the learning process. On the other hand, facing a series of problems in an unknown subject matter may arouse stress and anxiety. (Cratty [25], chap. 9); therefore, the issue of designing problems which are relevant to the individual is paramount and must be carefully handled.

The physical implications of this style are obvious. Students who are accustomed to offering new ideas through physical performance and who are emotionally fortified are quite free whenever called upon to present alternative physical responses in a game, in a sport, or in other movement situations. The wider the experience of the individual in problem solving in one area of activity, the greater the chances of transfer to other areas. The transfer here refers to the emotional and cognitive dimension upon which physical responses so often depend.

The cognitive process, at this point, exemplifies the individualized nature of learning. The cognitive dissonance, its amount and intensity, is private. The inquiry is personal. The response is unique and individualistic. Even when a group is engaged in seeking solutions to a mutual problem (relevancy to the group), and even though the cumulative solutions may be superior in quantity and quality to any one offered by an individual, the *very process of solving* is private and individualistic in character. It is only when the *individual* is ready to respond (emotional development), has a solution (cognitive development), is willing to communicate it (social development), and can demonstrate it (physical development) that the group has advanced.

This realization has an important role in the use of the problem-solving style in teaching team sports. It is important for the teacher or coach to identify the aspects of the sport which are best teachable through problem solving, because the more the individual members of the team are keen and able in seeing situations and relationships, the better will be the team.

This style also presents interesting implications for all other aspects of the teaching-learning situation.

Can you refer to Figure 3 and see what you can do in making decisions concerning the variety of adjustments needed? What adjustments are needed in class organization? What adjustments are needed in modes of communication? What adjustments are needed in your equipment distribution? Space allocation? Time duration and division? What adjustments are needed in the view of the structure of the course of study? The curricular structure? Supervisory procedures and purposes?

Can *you* suggest any other areas or dimensions that need to be studied in order to accommodate and develop the independence of students through the process of problem solving?

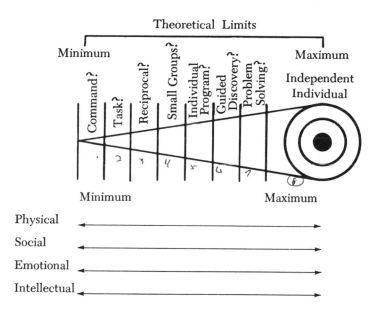

Figure 23. *Can You Find Your Own Position in the Spectrum of Styles and the Channels of Development?*

9

The Next Step—Creativity

Up to this point we have been discussing a process of growth, of freeing oneself, a process of emerging. This process is one that is to be consciously cultivated, and to that end I have proposed the delineation of the roles of both teacher and student. Interaction between teacher and student changes, dependency turns to independence, and the decision-making role constantly shifts. The growth process has been given theoretical limits so that it will be easier to visualize the concept of change in the student's learning behavior.

The teacher's behavior changes with each teaching style on the spectrum, and the focus in decision making shifts steadily from teacher to student. With each successive style on the spectrum, the role of the individual increases and becomes more intensified. This individualizing process is necessarily enhanced by the deliberate crossing of the cognitive barrier and the deliberate development of cognitive activity with its offspring—inquiry and discovery.

In viewing the changes in the anatomy of each style one realizes that in the problem-solving style all decision making is done by the student *except* the design of the problems! Despite the fact that the evolving subject matter is a result of the student's inquiry, discovery, and innovation, the learning umbilical cord is still attached to the teacher. The weaning process *is almost*, but not quite, complete!

Indeed, the next question is: Can the student ask the question by himself? Can the student identify the series of relevant problems, problems relevant to him and relevant to the subject matter confronting him?

This is the next step—the ability to *ask the question!* It is proposed that with this step we reach the *creative level of man*. This is the level where the individual sees what others do not see, hears what others do not hear, feels what others do not feel, thinks what others do not think, and does what others cannot do. Perhaps it is a matter of unique intuitive ability, or perhaps it can be developed and cultivated as psychologists are proposing. The important thing is that *it is*—it exists. This phenomenon exists as a part of human behavior, perhaps as a part of the behavior of every human being. May not the dreams, aspirations, and yearnings of each person be clues to some secret powers and abilities, suppressed and sealed? Doesn't each one of us have ideas never expressed, a wish which is never fulfilled, a statement which is never uttered, an image of movement never made? Are all these not signs of energy, emotional and intellectual, seeking to erupt, to be felt?

It is indeed creativity that enlarges boundaries, that is not afraid. At the creative level of behavior inhibitions evaporate, ideas are expressed, and questions are asked. This is the level where the new emerges, where the new must emerge. This is the level of courage that peers into the unknown, into the non-conventional. It is the level at which one is free and independent.

Can we teach creativity? Perhaps. One can learn to increase his ability to ask, to examine, to innovate. He can learn to look at a situation in new ways. He can learn to look at a *new* situation in a variety of ways. One can *learn to learn* in new and different ways, many of which are presented throughout the spectrum of styles of teaching physical education.

References

1. Abelson, Philip H., et al. "Creativity and Learning," *Daedalus* (Journal of the American Academy of Arts and Sciences) (Cambridge, Mass.), 1965.
2. Abercrombie, M. L. Johnson. *The Anatomy of Judgment.* New York: Basic Books, Inc., Publishers, 1960.
3. Anderson, Richard C. "Learning in Discussion: A Résumé of Authoritarian-Democratic Studies," *Harvard Educational Review,* XXIX (1959), 201–15.
4. ——, and Anderson, R. M. "Transfer of Originality Training," *Journal of Educational Psychology,* Vol. 54, No. 6 (1963), 300–304.
5. Anderson, Richard C., and Ausubel, David P. (eds.). *Readings in the Psychology of Cognition.* New York: Holt, Rinehart & Winston, Inc., 1965.
6. Andrews, Gladys. *Physical Education for Today's Boys and Girls.* Boston: Allyn & Bacon, Inc., 1960.
7. Ashton-Warner, Sylvia. *Teacher.* New York: Bantam Books, Inc., 1963.
8. Atkin, Myron J., and Karplus, Robert. "Discovery or Invention?" *The Science Teacher,* XXIX (1962), 45–69.
9. Ausubel, David P. "Creativity, General Creative Abilities, and the Creative Individual," *Psychology in the Schools,* I (1964), 344–47.
10. Berkson, I. B. *Education Faces the Future.* New York: Harper & Row, Publishers, 1943.
11. Bloom, Benjamin S. (ed.). *Taxonomy of Educational Objectives (Handbook I: Cognitive Domain).* New York: David McKay Co., Inc., 1956.
12. Brehn, J. W., and Cohen, A. R. *Exploration in Cognitive Dissonance.* New York: John Wiley & Sons, Inc., 1962.
13. Brown, George I. "A Second Study in the Teaching of Creativity," *Harvard Educational Review,* Vol. 35, No. 1 (Winter 1965), pp. 39–54.
14. Bruner, Jerome S. "The Act of Discovery," *Harvard Educational Review,* XXXI (1961), 21–32.
15. ——. "Needed: A Theory of Instruction," *Educational Leadership,* XX (1963), 523–32.
16. ——. *On Knowing: Essays for the Left Hand.* Cambridge, Mass.: Harvard University Press, 1962.
17. ——. *The Process of Education.* New York: Random House, Inc., 1963.
18. ——; Goodnow, J. J.; and Austin, G. A. *A Study of Thinking.* New York: John Wiley & Sons, Inc., 1960.

19. Bukh, Niels. *Primary Gymnastics.* 6th ed.; London: Methuen & Co., Ltd., 1941.

20. Carin, A., and Sund, R. B. *Teaching Science Through Discovery.* Columbus, Ohio: Charles E. Merrill Books, Inc., 1964.

21. Childs, John L. *Education and Morals.* New York: Appleton-Century & Appleton-Century-Crofts, Inc., 1950.

22. Christian, Roger W. "Guides to Programed Learning," *Harvard Business Review,* November-December 1962.

23. Collins, Barry E., and Guetzkow, Harold. *A Social Psychology of Group Processes for Decision-Making.* New York: John Wiley & Sons, Inc., 1964.

24. Cowell, C. C. *Scientific Foundations of Physical Education.* New York: Harper & Row, Publishers, 1953.

25. Cratty, Bryant J. *Movement Behavior and Motor Learning.* Philadelphia: Lea & Feliger, 1964.

26. David, Elwood C., and Wallis, Earl L. *Toward Better Teaching in Physical Education.* Englewood Cliffs, N.J.: Prentice-Hall, Inc., 1961.

27. Dewey, John. *Democracy and Education.* New York: The Macmillan Company, 1916.

28. ———. *Experience and Education.* New York: Collier Books, 1963.

29. ———. *How We Think.* Boston: D. C. Heath & Company, 1933.

30. Diem, Lisilott. *Who Can?* Translated, with an Introduction, by H. Steinhous. Frankfurt am Main, Germany: W. Limpert, 1957.

31. Festinger, Leon. *The Theory of Cognitive Dissonance.* Evanston, Ill.: Row, Peterson, 1957.

32. Flanders, Ned A. "Analyzing Teacher Behavior," *Educational Leadership,* XIX (1961), 173–80.

33. Fleischman, Edwin A. *The Dimensions of Physical Fitness.* (Technical Report No. 4, Office of Naval Research, Department of Industrial Administration and Department of Psychology, Yale University.) New Haven, Conn., 1962.

34. Ford, G. W., and Pugno, L. (eds.). *The Structure of Knowledge and the Curriculum.* Chicago: Rand McNally & Co., 1964.

35. Friedlander, Bernard Z. "A Psychologist's Second Thoughts on Concepts, Curiosity, and Discovery in Teaching and Learning," *Harvard Educational Review,* Vol. 35, No. 1 (Winter 1965), pp. 18–38.

36. Gagné, Robert M. *The Conditions of Learning.* New York: Holt, Rinehart & Winston, Inc., 1965.

37. ———, and Brown, L. T. "Some Factors in the Programming of Conceptual Learning," *Journal of Experimental Psychology,* LXII (1961), 313–21.

38. Gage, N. L. "Toward a Cognitive Theory of Teaching," *Teachers College Record,* LXV (1964), 408–12.

39. Gross, Ronald (ed.), *The Teacher and the Taught.* New York: Dell Publishing Co., Inc., 1963.

40. Guilford, J. P. "Three Faces of Intellect," *The American Psychologist,* XIV (1959), 469–79.

41. Hallman, Ralph J. "Can Creativity Be Taught?" *Educational Theory,* XIV (1964), 15–23.
42. Halsey, Elizabeth. *Inquiry and Invention in Physical Education.* Philadelphia: Lea & Febiger, 1964.
43. Harlow, H. F. "The Formation of Learning Sets," *Psychological Review,* LVI (1949), 51–65.
44. Hetherington, Clark W. *School Program in Physical Education.* New York: World Book Company, 1922.
45. *Individualizing Instruction.* (Association for Supervision and Curriculum Development Yearbook.) Washington, D. C., 1964.
46. Inhelder, Barbel, and Piaget, Jean. *The Growth of Logical Thinking from Childhood to Adolescence.* New York: Basic Books, Inc., Publishers, 1958.
47. Katona, George. *Organizing and Memorizing.* New York: Columbia University Press, 1949.
48. Kilpatrick, W. H. *Philosophy of Education.* New York: The Macmillan Company, 1951.
49. Kozman, H. C.; Cassidy, R.; and Jackson, C. O. *Methods in Physical Education.* Philadelphia: W. B. Saunders Co., 1958.
50. Krathwohl, David R.; Bloom, Benjamin S.; and Masia, Bertram B. *Taxonomy of Educational Objectives (Handbook* II: *Affective Domain).* New York: David McKay Co., Inc., 1956.
51. Kubie, Lawrence S. *Neurotic Distortion of the Creative Process.* New York: The Noonday Press, 1961.
52. Lindhard, J. *The Theory of Gymnastics.* 2d ed.; London: Methuen & Co., Ltd., 1939.
53. Maslow, Abraham H. *Toward A Psychology of Being.* Princeton, N.J.: D. Van Nostrand Co., Inc., 1962.
54. Miller, A., and Whitcomb, V. *Physical Education in the Elementary School Curriculum.* Englewood Cliffs, N.J.: Prentice Hall, Inc., 1963.
55. Morrison, Ruth. *Educational Gymnastics.* Liverpool: Speirs & Gledsdale Ltd., 1955.
56. Mosston, Muska. *Developmental Movement.* Columbus, Ohio: Charles E. Merrill Books, Inc., 1965.
57. Muse, M. B. *Guiding Learning Experience.* New York: The Macmillan Company, 1950.
58. Nash, J. B. (ed.). *Interpretations of Physical Education, Vol. I: Mind-Body Relationships.* New York: A. S. Barnes & Co., Inc., 1931.
59. ——. *Physical Education: Interpretations and Objectives.* New York: A. S. Barnes & Co., Inc., 1948.
60. NEA. *Schools for the 60's.* New York: McGraw-Hill Book Company, 1963.
61. NEA Project on Instruction. *Deciding What to Teach.* Washington, D. C., 1963.
62. Neilson, N. P., and Bronson, A. O. *Problems in Physical Education.* Englewood Cliffs, N.J.: Prentice-Hall, Inc., 1965.
63. Nissen, Hartvig. *A B C of the Swedish System of Educational Gymnas-*

tics. New York, Boston, Chicago: Educational Publishing Company, 1892.

64. *Perceiving Behaving Becoming.* (Association for Supervision and Curriculum Development Yearbook.) Washington, D. C., 1962.

65. Polya, G. *How to Solve It.* Garden City, N.Y.: Doubleday & Company, Inc., 1957.

66. Raths, Louis. "What Is a Good Teacher?" *Childhood Education,* XL (1964), 451–56.

67. Riccio, A. C., and Cyphert, F. R. *Teaching in America.* Columbus, Ohio: Charles E. Merrill Books, Inc., 1962.

68. Sanborn, M. A., and Hartman, B. G. *Issues in Physical Education.* Philadelphia: Lea & Febiger, 1964.

69. Schwab, Joseph J. "The Concept of the Structure of a Discipline," *The Educational Record,* XXXXIII (1962), 197–205.

70. Shaw, John. "The Operation of a Value System in the Selection of Activities and Methods of Instruction in Physical Education," *Fifty-ninth Annual Proceedings* (National College Physical Education Association). Daytona Beach, Fla., 1956.

71. Shoben, Edward Joseph. "Viewpoints from Related Disciplines: Learning Theory," *Teachers College Record,* LX (1959), 272–82.

72. Skinner, B. F. "The Science of Learning and the Art of Teaching," *Harvard Educational Review,* XXIV (1954), 86–97.

73. Smith, Othanel B. "A Conceptual Analysis of Instructional Behavior," *Journal of Teacher Education,* XIV (1963), 294–98.

74. ——. "The Need for Logic in Methods Courses," *Theory into Practice,* III (1964), 5–7.

75. Stebbing, Susan L. *Thinking to Some Purpose.* Baltimore: Penguin Books, Inc., 1961.

76. Taba, Hilda, and Elzey, Freeman F. "Teaching Strategies and Thought Processes," *Teachers College Record,* LXV (1964), 524–34.

77. Thomson, Robert. *The Psychology of Thinking.* Baltimore: Penguin Books, Inc., 1959.

78. Torrance, Paul E. *Education and the Creative Potential.* Minneapolis: The University of Minnesota Press, 1963.

79. ——. *What Research Says to the Teacher.* (No. 28, Creativity.) Washington, D. C.: National Education Association, 1963.

80. Vannier, M., and Fait, H. F. *Teaching Physical Education in Secondary Schools.* Philadelphia: W. B. Saunders Co., 1964.

81. Vannier, M., and Foster, M. *Teaching Physical Education in Elementary Schools.* Philadelphia: W. B. Saunders Co., 1963.

82. Weston, Arthur. *The Making of American Physical Education.* New York: Appleton-Century & Appleton-Century-Crofts, 1962.

83. Woodruff, Asahel D. "The Uses of Concepts in Teaching and Learning," *Journal of Teacher Education,* XV (1964), 81–97.

INDEX